D1007143

Snakes in Paradise

American River College Library
4700 College Oak Drive
Sacramento, CA 95841

American River College Library
4700 College Oak Drive
Sacramento, CA 95841

Snakes in Paradise

NGOs and the Aid Industry in Africa

Hans Holmén

Kumarian Press
An Imprint of Stylus Publishing

Snakes in Paradise
Published in 2010 in the United States of America by Kumarian Press, 22883
Quicksilver Drive, Sterling, VA 20166 USA.

Copyright ©2010 Kumarian Press.

All rights reserved. No part of this book may be reproduced or transmitted
in any form or by any means, electronic or mechanical, including photocopy, recording, or information storage and retrieval systems, without prior
permission of the publisher.

For permission to photocopy or use material electronically from *Snakes in
Paradise,* please access www.copyright.com or contact Copyright Clear-
ance Center, Inc. (CCC), 222 Rosewood Drive, Danvers, MA 01923, 978–
750–8400. CCC is a not-for-profit organization that provides licenses and
registration for a variety of users.

The text of this book is set in 10.5/13 Veljovic.

Editing and book design by Joan Weber Laflamme, jml ediset.
Proofread by Sue Boshers.
Index by Robert Swanson.

♾ The paper used in this publication meets the minimum requirements
of the American National Standard for Information Sciences—Perma-
nence of Paper for printed Library Materials, ANSI Z39.48–1984

Library of Congress Cataloging-in-Publication Data

Holmén, Hans.
  Snakes in paradise : NGOs and the aid industry in Africa / by Hans
Holmén.
    p. cm.
  Includes bibliographical references and index.
  ISBN 978-1-56549-301-8 (pbk. : alk. paper) — ISBN 978-1-56549-302-5
(cloth : alk. paper)
1. Economic assistance—Africa, Sub-Saharan. 2. Non-governmental orga-
nizations—Africa, Sub-Saharan. 3. Poverty—Africa, Sub-Saharan. I. Title.
  HC800.H64 2010
  338.910967—dc22

                                                                    2009019065

Contents

PART IV
ANOTHER WORLD IS POSSIBLE

Preface

Development partners are no longer the "solution" but also part of the problem.

—GÖRAN HYDÉN, 2008

This is a book about development—but also about the lack of it. More precisely, it is a book about one specific approach to development—the NGO approach. Ever since development and development aid became established issues in the 1950s and 1960s, a great many well-meaning individuals, organizations, and donors have made it their task to lift Africa out of poverty. Different approaches have been followed, some less successful than others. The so-called NGO approach to development has been the loadstar during recent decades.

Beginning in the 1980s sub-Saharan Africa has witnessed a veritable explosion of NGOs engaged in a multitude of efforts to develop the subcontinent. NGOs or CSOs (civil society organizations), as they are often called, represent a different approach to development. The Organisation for Economic Co-operation and Development (OECD), for example, recently declared that CSOs are often "particularly effective in reaching the poor and socially excluded . . . [and that] their strength lies in their . . . capacity for innovation" (OECD 2008, 2). This is a widespread view. Often praised for their commitment, flexibility, close contact with the grassroots, and ability to reach the poor, women, and other marginalized groups, NGOs/CSOs have become the darlings of donors and the UN system. During the same period rural Africa has sunk deeper into poverty and deprivation. Apparently, this massive NGO engagement has not led to any meaningful progress or "development." At the same time, it must be admitted that neither have other approaches. It is timely to ask why. Does development aid work at all? Or is this latest approach to promoting development not so different after all?

As the title of this book suggests, I am skeptical about much of the contemporary hype promoting organizations as a solution for underdevelopment in general—and for Africa in particular. But don't get me wrong. I strongly believe that organizations—peasant associations, producers' and consumers' cooperatives, labor unions, and other popular associations—have important roles to play in a development process. Indeed, they are indispensable—if not for development to come about, then at least to make it more humane and inclusive. This is a conviction that I share with a great many researchers, aid workers, and others who have a concern for the well-being of poor and vulnerable peoples and societies.

If the 1980s was the "age of NGOs" (Bratton 1989), this is even more the case in the early days of the third millennium. The number of organizations engaged in development in poor countries has grown immensely since the 1980s. But this is due not only to a greater number of players in direct development assistance. The conviction is widespread that a multitude of NGOs is vital for a healthy society. Organized citizens are seen as a necessary counterweight to power-hungry politicians and self-seeking bureaucracies. NGOs are also frequently seen as prominent players in international agenda setting and, not least, for promoting international solidarity and development in poor countries. There is a dilemma here. Self-organizing for shared interests may be seen as too slow and ineffective—or as misguided. Hence, it may be tempting to try to organize others and to do things for them in order to speed things up or to get people on the right track. When that happens, local initiative is lost and dependencies created or prolonged. It is the argument of this book that this is precisely what has happened with much of the effort to promote development in poor countries. Taken together, NGOs do not differ much in this respect.

As long as development has been a topic for study and implementation, there have been people proposing self-organization as a necessary instrument for its realization. At the time of formal political independence for most of Africa, in the early 1960s, René Dumont suggested that "a modernization of agriculture necessitates educated leaders in order to organize and animate cooperatives and mutual-aid societies" (Dumont 1964, 140). Since that time this opinion—and strategy—has been prominent among development theorists and practitioners both in Africa and among Northern development promoters. Emphasis has shifted, however, about the role of organization. Gradually, it came to mean assisted organization and even organization from abroad. Early on, cooperatives and other rural organizations often lost their character as self-help instruments. Instead, they became part of donor-supported and government-led nation-building projects and were thus seen as tools for implementation of long-term plans. Development, in those days, was often looked upon as a straightforward modernization project, with underdevelopment merely "a stage in societal evolution" (Amutabi 2006, 67); the issue was just a question of catching up with the West (or with the East, according to some proponents). Today, much development theory has abandoned this replicate or catching-up paradigm and instead tends to emphasize plural approaches and the need to find local solutions to local problems.

The previously common state-initiated "cooperatives" left little initiative to local people and increasingly came to be seen as failures. With the critique of the state that intensified beginning in the early 1980s, focus has shifted and many supporters of organizations have since that time pinned their hope on independent organizations as the only viable cure for underdevelopment. Not least, donors claim they have encouraged independent organization building at various geographical levels (local, regional, and national) in Africa. A great number of Northern NGOs have been quick to jump on this bandwagon, partly as a long-sought opportunity to be helpful and partly because they have found new opportunities to enhance their own importance and boost their own careers. During the last two decades of the second millennium the world saw a virtual explosion in the number of organizations engaged, in one way or another, in development in Africa and elsewhere.

To a large extent I share the optimistic view about the potential of popular organizations as vehicles for social and economic betterment. But I do not believe that they represent a panacea for development. Important as they are, there are no simple organizational "fixes" to the dilemma of poverty and underdevelopment

(Holmén and Jirström 1996). The process of development is much too complex to be solved by any kind of magic bullet. My skepticism derives from observations of how organizations often have been initiated and supported, and because much of the hype for organizations is based on assumptions rather than knowledge about their potential as development vehicles. There is a lot of wishful thinking around and many misconceptions about which associations can accomplish what, when, and where.

Much has been written about NGOs and other organizations, as noted, for example, by Igoe, who writes: "Much of what is known about NGOs is based more on what is believed about them than on empirical observations of what NGOs actually do in practice" (2005, xi). Others point out that "much of the knowledge that we have on NGOs work in Africa is artificial, as it has come from evaluation of carefully selected and choreographed reports and brochures and ideas generated from the pro-NGO western media and scholarship" (Amutabi 2006, xxiii). In particular, "there is a noticeable lack both of empirical case studies and analysis of INGO interaction with Southern social movements" (Earle 2007, 3). There is thus a need to dig deeper into the matter and, rather than presenting just another case study, to find out what is actually known about the subject. In this pursuit I have made an extensive literature review about what different kinds of organizations do and do not do, as well as about their successes and shortcomings.

From this I have tried to determine what is common and allows generalization. I have found an abundance of disparate and scattered information on NGOs and, to a lesser extent, on local organizations and peasants associations in Africa. Some of this information has broad relevance. However, much is unsystematic and/or locally specific, often contradictory, and not always easily accessible. This contributes to the confusion surrounding common knowledge about organizations and development. My ambition has been to bridge this knowledge gap, to reach beyond "myths" of organizations by putting together and systematizing a large number of empirically founded reports about organizations, development, and the environments in which these organizations operate in Africa south of the Sahara. Assembling such a large amount of information allows one to observe patterns and commonalities and eventually to see the forest despite all the trees.

Despite its contemporary popularity, the term *NGO* represents a complicated concept. To begin with, it is a negative term. It does not reveal what kind of organization we are dealing with; it merely says what it is not. And even that is not always true. Governments both in the global North and South have sometimes been active in establishing NGOs, in literature often referred to as GONGOs (government-organized NGOs) or QUANGOs (quasi-NGOs). Even if such NGOs are excluded, the term appears to be broad and all-inclusive, designating a wide spectrum of associations ranging from cooperatives and trade unions to bird-watcher societies and football clubs, that is also how it was initially used—as an alternative to government-led organizations. Over time, however, the concept has been narrowed and now commonly designates *intermediary* organizations, which in one way or another support groups and local organizations in less developed countries. Even if there is no consensus that this is the correct interpretation, this is how the term *NGO* is most often used today.

The focus on sub-Saharan Africa is motivated by the fact that NGO involvement in development efforts is particularly marked in Africa (Atampugre 1997). A further reason is that sub-Saharan Africa—the arena in which these organizations perform—is still the part of the world that Westerners know the least about. I find this assemblage a long overdue task. Possibly, it will allow us to harbor more realistic expectations about the role of organizations in development and to devise more appropriate means for support when that is appropriate—but also to accept that on many occasions a hands-off policy might be the best.

The information obtained from written sources has been complemented with my own observations, discussions, and interviews with researchers, NGO personnel, and activists engaged in African associations, as well as with field visits to local groups and community associations in Malawi, Senegal, Tanzania, and Uganda. Necessarily being founded on the observations, interpretations, and narratives of others, it is based on a wide spectrum of secondary sources: books, articles, research reports, working papers, conference contributions, and unpublished evaluation reports of varying content and character. This obviously limits the generalizations that can be made. Some of the documents used aspire to be neutral and detached. Others are to some extent colored by the affiliations and engagements of individual authors. Much has been written from within the organizations or by people who have some kind of stake in the organization written about. To report about what one is part of and/or believes in invites blindness, and a literature review always has difficulty evaluating such works. Sometimes biases are obvious, but often they are not. It is also difficult to analyze what might not have been included in written materials. This is not to say that I suspect the authors I have relied upon of being dishonest or secretly propagandistic. Yet a certain amount of uncertainty is inescapable.

Also, the main interest of this study is rural local organizations, and these are the least documented of all types of organizations in Africa. More is written about intermediary types of organizations—INGOs—than about small and dispersed farmers' organizations at the grassroot level. These, and their activities, successes, and failures, are comparatively invisible. That is unavoidable since many are small, informal, unregistered, and, perhaps, short lived. Our information about them is scattered and almost exclusively indirect.

This poses a special difficulty to a literature-based study. Organizations in Africa have been studied not only with different methods, but particularly from various theoretical perspectives and frequently through different ideological lenses. This has led some authors to be overly critical while others seem satisfied with presenting success stories, apparently with the hope that others will follow these examples. However, organizational models are not easily transferred from one socioeconomic or cultural-institutional environment to another.

While those writing success stories devote much effort to demonstrating what was done and how activities were structured, they often reveal little about the contextual factors that made the endeavor a success, or what made it come about in the first place. This is disturbing because "African civil society . . . is a murkier and less stable space than most civil society theories would suggest" (Igoe and Kelsall 2005, 3). Hence, although much has been written about NGOs, and to some extent about small, rural, grassroots organizations, far too little is known about what actually goes on where and why. That this was the case when the NGO scramble for Africa set in during the 1980s makes one wonder about the foundations of development assistance in the first place. It is also disturbing that "NGOs only rarely support scholars who collect data" (Nunnenkamp 2008, 208), the obvious reason being "a lack of space to properly debate these issues within an NGO setting" (Lockwood 2005, vii). Hence, it is still the case that common knowledge about associations in Africa remains clouded by what many stakeholders want us to believe about them.

Some demarcations have been unavoidable. Due to limited linguistic competence, I have confined the literature search almost entirely to texts written in English. Moreover, NGOs are of many kinds and pursue a wide range of activities: campaigning, relief and charity work, emergency assistance, capacity building, and development. Some NGOs are more specialized than others, and even though many NGOs display a bundle of activities and cannot easily be categorized as either/or, my focus has been on development-oriented NGOs and therefore I have given less attention to campaigning organizations like Greenpeace, Grain, Human Rights Watch, or relief organizations such as Save the Children and Médécins Sans Frontiers. Even without them, the task is big enough.

I have also found it necessary to restrict readings (although not completely) to more recent writings. This doesn't mean that I have lost the historical perspective on NGOs and other organizations. Important earlier studies on NGOs in general or with a specific focus on Africa have been provided by, for example, Hydén (1983), Esman and Uphoff (1988), Fowler (1988), Edwards and Hulme (1992), Farrington and Bebbington (1993), Wellard and Copestake (1993). They were all written during the 1980s and early 1990s, and I see no reason to repeat that exercise again. My interest concerns what has happened since then. This is partly for practical reasons and partly in order to present a state-of-the-art report of NGO presence and practice during the first decade of the third millennium, that is, at a time when many NGOs have come of age and gained the experience necessary to enhance their efficiency.

In addition, in recent years the tone in writings about organizations and African development has changed somewhat. In the

1980s and 1990s articles were generally optimistic, sometimes naively so. Over time, they have become more nuanced and contemporary narratives about NGOs are more dissonant than previously. Earlier, NGOs themselves were the main source of information about NGO activities and accomplishments. With few exceptions, there has long been a lack of evaluations and critical, or at least detached, reports on NGO activities and performance. To some extent this adversity has been overcome, and there is now available a growing number of independent and less partisan reports—but only to some extent. Hopes and expectations about what associations are and do still sometimes have a strong influence on what is being reported. Igoe and Kelsall grouped authors' expectations on NGOs[1] and African development as follows:

> *Liberals,* dissatisfied with the insatiable, undemocratic and non-developmental State, tend to see NGOs as its antithesis, *Viz* as 'close to the people.' democratic and as 'schools of civilized politics.' Being the constituent units of civil society, NGOs are viewed as the voice that can (and will) admonish the State when it makes inappropriate policy or discharges its duties poorly. According to liberals, NGOs are authentic, self-propelled vehicles of emancipation.
>
> Also *communitarians* are completely convinced by liberal claims about the NGOs liberal mission—they just don't like what they are trying to do. Whereas liberals see NGOs as a vehicle to foster horizontal, contractual forms of association and as a means to eliminate old ways of life, old communities, and old institutions—communitarians want to preserve them. They resent the ways in which (some) NGOs try to reconstruct Africa on a western template and regard 'African communities' and 'indigenous associations' as endangered species.
>
> *Marxists* embrace elements of the communitarian critique. However, it is not the erasure of 'traditional' communities that they are unhappy about, it is that the liberal agenda preempts the possibility of socialist emancipation. They doubt NGOs' developmental capabilities and see them as plagued by lack of coordination, amateurism, and narcotic religious zeal. Because they divert donor funds from

governments, Marxists regard NGOs as complicit in an international project to undermine the State, paving the way for global capitalism. They would much rather prefer genuine social movements made up of peasants, workers and the unemployed. (Igoe and Kelsall 2005, condensed from 12–15)

Conclusions about African associations and foreign organizations active in Africa tend to be wrestled into the straitjackets of (often Western made) pre-constructed theoretical categories and/or are colored by beliefs and expectations that may have little to do with on-the-ground realities. While "schools" of NGO promoters and interpreters point at both difficulties and diversity, they all have in common a tendency toward broad and ideologically motivated generalizations about what associations are, why they emerge, and what they can accomplish.

The contextual factor is often overlooked. The geographical tradition offers a perspective that is particularly relevant for explaining organizational development in the real world. Geography is not primarily preoccupied with constructing abstract models or with developing theories of supposedly universal applicability. The discipline rather strives to explain *why things happen where they do*. This cannot be done if the objects of our interest are taken out of the context where they are found. To the contrary, "everything which is present in a bounded part of the world has to be recognized as [potentially] playing a role there" (Hägerstrand 1983, 378).

Organizations in Africa are not always formed for the reasons or with the objectives that Western supporters assume. If the "organizing context" (Baume 1996, 17) rather than the "organizational landscape" (Temudo 2005, 273) is the ground where development takes place, it follows that it will not be enough to focus studies on organizations only. More attention must be directed toward this ground—or, rather, arena (Holmén 1991; 1995)—where associations are formed, perform, alter or preserve their purpose, and eventually, cease to exist. Not only is it essential to acknowledge that the organizational landscape—and the reasons for forming organizations—is much more multifaceted than the "schools" tend to admit. It is also crucial to go beyond "the historical processes of transformation of local societies and

their many forms of resistance to understand [organizations]"
(Temudo 2005).

Many writers, like Temudo, tend to emphasize resistance,
which might reflect a Marxian or a communitarian bias. Even if
local organizations in sub-Saharan Africa sometimes are created
as a means for resistance, this seems to be exceptional (although
this idea appears to be more common among Northern intellectuals, activists, and political academics). Most African local organizations and NGOs are instead created to make use of
opportunities. Hence, it is not enough to highlight resistance. It
is, rather, crucial to study *both* the historical processes of transformation of local societies—that is, the organizing context—*and*
the many forms of organizational appearance—that is, the variegated organizational landscape—in order to understand organizations, their potential, and their limitations in the environments
where they were created.

Such studies are hard to come by, and this unavoidably colors
the present study. Nevertheless, an effort will be made to go
beyond organizations and to highlight different contexts and how
they facilitate or constrain impacts on the different kinds and
degrees of success of the organizations included in this study.

My ambition has been twofold: on the one hand, to make an
assessment of the presence, activities, and potential of farmers'
organizations in Africa, and, on the other, to determine whether
local organizations in some parts of Africa are more effective—
have a better record—than local organizations in other parts, and,
if so, to try to determine why. Against the above mentioned background, this may seem like an impossible task. Here too, the
documents used vary greatly in regard to the kind of information they provide.

A specific problem has been how to measure success. This
can be done, for example, by comparing the effects of local organizations on members' or communities' wealth (to the extent
that it is possible to isolate this variable). Or one can look at
spread effects either in space or in the number of members or
beneficiaries over time. Changes in the scope and number of
activities undertaken by an organization can be documented (although more, of course, is not necessarily better). Another possibility is to check whether negotiating power and political
influence have improved. And, of course, members of organiza-

tions may have (or may develop) other reasons for joining (or remaining) than the founders. Here too, the documents used vary in quality. Different writers use different criteria for determining success or failure, but they are not always clear about how these criteria have been used. Data are not always comparable and, in any case, it seems impossible to construct a scale where "effectiveness" can be rated, say, from one to ten.

Therefore, what this study offers is impressionistic evidence more than hard facts. With this reservation in mind, it is nevertheless my hope that it will fill some gaps in our body of knowledge and contribute to an improved understanding of what kinds of associations we are dealing with, why they emerge (or do not), as well as the conditions under which NGOs and local organizations in rural Africa operate and what can realistically be expected from them.

Because most of the sources I have used are written by Westerners (sometimes with many years of Africa experience) and/ or emanate from Western organizations, and therefore have been criticized for being biased, I take pride in presenting texts and interpretations from African writers. This is not necessarily because they are better informed, but because they often see things from a different perspective. This, however, is not to say that I have assumed the role as spokesman for Africa or that I (without being asked to do so) purport to represent the "African viewpoint." For one thing, "Africans" are a much too heterogeneous group to make such an endeavor possible. All I can offer is my own interpretation. But I hope I have been able to balance the often simplified and uncritical vision of NGOs' role in development that Westerners have become accustomed to being served.

Acknowledgments

During the work on this book I have in various ways benefited from the knowledge and experience of a great number of people. For their encouragement and willingness to share information, to discuss different issues, and/or to give valuable and sometimes critical comments on earlier versions of this text I am indebted to Charlotte Billgren, Göran Djurfeldt, Christer Gunnarsson, Göran Hydén, Iddi Hussein, Magnus Jirström, John Kadzandira, Zachary Kinaro, Roger Kirkby, Patrik Kormawa, Kilama Luwa, Enrico Luzzati, Gaby Mills, Elias Mtinda, Nathan Mugerwa, Frank Muhereza, Ruth Onyang'o, Lars Rahm, Astrig Tasgian and, last but not least, some African NGO employees who prefer not to have their names mentioned. It goes without saying that their contributions have greatly improved the outcome of my undertaking. Any errors are, of course, my own responsibility. Financial support from the Swedish Development Cooperation Agency (Sida) is gratefully acknowledged.

Abbreviations and Acronyms

APFOG	Apex Farmers' Organization of Ghana
APT	Association des paysans de Tukar (Senegal)
AVAPAS	The Association for the Popularisation of and Support to Agroecologists in the Sahel
CBNRM	community-based natural resource management
CBO	community-based organization
CDD	community-driven development
CIG	common-interest group
CNCR	Conceil National de Concertation et de Coopération des Rureaux (National Council for Rural Dialogue and Cooperation, Senegal)
CO	community organization
CSO	civil society organization
DDD	demand-driven development
ECIDP	European Community International Development Programme
ESA	Eastern and Southern Africa
FADC	focal area development committee
FDSC	Civil Society Development Foundation (Romania)
FOCAC	Forum on China-Africa Cooperation
FO	farmers' organization
FONGS	Féderation des ONGs Sénégalaises
GDPRD	Global Donor Platform for Rural Development
GONGO	government-organized NGO

ICA	International Co-operative Alliance
ICCO	Interchurch Organisation for Development Co-operation
IDRC/CRDI	International Development Research Centre/ Le Centre de recherche pour le développement international (Ottawa, Canada)
IDS	Institute for Development Studies
IFAD	International Fund for Agricultural Development
IFAP	International Federation of Agriculture Producers
IFI	international financial institution
IIED	International Institute for Environment and Development
ILO	International Labour Organization
INGO	international nongovernmental organization (often Northern)
INTRAC	International NGO Training and Research Centre
KDDP	Killifi District Development Programme
KENFAP	Kenya National Federation of Agricultural Producers
LACCU	Lubulima Agriculture and Commercial Cooperative Union
LO	local organization
MO	market-oriented organization
NAADS	National Agricultural Advisory Service (Uganda)
NALEP	National Agricultural and Livestock Extension Programme (Kenya)
NEPAD	New Economic Partnership for African Development
NGO	nongovernmental organization
NRM	natural resource management

ODI	Overseas Development Institute
OECD	Organisation for Economic Co-operation and Development
PMA	Plan for Modernisation of Agriculture (Uganda)
PO	producers' organization
PRS	poverty reduction strategy
PRSPs	poverty reduction strategy papers
QUANGO	quasi-NGO
RELMA	Regional Land Management Unit (Kenya)
RIMISP	Latin American Center for Rural Development
ROPPA	Réseau des Organisations Paysannes et de Producteurs de l'Afrique de l'Ouest (West African Network of Peasants' and Producers' Organisations)
SACCO	savings and credit cooperative
SAP	structural adjustment policies
Sida	Swedish Development Cooperation Agency
SSA	sub-Saharan Africa
VO	village organization
WUA	water-use(r) association

Part I

INTRODUCTION

One

Development and Peasants' Associations in Sub-Saharan Africa

> The danger for many Africans is that the erosion of our ways by the aggressive ways of others, our own values by foreign values, will destroy our sense of responsibility for solving our communities' problems.
>
> —BERNARD OUEDRAOGO, FOUNDER
> OF THE NAAM MOVEMENT

> Any change in the social sector requires champions who are willing to be unpopular with changing from the known to the unknown
>
> —KENFAP, 2005

An African Dilemma

This study is about building organizations for development. The above two quotations—taken from different African farmers' associations—reflect part of the "development dilemma" with which the predominantly village-based and agriculture-dependent population of sub-Saharan Africa is presently confronted. Development always entails a break with the past. Whereas it may solve certain problems, it also creates new ones, some of which might not become manifest until after considerable time has passed. But development also has a more immediate price—institutions, established knowledge, social security systems, and ways of doing things as well as peoples' identities, relationships, and social

3

positions are all in flux. While there are winners, there are also losers—at least in the short run. Development, therefore, may not even be desired. It often meets resistance, especially when initiated or orchestrated from "above" or outside.

In order to reach a theoretically anchored understanding of what organizations are and what they can do—and under what circumstances—in order to benefit development, it is necessary to problematize everyday phenomena and scrutinize processes that we often take for granted. It is not only about NGOs that more is believed than known. This chapter, therefore, discusses assumptions about some phenomena, concepts, and processes that are fundamental to the problematic under study and that have a bearing on organizations' performances, accomplishments, and lack of accomplishments. The ambition is to go beyond intuition and politically correct interpretations in order to eliminate wishful thinking and arrive at a more realistic conception of what can be expected of organizations as instruments for development. Focus is directed at seemingly unproblematic concepts such as development, organization, civil society, community, nation building, and good governance. It is, however, not sufficient to scrutinize them one by one. They must also be fitted together to form an understandable whole, in the light of which the parts acquire meaning.

Development—What's in a Word?

Poverty is widespread in contemporary Africa. Half the continent's population ekes out a living below the poverty line. Poverty is also in large degree a rural phenomenon. In order to improve this situation, economic growth, diversification, and development are necessary. This seems to be a straightforward and uncontroversial statement. Unfortunately, it isn't. It is, for example, striking how discredited concepts like *modern* and *modernization* have recently become.

Development is a hotly debated issue, which more often than not concerns what various authors would like development to be rather than trying to establish what it is. While it is true that development does not mean simply catching up or Westernization—and that it is necessary to "move away from taking Europe as the theoretical and normative reference point" (Power, Mohan, and Mercer 2006, 231)—many today are reluctant to spell out what an alternative could be (apart, of course, from saying that it must be democratic, participatory, and transparent). To try to say what development is, rather than what it ought to be, obviously means walking on thin ice. Whereas we are, on the one hand, required to "think more critically about what development means" (ibid., 2006, 233), it is also suggested that development "cannot be thought of in abstract and universal terms" (Bignante, Dansero, and Scarpocchi 2007, 9). This post-modern stance is fairly widespread today, and consequently much more energy has been devoted to propagating "development as project" rather than to understanding "development as process." This may explain why so many projects and programs do not live up to expectations. What few writers would disagree with, though, is that development implies enhanced supportive capacity (that is, economic growth plus structural change), but it is a complex issue, which may take many forms and directions.

A lexical definition of *development* is "unfold." This refers to an inner potential (a rosebud opening up to become a flower; realizing one's true self). Whereas in principle development is open ended, at any point in time the options available are limited. Whatever its form and direction, development always has a starting point—a place, a culture, an economic system, an institutional order, and so forth. This offers both possibilities and constraints. North (1990) talks about "path-dependence," meaning that once a direction is embarked upon the number of alternatives will be restricted, sometimes severely so (see also Harris 1979).

Aristotle saw development as organic growth. He thought that individuals had a potential for development, a potential that would or would not be realized. In his view development is the realization *(energia)* of or transgression from potential matter *(dynamis)* to actual form *(enteleki,* from *telos,* "purpose"). Hence, all individual "things" have a potential that can be realized, but they cannot become *anything* (a man can become a hero or a traitor, and a piece of clay can become a pot or a statue, but they cannot become other species or materials). Moreover, this potential will not be realized without external stimuli *(causa efficieus),* for example, an assault or a child playing with clay. Hence, isolation holds development back. Because crowds offer more stimuli, it is easier for human beings to realize their potential in groups than in solitude. Accordingly, Aristotle saw the city-state *(polis)* as the highest form of interaction (Aspelin 1977a). It is this unfolding or realization of inner potential that has a semblance with development from below rather than importation of a perhaps ill-fitting form.

An analogous interpretation of development (Herbert Spencer) says that, whatever its precise configurations in time and space, the local becomes integrated into a larger and more complex whole, and that the parts of this whole become increasingly differentiated and functionally interdependent (Aspelin 1977b; von Wright 1994). Among other things, this implies that local autonomy is reduced or even lost during a development process. It is therefore likely to meet resistance, at least during the early stages of the process.

From an economic point of view modern economic growth entails both a long-term rise in supportive capacity and diversification of goods and activities. Important to note is that "this growing capacity [is] based on advancing technology and the institutional and ideological adjustments that it demands" (Kuznets 1973, 247). These adjustments entail a high "speed of structural transformation in the economic, institutional, and perhaps even in the ideological, framework [of society]" (ibid., 1973, 249). Hence, whatever their specific nature, uncompetitive ways of doing things and outmoded modes of organization will have to give way to more effective innovations—what Schumpeter (1951) called "creative destruction." This is an inevitable part of the process. Development, therefore, is always contested, at least in the short term.

From a sociological perspective it has been emphasized that (modern) development implies a transition from *Gemeinschaft* (community) to *Gesellschaft* (society) relations. *Gemeinschaft* here represents a small local community characterized by intimate relations among its inhabitants. Social control is upheld by tradition and group norms. *Gesellschaft,* on the other hand, refers to a large (urban) society characterized by impersonal and contractual relations. Social control is based on written laws and a formalized normative system (Tönnies 1963). In Durkheim's terminology development implies an alteration of people's relations from *mechanical* to *organic* solidarity. In the local, "traditional" community, where division of labor is limited, where anonymity is absent and people feel very much alike, mechanical solidarity characterized by cooperation, unity, and a "collective conscience" dominates. Organic solidarity, on the other hand, has its roots in the differences among people, which tend to be more accentuated in societies with more division of labor and, perhaps, individualism. In a society characterized by organic solidarity, people depend on one another because they are different. They unite and interact according to their occupational and economic positions and need not be personally involved (Østerberg 1978). Seen this way, development always has tradeoffs, and it may not come about as easily as is often assumed. From a local point of view it may not even be desirable.[1]

When, then, does development from below come about? It can be said that development is an incremental process that happens all the time. For most of human history that has been the case, albeit at a very slow rate. Sometimes, however, development seems to speed up and be a rather concentrated event (see, for example, Mabogunje 1989). Apparently, there has to be a not insignificant pressure for change and development as a more tangible occurrence takes place only when known lifestyles and established modes of livelihood are threatened. Significantly, the Greek word ουσιαστιχό translates as both "crisis" and "development." It is in situations of prolonged crisis that institutions—the putty that holds society together—are weakened, which allows a more massive search for new solutions.

For the sake of convenience I limit this discussion to preindustrial societies. The classical trigger is population growth (actually, lasting food deficits), which, when emigration is not an option, forces people to become innovative, to experiment with technology, and to intensify land use in order to enhance food production (Boserup 1965). It is important not to place too much emphasis on population itself. Boserup analyzed development as an endogenous process, but it can of course have exogenous causes as well. What is important is that the supportive capacity of a social system comes under pressure when population grows. Other threats to livelihoods and known ways of life are, for example, environmental degradation (Harris 1979), threats of war (Herbst 2000), or a combination of these forces (Holmén 2005). The familiar proverbial expression is that need is the mother of invention. In that sense—in a situation where governments have been forced to retreat, where the private sector is poorly developed, when extension services are collapsing, and when traditional livelihoods no longer suffice to feed a growing rural population—it can be argued that the time is ripe for local initiatives and for local organizations to be at the forefront of African development.

A pressure for change has slowly been building up in Africa's smallholder sector. Africa has long been considered underpopulated and extensification of agriculture has been a common option. However, due to population growth, in large parts of Africa the land frontier has now been reached or is about to be reached (Larsson, Holmén, and Hammarskjöld 2002; Djurfeldt et al. 2005). This, following the logic of Boserup, forces people not only to intensify land use and improve production techniques but also to find new organizational forms for individual and collective revenue generation. Moreover, since SAP (structural adjustment policy) was introduced in the 1980s, many marketing boards and state-controlled cooperatives have been liquidated or significantly reduced both in scope and geographical presence. This has left large rural areas with an organizational vacuum that needs to be filled (Holmén and Jirström 1999). Due to local contingencies, this filling is likely to take place for different reasons and to give rise to local organizations with different characteristics, objectives, and development implications.

Development from Below

Self-help is the name of the game. Widespread disappointment with the modernization paradigm, with ineffective foreign development aid, with top-down mobilization and extension strategies, and with Africa's often anti-developmental governments has led to a radical change in the last decades' development discourse and, to some extent, practice. Rather than relying on centrally designed projects for rural development, it is now emphasized that development—if it is to be realized at all—must come from below, from the grassroots and by the grassroots, if and when they so decide. Twenty-five years ago Borgin and Corbett wrote: "Practically all the difficulties Africa is encountering stem from the fact that the Africans have been forced into a development that is not of their own choice" (1982, 179) and concluded that Africa should perhaps be left alone to find its own viable solutions to perceived problems. Since then development aid has been reduced, as has the role of the state and "experts." Instead, we have witnessed a veritable explosion of NGOs and CSOs as vehicles for development. Apparently, with the change of the millennium, the door was finally opened for a genuine process of self-reliant development from below in sub-Saharan Africa. Many, therefore, have expressed strong hope that local farmers' organizations will constitute effective tools for development.

Africa, however, has not been left alone. Instead, whereas development aid has been reduced and donors to some extent have abandoned Africa, since the 1980s aid conditionalities and SAP have been forced upon Africa from outside.[2] Even if they aim inter alia at widening the scope for private entrepreneurs and local initiatives, this does not necessarily mean that empowerment and self-reliance have become prominent on development agendas. Donors and international institutions, before deciding on aid and debt relief, scrutinize "domestic" policies to make sure that these are in line with external priorities. As pointed out by Smith, there is a clear risk that the contemporary trend toward donor collaboration and streamlining of strategies—the joint donor platforms—will "homogenise development thinking" and thus reduce the scope for domestic solutions and independent local organization building (2006, 1; see also Pollard and Court 2005).

During the same period Africa has been flooded with a myriad of foreign NGOs aiming to speed up development. Many of them claim that they represent the alternative development paradigm. Indeed, "advancing an alternative development paradigm in the interest of the global majority has been the distinctive mission of development NGOs" (Eade and Ligteringen 2001, 12). It is, however, not always clear what this means. Various ideas and approaches have been lumped together under the banner of alternative development. In an effort to bring clarity to the matter, Tandon (2001) summarizes the alternative paradigm as being founded on the following five principles:

- Development is to occur at the local level and to be based on local priorities.
- Projects are small scale.
- Development requires an integrated approach, which looks at the community as a coherent whole where all will benefit from projects implemented.
- If development is not built on principles of participation, it fails.
- Projects should emphasize the marginalized sections of society, socioeconomic equality and justice.

The ambition behind the alternative paradigm is credit worthy. However, it rests upon a number of taken-for-granted assumptions about the local level, about the nature of communities, and about the abilities of grassroots—assumptions that may not be very realistic. Moreover, it disregards the context, that is, the different environments in which grassroots struggle to make ends meet.

NGOs, moreover, are a very heterogeneous family, and not all NGOs see themselves as representatives of alternative development, even though group-based approaches and local organizations have become prominent elements of virtually all NGO projects. While many strive to integrate smallholders with emerging markets, and in the process enhance smallholders' bargaining capacity, management, and marketing skills, others are "distinguished by their antipathy to markets" (R. Tripp 2001, 7). Some are genuine promoters of local initiative, project ownership, and empowerment, whereas others, due to their strong ideological motivation, are weak on empowerment (Michener 1998; Botchway 2001) and tend to impose preconstructed solutions and to make their clients see things the outsiders' way (Schmale 1993; Holmén and Jirström 1996; Lockwood 2005). NGOs tend to be strong on participatory rhetoric but weak on its practice (Oakley 1999; see also Edwards 2005). For all their virtues, NGOs may undermine local initiatives as well as facilitate them.

The reason seems self-evident. Sub-Saharan Africa appears not to have developed since independence. A majority of the population still lives under the poverty line, and 27 percent are undernourished (African Union 2005). Most writings about sub-Saharan Africa and its development potential are permeated with pessimism. Marginalization is increasing, and instead of developing, African societies are seen as being caught up in a quagmire of de-agrarianization (Bryceson 1999; 2002). African governments are generally considered too weak, corrupt, or disinterested to take the lead in a development process (Bayart, Ellis, and Hibou 1999; Fukuyama 2004; Herbst 2000; Lockwood 2005). Hence, donors and international institutions have found it necessary to strengthen organizations outside of government. Accordingly, Platteau (2000), and many with him, suggests that communities and local organizations are likely to be the key actors and development promoters in the African arena in coming decades.

However, besides weak governments, sub-Saharan Africa is also found to be the home of a weak civil society (Driscoll and Evans 2005; Lockwood 2005; Milligan and Binns 2007) with weak or absent farmers' organizations (Gyimah-Boadi 1996; CBR 1994; Golooba-Mutebi 2005). Apparently, SAP has offered them few stimuli. Consequently, Hydén (1995) asserts that, rather than engaging with the new situation in a constructive way, many smallholder peasants have retreated into a primordial, premodern, and subsistence oriented "economy of affection" as a result of SAP implementation.[3] The unanswered question is, however, Is Africa poor and underdeveloped because its civil society organizations are weak, or are these organizations weak because Africa is poor and underdeveloped? If so, can they be the vehicle of change?

The contemporary situation is unclear, and we need to know more about the characters, activities, and potential of local and farmers' organizations as effective tools for sustainable development in contemporary Africa—especially since there are also other and more encouraging stories told. Hydén's observation is now more than a decade old, and things may have changed since then. Notwithstanding the range of difficulties many peasant households are presently facing, Toulmin and Guèye, reporting from West Africa, find that SAP has also "brought benefits to the farming sector and provided a boost to the millions of smallholders making up this sector." They further find that "liberalisation has certainly created space for the multiplication of economic actors . . . and has helped open up many new possibilities to farmers" (2003, 23). Not everyone is benefiting from liberalization, however, and those that do, do not benefit equally. Nevertheless, according to Toulmin and Guèye, "family farms have been able to adapt and intensify" (ibid., 33) and, moreover, "for a decade or more, throughout West Africa, a range of producer organisations (POs) have established themselves and strengthened their position, at local, national and sub-regional levels" (ibid.). Also, for example, Bingen (1998), IFAD (2001), and McKeon, Watts, and Wolford (2004) find that accomplishments by West African organizations are in many ways outstanding. It thus seems as if organizations in West Africa have quite different experiences and a much more positive development impact than do organizations in Eastern and Southern Africa.

In many respects sub-Saharan Africa remains a "white spot" on our mental maps. Whereas much has been written about NGOs and development, comparatively little is known about local and community-based organizations. Apparently, however, neither the present nor the future needs to be painted in such dark colors as is commonly, even routinely, done. The above observations force us to question the common apocalyptic narratives about African development and formulate questions that might clarify the situation. The focus of what follows is on peasants' associations and rural NGOs, and on factors and circumstances inhibiting or facilitating their evolution. The purpose of this study is to find answers to the following questions:

- What are the activities, characteristics, strengths, and weaknesses of farmers' organizations in contemporary Africa south of the Sahara?
- Do indigenous organizations in sub-Saharan Africa have the same priorities as their supporting foreign organizations (donors, Northern NGOs)?
- Do indigenous local organizations and NGOs in West Africa have a better record than similar organizations elsewhere in sub-Saharan Africa?
- If so, are there important lessons to be learned about the West African experience that could be of value for enhancing development in other parts of Africa?
- What do the findings imply for donor engagement with organizations in Africa?

Organizations
and Development

Over the years far-reaching expectations have been placed upon local and member-based organizations, and the belief is widespread that they are, in some sense, ideal for realizing development. Firtus asserts: "Almost all countries that carried out successful agrarian transformations relied heavily on cooperative institutions" (1999, 1). The World Bank, in its flagship publication *World Development Report*, makes a strong plea for rural producer organizations as the key to development (World Bank 2007). Esman and Uphoff summarize what may be called the prevailing paradigm for rural development:

> A vigorous network of membership organizations is essential to any serious effort to overcome mass poverty under the conditions that are likely to prevail in most developing countries for the predictable future. . . . While other components—infrastructure investments, supportive public policies, appropriate technologies, and bureaucratic and market institutions—are necessary, we cannot visualize any strategy of rural development combining growth in productivity with broad distribution of benefits in which participatory local organizations are not prominent." (Esman and Uphoff 1988, 40)

This is an important observation. However, it is also the other way around. In order to realize their potential, local organizations depend on the presence of transport and communication infrastructure, on supportive public policies, and on access to information, technologies, markets, and so forth. After all, local organizations do not operate in a vacuum.

Organization means cooperation for a common purpose, such as communal projects and/or provision of local public goods, such as a seed bank, a school, or a health clinic. Or it can refer to a joint effort to realize individual benefits, for example, banding together in order to achieve enhanced negotiating power when dealing with political authorities and/or private traders. Such collective efforts can be pursued in more or less formal ways. For example, literature dealing with cooperatives and development typically distinguish between formal cooperatives and pre- or proto-cooperatives. Such distinctions are, however, of minor importance in this study. But a comment still needs to be made about the word *cooperation.*

Africa has a relatively long history of formal, often nation-wide and state-run cooperative organizations (see, for example, Holmén 1990). They generally have not worked well, and most have been reorganized or liquidated as a consequence of structural adjustment policies imposed upon African governments in the 1980s. Great efforts are instead made (primarily by donors and NGOs) either to create new organizations or to motivate grassroots to establish their own organizations. In order to do this, smallholders must cooperate.

Birchall states, "In reality many development agencies are actively engaged in promoting cooperative-type organizations but use a variety of alternative terms, without recognizing that they are in fact promoting cooperatives" (2003, iv). Language, however, need not be a sign of ignorance. The words *cooperation* and *cooperative* have become polluted and acquired a bad reputation due to the negative experiences with state-controlled formal co-operatives. Other concepts such as club, common interest group, mutual benefit organization, farmers' association, or producers' organization are currently preferred in order to circumvent this historical bias. "Whatever they may call themselves," say Bélières et al. "farmer and rural organisations are mainly concerned with two issues: the creation and management of services to agriculture; and the representation and defence of farmers' interests" (2002, 31).

During the first decades after independence much hope was placed on cooperative organizations as engines of development in Africa, and donors actively supported the building of nationwide cooperative structures. However, member influence dwindled as both donors and African governments increasingly saw these structures as tools for control and for channelling predetermined projects and programs for development from above. More often than not, they were used to tax agriculture. Cooperation came to mean vertical rather than horizontal cooperation, that is, it did not primarily imply cooperation among peasants but rather that peasants should cooperate with central planners and bureaucrats in programs and projects on which they had little influence (see, for example, Mabogunje 1989). In terms of participation, empowerment, agricultural productivity enhancement, and local revenue generation these cooperatives were virtually never successful (Holmén 1990). Hydén (1983), among others, reported that smallholder peasants, rather than participating, often preferred the exit option and retreated into meager but free informal and/or subsistence sectors.

Due to disappointing experiences with development from above, development theory came to emphasize development from below (Stöhr and Taylor 1981), an approach where local and member-based organizations were expected to have a prominent role. As summarized by Hoogvelt, "'Empowerment through participation' became the clarion call of development practice" (2001, 53)—or, at least, theory. This theoretical U-turn was further strengthened by neo-liberal ideology with its declaration that less government is good government. Henceforth, the invisible hand of the market was expected to take care of it all.

This not only laid the ground for the imposition of SAP all over Africa—since nongovernmental was by definition good— but it signaled the heyday for almost any kinds of NGOs. For example, the World Bank, which previously had seen cooperatives and other organizations merely as links in delivery chains (Kirsch, Benjacov, and Schujmann 1980), now increasingly emphasized that cooperatives are "business entities" (Braverman et al. 1991) and that development should be "community driven" (Salzer 2003). A recent joint donor platform stresses the paramount importance of "local bottom-up processes and local groups and organizations" (Woltz 2005, 47), and, for example, the Swedish aid agency (Sida) finds that "the possibility to organise is . . . essential to enable poor people to exert an influence and to change their lives" (Sida 2004, 1). Also the European Union now underlines the importance of "support to Southern civil society organizations" (ECIDP 2001, 1).[4]

Whereas there seems to be a widespread consensus both among development researchers and donor agencies that development must come from below and that it must be accomplished collectively through smallholders' and rural inhabitants' own organizations, little has so far been said about which these organizations are, about their capabilities, and about the circumstances under which they are likely to emerge. Even more so, the questions whether, where, or under which conditions these local organizations will assume the role of change agents—and thus challenge established power structures and ways of doing things—so far remain unanswered.

With Whom Are We Dealing?

The world of organizations is a heterogeneous one. It is made up of large and small, formal and informal, indigenous and foreign, political and apolitical associations with different management styles and modes of operation that engage directly or indirectly in a wide spectrum of activities, including development, child and maternity care, health, education, agricultural extension, environment conservation, savings, credit provision, small-scale industry, political and/or human rights advocacy, and sensitization.

Literature and debate invariably refer to NGOs as if they were one of a kind. Sometimes, although this is even less clarifying, the preferred label is civil society organizations. The term *civil society* has an immediate appeal. Not only does it allude to civilized, but it also sounds all-inclusive and inherently democratic. Weinberger and Jütting claim that CSOs constitute a distinctive social sphere and that "while the state depends on the rule of law and regulations which are backed by coercion, the market is driven by utility maximization, and civic organizations are mainly bound together by engagement of volunteers, self-interest and solidarity" (2001, 1392). This, however, is more idealizing than clarifying. But it is a good illustration of the self-image held by many who see themselves as representatives of civil society. The influence of CSOs is sometimes great, and donors tend to "view civil society as a uniformly positive force" (Duhu 2005, 52). However, in many cases civil society simply reflects the local situation, which may be neither solidaric nor democratic.

A common distinction is to say that civil society constitutes a third sector in society, separate from both the political and the private business spheres (the first and second sectors). At the very basic level individuals and households make up civil society, but mostly the term refers to entities situated beyond the household, namely, organizations (FDSC 2001). However, not all civic organizations fit, and there is a certain ambiguity over how to define a CSO. As Onsander points out, NGOs "do not represent the entire civil society. They represent smaller or larger interest groups with often very specific agendas" (2007, 12). Nevertheless, more often than not, civil society is equated with NGOs (see, for example, FDSC 2001). Civil society is often depicted as morally superior, represented by nonprofit organizations. In reality this is, of course, not always the case. There are also other ambiguities connected to the use of the concept, and there are many different understandings of civil society. Based inter alia on Putnam (1993), it commonly excludes family, kin group, or clan, and instead preserves "civil society" for groups that bridge or cut across primordial ties of kinship and clan. Moreover, they are voluntary associations.

Civil society, then, according to many interpreters, belongs to modernity. The concept was coined in the West during its transition from local-rural to large-scale urban-industrial society and was developed by thinkers such as Hegel, de Tocqueville, and Gramsci, who all gave it different interpretations. Currently, the most common view goes back to de Tocqueville, who saw civil society as a counterbalance to the increased capabilities of the modern state (Whaites 2000). This interpretation fits well the neo-liberal agenda, which tends to see the state—particularly in Africa—as corrupt and all powerful, if not monstrous.

Putnam (1993) opined that democracy is strong where civil society is strong and weak where there are few cross-cutting organizations. The question, however, is whether democracy is the result of the presence of a multitude of CSOs, or whether it may rather be the case that both the emergence of nontraditional (bridging) associations and of democracy are caused by other processes reshaping society. Many donors and foreign NGOs assume a clear and simple causality and are presently trying to promote "good governance" and to build civil society in countries where it appears to be weak or nonexistent, notably in Africa. However, this may well be a fallacy. Not only has it been claimed that this Western notion of civil society is "inadequately fitted to the realities of the continent" (Murunga 2000; see also Lyon and Porter 2005), but others have questioned whether it is meaningful to try to export a time- and space-specific type of organization to a context in which it did not evolve (see, for example, Lewis 2001).

Such doubts emerge because there are good reasons to believe that organizations mirror their environment more than they reshape it. To accept this is not to take a deterministic stance (see Giddens [1984] on structure and agency) but to accept that social change tends to be a slower process than we sometimes wish it were. Following North (1990), it is institutions that make up society. Institutions are the rules of the game and organizations are created to make use of these rules (ibid). Whether society is strong or not largely depends upon the strength of its institutions and where they are strong, imported organizational solutions are likely to be captured and "perverted" or at least to "under-perform." Of course, this can be blamed on the "inadequate" context, but that wouldn't help us much.

In accordance with the above reasoning—that civil society belongs to modernity—Karega concludes that "civil society is an alien term in the African setting. . . . This is because Africans do not operate in isolation of African traditions and traditional institutions" (2002a, 1). Nkwachukwu contends: "Because many organizations in African social formations do not meet the 'civility' criteria set by this notion, it excludes most part of Africa's rich associational life from the civil society" (2003, 4). Hence, support to "civil society" in Africa would represent less an expression of solidarity and more an effort to reshape African institutions and organizations to fit alien and predetermined categories. However, doing so will likely "cut-off these organizations from the social bases which they are meant to serve" (ibid., 4–5).

However, if the term *civil society* were used less as a normative concept and more as an analytical tool, one would have to admit that there is a variety of civil societies in contemporary Africa. The implications of this is that "the idea of civil society cannot . . . simply be exported by Western donors and used crudely to build good governance in developing [countries]" (Lewis 2001, 11). Also, although *CSO* and *NGO* are often used synonymously in literature dealing with organizations and development in Africa, it is far from clear which NGOs authors think belong to (modern) civil society and which do not. Being a literature-based study, this is reflected also in the present narrative, and in what follows *CSO* and *NGO* will be used inter-changeably to reflect the different authors' use of language but without hidden implications. Distinctions will, however, be made when necessary.

Among NGOs—intermediaries in development—we find both Northern and international organizations, which in some ways are involved in implementing development projects and pro-grams in more or less close cooperation with indigenous organi-zations of various kinds. To varying degrees they emphasize empowerment and pursue more or less participatory activities. They often channel donor funds and foreign expertise and thus in various ways fulfill their roles as intermediaries. Among in-digenous NGOs there is likewise a wide array of organizations operating for different purposes and at different levels of soci-ety. Many are urban based but fulfill similar supportive roles as INGOs in rural settings and thus also assume roles as intermedi-aries. The number of such organizations supporting various kinds of local organizations (LOs) has grown rapidly during recent decades. Although rhetoric sometimes suggests the opposite, their role, invariably, is to introduce modern (and sometimes post-modern) ideas and to enable local populations to engage more profitably with an increasingly capitalistic social and economic environment.

Below this intermediary level a heterogeneous mass of orga-nizations is found, in literature variously referred to as local or-ganizations, voluntary organizations, member organizations, grassroots organizations, women's organizations, and community-based organizations (CBOs). They operate at local or regional levels and are expected to be spontaneously evolving, although many NGOs not only support such groups where they exist but also try to establish them where they do not. NGOs, foreign as well as indigenous, often see themselves as catalysts of develop-ment. This apparently is so because—despite the emancipatory rhetoric surrounding local and community-based organizations—in reality not much seems to be expected from them (see, for example, Carroll 1992; Holmén and Jirström 1996). Or, at least, that used to be the case.

Another distinction that needs to be made is between the kinds of grassroots' involvement in the different kinds of organizations. NGOs not only tend to be urban based and sometimes of foreign origin, but they also tend to be run by professionals. Hence, as pointed out by Farrington and Bebbington (1993), membership organizations are staffed and elected by those people they are meant to serve, whereas in nonmembership organizations, by contrast, functionaries are appointed and staff is made up of people from entirely different backgrounds. This leads to very different relations within organizations, where the poor may be members of LOs and CBOs but clients of NGOs.

When the "NGO scramble for Africa" took off in the 1980s, NGOs were—and still are—expected to be different from—and hence better than—governments in a number of ways. They were seen as more democratic, flexible, and participatory in project formulation and implementation. They were viewed as particularly effective in reaching the poor and, hence, as ideal organizations for capacity building and for empowerment of the powerless (for a review, see Holmén and Jirström 1996). NGOs engaged in a variety of activities, from microcredit schemes, small-scale business projects, agricultural extension, training campaigns, and women's emancipation, to lobbying and human rights advocacy, to name just a few. Underlying both the switch in donor funding and the high expectations was a strong and widespread "belief in the altruistic motivation of NGOs" (Fafchamps and Owens 2006, 1).

In contrast to such assumptions, in the early days of massive NGO involvement in African development (the 1980s and early 1990s), NGOs were often found not to be the democratic institutions they were expected to be, and behind their rhetoric of participation and empowerment one often found a desire to control and direct. *Conscientization* often turned out to be an euphemism for making grassroots see things the outsider's way (Holmén and Jirström 1996). This negatively affected the possibilities for grassroots and their organizations to function as vehicles for development from below—especially when NGOs carried external funding and competed with local initiatives. This only created or prolonged dependency syndromes and, in fact, NGOs have been found to establish new forms of patron-client structures (Holmén and Jirström 2009).

This is not to say that NGO involvement always is negative for local efforts at organization building from below. As we shall see, there is also evidence to the contrary. And some indigenous organizations in Africa have now come of age and are becoming increasingly professional. But it does highlight that external support often turns out to be a double-edged sword. One question that begs an answer is thus whether such tendencies toward external control over local organizations were merely a sign of "child diseases"—equally common among supporting organizations and newly established local organizations, both of which were lacking necessary skills and experience—or whether this is a persistent problem?

Community-driven Development

Many writers on the subject put their hope on "true" development from below in the form of CBOs and community-driven development (CDD). The idea is that communities are (or should be) subjects of change in their own right and that those making up a community should initiate, design, and own any development project implemented in the community. Local people should be empowered to "decide for themselves the kind of development they are striving for and to . . . mobilize the resources to pursue their own development agenda" (Närman 1995, 33). CDD, says Perrett, "is a leitmotif of current development practice" (2004, 1)—a rather surprising observation since "much remains to be learned in designing and implementing CDD projects" (World Bank 2007, 256). Actually, literature, donors, and NGOs all are ambiguous about the meaning of *community*. Depending on whom one asks, a community can encompass anything from a whole village down to a ward or a user group within a village. It is, however, rather common in literature to omit sub-village groups and to preserve *community* for whole villages or *localities,* which are thought of as being characterized by "shared identity, associational ties and mutual support" (Bryceson 1999, 42). A definition that is useful for the present task is provided by Pantanali:

> A community is a village (small, medium, relatively large, not a small town), and comprises a group of rural people resident in a territory they recognize as their own, such group recognizing as well some form of governance of their collective affairs. . . . Associated with the idea of a group of

people, a territory, and some common institution, is the idea of a community as a locus where direct *participatory* democracy (as distinct from "representative" democracy) is a practical option. (2004, 8, emphasis in original)

Expectations about the aims and abilities of CBOs vary greatly, however. While some expect that LOs will be instrumental in fostering ownership of mainstream development at the local level, others hope that CBO-based development will be an alternative to development as usually understood, that is, egalitarian, culturally appropriate, and ecologically sound.

The former category normally leaves the outcome of development aside (that is, it is taken more or less for granted) but stresses that "without some form of self-organization by the poor, wider development would not be sustainable" (Birchall 2003, x). The latter point out not only that Africa has a long tradition of mutual aid and self-help institutions (Pimbert 2005), but also that "experience shows that communities, even in the remotest rural areas, can organize themselves according to democratic principles and can greatly contribute to their own social and economic development" (Salzer 2003, 1). This, apparently, is so because "democratic ethos and practices are engrained in Africa at sub-national levels" (Cheru 1995, 52–53). In this camp it is also pointed out that "social harmony is a high priority in rural communities" (Metcalfe 1997, 275), and that in Africa communitarian links "constitute the basic texture of society" (Luzzati 1999, 138). Hence, CBOs and community cooperatives "offer the breeding ground for the successful operations of new communitarian enterprises" (ibid., 139) where "social motivation (group solidarity) over-rides the strictly economic one" (Cracknell 2000, 6). Community-based or communitarian LOs, it is thus hoped, can avoid subordination under oppressive governments and, at the same time as they further local development, can act as a buffer against or even constitute an alternative to encroaching capitalism.

It is quite possible that expectations for communities and CBOs are too high. For one thing, "there is surprisingly little empirical information about CBOs in . . . Africa" to base such expectations on (Manji and Naidoo 2006, 5). Luzzati (1999) admits that community cooperatives tend to suffer from an economic disadvantage compared to private enterprise. They often do not aim at being effective business organizations (maximizing profit) in the first place, but also—or rather—they take on community objectives. "When a surplus is obtained, it is partly destined to the creation of local public goods, or to the redistribution inside the community" (Luzzati 1999, 139; see also Soulama 2003). However, the extent of solidarity and community may be exaggerated. Haubert warns against the common abuse of the word *communitarian*, because it "risks reflecting an ideology that presents development as a harmonious process without conflicts between social categories and without social costs" (2002, 98). This is a timely remark, because "many foreigners have romantic notions of communal altruism in developing countries" (Michener 1998, 2113).

"Community," says Kumar is often assumed and referred to in "a ritualistic manner" (2005, 275) that may have little to do with real life. Brent finds that "community is a desire constantly invoked [by utopians] as an 'answer' to problems of power, voice and social peace, yet never arrives" (2004, 213). Proponents of community tend to assume a great extent of social harmony, neighborliness, and egalitarianism in small settlements but overlook "inequality, oppressive social hierarchies and discrimination" (Kumar 2005, 282). Coquery-Vidrovitch (1997), Murunga (2000), and Mafeje (2003, 11) likewise underline that kin or group solidarity does not imply absence of exploitation and social dominance.[5]

Bayart, Ellis, and Hibou state, "Contrary to what is often said, African societies are characterized less by their communalism than by the almost frenetic individualism of those who comprise them" (1999, 34). Hydén's characterization of village life in Africa as constituting an "economy of affection" (1983, 39) they dismiss as "a rather unfortunate misnomer."[6] In contrast to idealizing notions of community, Golooba-Mutebi writes about African villages "plagued by disharmonious social relations" (2005, 938) where the willingness or ability of the poor to participate or self-organize is weak. Mana finds that the "democracy of consensus," which is sometimes believed to govern village life in Africa, is "the democracy of the lords and the chiefs" rather than of the community (1995, 24).

It is nevertheless correct that Africa has a long tradition of mutual aid, reciprocity, and self-help arrangements, ranging, for

example, from food gifts and work-exchange groups to burial societies, local seed banks and rotating saving clubs. At the micro
level the "economy of affection" is often stronger than formal
institutions (Duhu 2005). However, exchanges are neither immediate nor precise, and the result is "a continuous give and
take that reinforces relationships" (ibid., 43)—even if these relationships are unequal and exploitative. As with community cooperatives (see above), the economy of affection "blends
economic and social rationality" (Hydén 2006, 3). The relations
of mutual support that it fosters "are sometimes lateral (among
equals) at other times vertical involving a relationship with a
patron" (ibid.). Tokuori finds: "Through its formal institutions,
the economy of affection facilitates business transactions and
faster networking. At the same time, it encourages relatives and
friends to become dependent on the entrepreneurs and limits
their chance of succeeding. They become, if not parasites, at
least a burden that entrepreneurs have to cope with" (2006, 1).

Hydén (1983), moreover, pointed out that these mutual aid
arrangements are often occasional creations and should be seen
as latent or proto-organizations, some of which may lay dormant
for long periods only to be activated on special occasions. Hence,
while they doubtlessly display a propensity for mutual aid and
solidarity, they should perhaps better be seen as survival techniques and coping mechanisms rather than as instruments for
change—and therefore as more likely to preserve the status quo
rather than to promote development. Even so, these communitarian organizations can acquire a new and different function—if the overall situation/environment changes. In most
cases, however, such a reorientation is likely to require a shift
of power within the community, often implying a younger
generation's ascendance to prominence. For this to happen—
for preservationist organizations to become vehicles of change—
external pressure for change will, most likely, be a necessary
precondition.

Good Governance

Due to the perceived dysfunctionality of the African state, "good
governance" is proposed as a prerequisite for development. It is
high on the agenda of most aid agencies, governmental as well

as nongovernmental. It is, however, not self-evident what good government means. In its simplest neo-liberal form, it merely means less government. Calls for good governance have been aired because more often than not African governments have been regarded as obstacles to development. Conventional wisdom maintains that political and economic life has become overly centralized, corrupt, and ineffective. Africa, moreover, is perceived as being governed by crooks and kleptocrats, who plunder their countries (see, for example, Bayart, Ellis, and Hibou 1999; Fukuyama 2004). Consequently, donors and international financial institutions have found it necessary to roll back the state. Good governance, in this interpretation, not only means less government but it commonly also means formal democracy.

> On the whole, good governance implies an efficient and predictable public sector incorporating participation and the rule of law, i.e., with the characteristics of democratic governance. . . . Emphasis is placed on central democratic institutions like a democratic constitution, a parliament, general elections, participation and an active civil society, as well as human rights. (Sida 2002, 2)

NGOs and CSOs are believed to fulfill important roles in this regard as watchdogs, partners, and more flexible service providers (see, for example, Bernstein and Woodhouse 2001; Sida 2007). Many NGOs believe that they have a democratizing impact in countries where they operate. Typical positions when it comes to governance are that consensus is a precondition for development to be acceptable. Bignante, Dansero, and Scarpocchi thus find that "local development is . . . a process of interaction between local actors . . . who, implicitly or explicitly, share a vision of how territorial resources, be they tangible or intangible, can be developed" (2007, 4).

The Civil Society Consultation on the *World Development Report 2008*, maintains that

> government requires close and constant engagement with all relevant stakeholders and transparent and accountable processes of decision making. In this regard the voices of the poor, rural women and marginalized groups must be

heard and responded to in formulating national policy frameworks. Much needs to be done to develop representative, democratic, accountable and competent producer organizations that can engage effectively with policy issues at local and national levels, as well as effective participatory planning systems that bring the voices of communities into mainstream planning and resource allocation processes. (RIMISP, ICCO, and IDRC/CRDI 2007, ii)

Is this what development requires? No doubt, it is safe to call for good governance. Who wants bad governance? But, as pointed out by Moore, "because notions of 'good government' strike a responsive chord in most quarters, there is a danger that . . . critical questions about what is going on behind this 'façade' will not be addressed" (2006, 52).

"Good government" rests upon a number of assumptions—about development, about the African state, about civil society, and about organizations—which may have little resemblance in real life. It appears to have more to do with what donors wish the world were like than with how it is. Despite the well-meaning intentions, good governance may well be putting the cart before the horse. Good governance is presented as a precondition for development, when instead there are good reasons to expect it to be a result of development. Otherwise expressed, by manipulating the superstructure, donors and INGOs hope to alter the base. It is questionable whether this is how development takes place. There is, for example, little evidence that democratization improves service delivery (Conyers 2007). Neither is it clear "whether group-based organizations always increase efficiency and equity" (Weinberger and Jütting 2001, 1391). The "empirical relationship between democracy and development remains complex and ambiguous" (Fukuyama 2004, 37), and, in fact, "'good governance' has not proven its relevance as a development strategy" (Meisel and Aoudia 2008, 44). Moreover, there is "nothing inherent about civil society organizations that makes them opponents of authoritarianism and proponents of democracy" (Ndegwa 1996, 6).

It appears that calls for good governance attacks symptoms rather than causes. While many African governments have been criticized for being undemocratic, we must, with Mazrui, ask: "Is

Africa underdeveloped because it is primarily undemocratic? Or is Africa undemocratic because it is primarily underdeveloped?" (2002, 2). The answer to these questions will have far-reaching consequences for the kinds of intervention or assistance that may be required.

One would expect donors and INGOs not to be only knowledgeable about the intricacies of development but also to be sensible about social and cultural diversity, and hence to be prepared to allow for a wide range of solutions to difficulties encountered. That appears, however, not to be the case. Despite a jargon that indicates the opposite, the West (as interpreted by Western donors and aid agencies) remains the model others should copy. Implicitly, say Meisel and Aoudia,

> "good governance" assumes a homogenous world in which poor countries have the same institutional characteristics as wealthy countries but are affected by pathologies that prevent them from catching up to wealthy countries (corruption, lack of democracy, State failures, market failures, etc.). To attenuate these pathologies (i.e. applying 'good governance') is to foster their catch-up. (2008, 44)

Many advocates of good governance believe it to be "a sort of 'global policy' based on the universality of democratic principles" (Bignante, Dansero, and Scarpocchi 2007, 7). Löwenheim, commenting on the tendency among international actors (donors, international financial institutions [IFIs], INGOs) to rate and rank performances and governance capacities of states, contends that these "governance indicators establish a discursive field of state legitimacy and normalcy and 'responsibilises' states: constructs them as ethical actors that are capable of correct and responsible choices and policies" as if their context didn't matter. This is a convenient practice because it "enables the powerful to disregard or diminish their own responsibility for various global injustices and inequalities" (2008, 255, 257).

Calling for good governance can serve many purposes. In the worst case it simply means Westernization, that is, an expression of cultural imperialism. As underlined by Fukuyama, "At issue is whether the institutions and values of the liberal West are indeed universal, or whether they represent . . . merely the outgrowth of cultural habits of a certain part of the northern European world" (2004, 3). It may be worth remembering "Europe could develop its various forms of democracy only after having reached a relatively high level of economic development" (Dumont 1964, 203). The same goes for the so-called miracle economies in east Asia, where calls for democracy and transparency came after the economic break-through, that is, when the new socioeconomic system was firmly established, allowing no escape but requiring new modes of interaction.

Calls for good governance also serve the self-interests of the aid industry. Europe has long been plagued by "aid fatigue" and in the 1990s development aid "fell to [its] lowest ever level" (Earthscan 1997, 3). At the same time, "foreign aid [was] losing its domestic political constituency in the USA. Notions of good government, including democracy and civil rights, do however strike a positive chord with parts of the American electorate. The good government agenda thus reflects in part an attempt to recreate a domestic political base for foreign aid" (Moore 2006, 51). Calls for good governance likewise serve to legitimate much NGO activity, especially since NGOs (or civil society) are seen as watchdogs, safeguarding governments' good behavior. But, as a universal receipt for development, good governance totally disregards the context in which policies are to be implemented.

Development strategies cannot be freely chosen (Hettne 1971). Neither can modes of governance. The freedom of governments to choose development strategy or mode of governance will always be constrained by geopolitical imperatives, prevailing social structures, institutions, and the distribution of power. It follows that what may count as good government in one context may be bad government in another. If Otto von Bismarck's statement that politics is the art of the possible is correct, then much of contemporary demands for good governance is naive and, possibly, undermines development.

Governance in sub-Saharan Africa is frequently labeled neopatrimonial and undemocratic and sometimes despotic, repressive, and predatory. More often than not, focus is on the "misbehavior" of governments (see, for example, Bayart, Ellis, and Hibou 1999; Tangri 1999; Mbeki 2005; Calderisi 2006). However, as Beckman points out: "Too much current writing on the

African state substitutes tales of corruption and mismanagement for an analysis of social forces and processes" (1988, 26), which could explain such behavior. To begin with, in most of sub-Saharan Africa the state is an alien entity, initially imposed by colonial powers in order to control and exploit—but seldom to develop—Africa. Because the state did not evolve as a consequence of internal processes, it had—and still has—a very weak social base. It is still not structurally rooted in the society it is supposed to govern and commonly only controls part of the national territory, often indirectly so. Governments do not represent a corporate class whose development purpose they could be instrumental in fulfilling (Hydén 1995). The "uncaptured" and still fairly subsistence-oriented smallholder peasants—still the majority of Africans—own their means of production and enjoy a comparatively high degree of independence from government or "higher" social classes. The state in Africa, therefore, has limited ability to influence what goes on locally. In many cases it has not been able to monopolize the use of power. Instead, it "sits suspended in 'mid-air' over society and is not an integral mechanism of the day-to-day productive activities of society" (Hydén 1983, 6).

Neo-patrimonialism is a term often used to characterize African governance. This concept is commonly understood to mean a system of clientelism (Lockwood 2005). However, it is not a traditional system or mode of governance but a quasi-modern hybrid—or, rather, transitory—regime "in which relationships of a broadly patrimonial type pervade a political and administrative system, which is formally constructed on rational-legal lines" (Clapham 1985, 48). A neo-patrimonial regime consists of, "on the one hand, an exterior modern, formal rational-legal state, and, on the other hand, a patronage system or spoils network in which a highly centralised administration obtains political support by pilfering the state resources to distribute jobs, rent-seeking opportunities, and resources through personalised relationships to clients" (deGrassi 2005, 12). Although neo-patrimonialism has misleadingly been characterized as "criminal" (see, for example, Bayart, Ellis, and Hibou 1999), it seems fairer—and more correct—to regard such traits as transitory, surfacing when the state is caught between two systems' rationalities without fully belonging to either of them.

Nation building is still an unfinished project in most of Africa. In this situation the urge to roll back the state was perhaps not the best policy. The African state is not as powerful, and perhaps also not as dysfunctional, as is often believed. But it serves a different purpose than commonly assumed. And it has to a not insignificant degree been captured by the "economy of affection." The influence of the economy of affection "stretches right from the grass-roots to the apex of society" and it "imposes social obligations [such as tribalism and nepotism] on individuals that limit their interest and capacity to support public concerns outside their community" (Hydén 1983, 9, 17). In order to gain legitimacy and increase their sphere of influence, African governments have resorted to patronage and cooptation of local chiefs into clientelist structures.

Indirect rule is still a common feature in sub-Saharan Africa. This may be rational if the primary objective is to acquire or remain in power, but from a developmental point of view it has been disastrous. Instead of imposing its hegemony in the national territory, African governments have bought their way into the countryside. This was (is) not done without tradeoffs, and the state has become a target in factional struggles and a resource to be tapped by primordial groups in a game where "winner takes all" (Hydén 1983, 1995). Hence, "rather than being guided by a forward-looking purpose and executing corporate power, African states—permeated by neo-patrimonial rule and the informalization and personalization of power—were typically looted by their servants in order to honour obligations towards sub-national communities such as tribe and kinship" (Holmén 2005, 90).

If the above interpretation holds, it turns much established wisdom upside-down. It has far-reaching implications for what should be counted as rational or good behavior. Primarily, it calls for precaution when it comes to labeling behavior as corrupt and for more down-to-earth expectations about who can do what, when, and where.[7] This has implications not only for the available room for maneuvering of governments but also for organizations.

Development from below and, in particular, local organization building for development appears to be considerably more complex than what is often assumed. Primarily, it seems to be a much slower and contingent process than many supporters are willing to accept. Important questions are, for example, whether African communities constitute steppingstones or stumbling blocks in a development process that, in whichever case, needs to become more indigenously owned. Can modern organizations be built on these proto-organizations, or do they need to find new foundations? Is external engagement in organization building a blessing or a curse? In order to grasp the problematic concerning the possibilities for local self-organization for development a little better, we need to theorize under which circumstances it may be likely to occur and then check whether our assumptions are corroborated or not.

Organization Building from Below— When, Where, and Why?

When, where, and under what circumstances do local development organizations evolve "spontaneously" from below? This seems pretty much to be a "black box" in development research. Literature is divided on the topic, and more research seems to be needed. Two opposing viewpoints—the market-induced organizational development theory and the remoteness as trigger of organizational development theory—form the basis for the discussion below.

Market-induced Organizational Innovation

Laidlaw, among others, underlines that "traditional and informal kinds of cooperation are not at all the same as formal cooperation . . . and the latter does not necessarily evolve from the former" (1978, 71). As the World Bank points out:

> In all rural societies, traditional organizations have an inward-oriented or "bonding" function to facilitate collective actions that mitigate against the uncertainties of production, and regulate relationships within the group. In contrast, formal producer organizations perform a "bridging" function to organize relationships between the group and the outside world. In the context of [Africa], rural producer

organizations typically include elements of both traditional and formal organizations. . . . Inclusion is characteristic in traditional groupings, where everyone is inherently a member, but formal producer organizations tend to be more exclusive. (2004, 1–2)

Much writing about LOs in Africa is not very clear on this distinction between bonding and bridging functions. It should come as no surprise, therefore that although some reports give the impression that contemporary Africa is flooded with rural grassroots organizations, local *development* organizations are reportedly few in Africa (see, for example, Wellard and Copestake 1993; Holmén and Jirström 1996; Larsson 2005). This could be a misinterpretation, however, since many LOs are likely to be less formal and, hence, unregistered. The (apparent) absence of LOs has often been explained as a consequence of lack of capitalism and weak market penetration in sub-Saharan Africa. "Modern" (bridging) organizations, for example, cooperatives—that is, organizations founded to safeguard their members' (economic) self-interest—are often considered to depend on economic diversification, markets and (emerging) class relations to evolve (Hydén 1970; Harvey et al. 1979; Braverman et al. 1991; Gyllström 1991).

For most of the post-independence period African markets have been neglected or suppressed (Bates 1981; Lipton 1989; Holmén 2005), and class has been deemed an inappropriate variable to characterize African societies (Clapham 1985; Mafeje 2003). Instead, family, kin, and patrimonial structures dominate the scene. Hence, the preconditions for "modern" or at least unconventional organizations to evolve may not have been present for most of the independence period—at least not to any significant degree. As suggested above, this may well have changed during recent decades.

Although markets have been slow to develop in the aftermath of SAP, they do develop, albeit unevenly. The market itself is a formidable pressure for change, which induces people to organize in nontraditional ways. With markets come new goods, information, and opportunities, as well as competition and unfamiliar challenges to established ways of doing things. In order to learn about and influence the emerging new rules of the game, to gather and disseminate information, to gain bargaining power in regard to private traders and enhance competitiveness, smallholders need to pool resources. As explained by Ruttan and Hayami, in a market economy

> farmers are induced by shifts in relative prices to search for technical alternatives that save the increasingly scarce factors of production. They press the public research institutions to develop new technology and demand that agricultural supply firms supply modern technical inputs that substitute for the more scarce factors. . . . The dialectic interaction among farmers and research scientists and administrators is likely to be most effective when farmers are organized into politically effective local and regional farm "bureaus" or farmers' associations. (1998, 169)

This, however, presupposes a fairly advanced market economy. In Africa, such are only found near big cities and in more densely populated areas where markets are larger and more diversified and communication infrastructure comparatively well developed. Since independence, a bimodal agrarian structure has evolved in Africa with a small group of large and well-connected commercial farmers at one end of the spectrum and a mass of semi-subsistence-oriented smallholders at the other (Lipton 1989; Larsson 2005). The former tend to be more common in high-potential areas, and the latter, while numerous everywhere, dominate in less well-endowed environments. The impact of the market as an inducing force is, therefore, quite unevenly distributed, both in space and socially. More or less modern organizations, it can be hypothesized, are thus likely first to evolve in already relatively well-endowed, high-potential areas and, perhaps, among more well-to-do farmers.

Everyone, therefore, does not enjoy the same possibilities to exploit the new opportunities offered by development. This is one reason why many put their faith in the poor's and the smallholders' abilities to make use of organizations. The poor, however, have limited resources to pool, are more vulnerable, and "tend to look upwards rather than sideways for cooperation" (Verhagen 1984, 177; see also Yaro 2006). Hence, as for example Scott (1985) observed in Asia, it is in the poor's interest to preserve patron-client structures, at least during the early phases of a transformation process (Holmén 1990). At the same time, it is likely that the few capitalist farmers and the patrons (often the same persons) will be the first to seize the new opportunities (because they can afford to take risks and they also tend to be the first to obtain information about new possibilities). In this situation the relatively wealthy and well connected find more profitable opportunities in the emerging new economy, tend to fail to fulfill their roles as patrons, and the old social fabric crackles (Verhagen 1984; Arn 1988; Holmén 1990, 1991). These emerging capitalists may or may not establish their own class-based organizations (locally they may be too few to organize and/or these "entrepreneurs" may value being self-made and independent too much to do so). But this "social failure" also spreads incentives to organize to the less advantaged groups and social strata.

It is thus not only an emerging, market-oriented peasant class that is likely to form more or less "modern" organizations when market penetration and other pressures for change accumulate. Other groups also will be forced, albeit with some delay, to organize in nontraditional ways, perhaps in their own organizations. But these pressures to organize are not evenly distributed geographically. Following Boserup (1965), the pressure to intensify agriculture first manifests itself where population densities increase most (relative to the land's supportive capacity). Markets, likewise, tend to evolve first near major towns and in more densely populated areas where land scarcity is manifest, where there are more customers within short range, where the economy is more diversified than in more remote and sparsely populated areas, where it is more costly to invest in transport and communication infrastructures, and where private traders may not find it worthwhile to establish business.

Remoteness as Trigger for Organizational Innovation

Accessibility and market inducement as triggers for organizational innovation stand, however, in stark contrast to Esman and Uphoff's finding that "a number of environmental conditions generally thought to be undesirable [difficult topography, poor resource endowment, lack of physical infrastructure] correlate with better LO performance" and that "LOs facing difficult physical circumstances can . . . perform as well on the average as local organizations more benignly located" (1988, 110; see also Krishna, Uphoff, and Esman 1997). This is also opined by Lyon, who suggests that "group activities in remote rural areas can contribute to community development and reduce poverty through allowing members to have greater control of their own livelihoods" (2003, 323). Also, Luzzati proposes that it is in the less favored areas, "where the presence of poor people is greater, [that] new organizations, which can be called associations or cooperatives (formal or informal) are being created." What is happening, he states, "is a genuine and culturally appropriate effort of deprived populations to find a way out of their difficult situation; . . . the basic aim of these organizations is to counteract the rent seeking and exploitative behaviour of traders and capitalists [to the extent that these are present in peripheral areas] or to *substitute non-existent markets*" (1999, 136–37, emphasis added).

Why difficult physical circumstances and/or remoteness should present a more favorable environment for local organizations to develop is less clear, however. Esman and Uphoff were not able to explain their observation, merely finding it "curious," but suggest that "perhaps [LOs] are spurred on by unfavourable conditions" (1988, 110). This is probably because the authors place too much emphasis on the *physical* environment. We must, however, not limit our view of environment to include only the physical endowment but rather take a holistic approach to environment and include also the presence of other features and actors. As argued above, difficulties or crises tend to be triggers of development. Different environments present different kinds of difficulties. It is well known that, for example, bureaucratic paternalism has often inhibited the development of effective popular organizations. In Africa, before SAP, some governments prohibited unauthorized meetings of more than a few people and thus effectively undermined board meetings and other gatherings in those LOs they considered competitors or potentially subversive (Holmén and Jirström 1994).

As argued by Holmén and Jirström (1994), the presence of the state, its control attempts, and so forth have been much more accentuated in more densely populated areas with high production potential and comparatively good infrastructure. In these areas state and bureaucracy have laid their heavy hands over independent organizations. However, the influence and hence effective control is and has been geographically limited. Herbst (2000) underlines that African governments often only control minor parts of the national territory, most commonly the most accessible and high potential areas. Outside these limited areas, that is, in the national peripheries, there is considerably more room for maneuvering for independent LOs and self-help associations. The statistical correlation between unfavorable physical environment and LO effectiveness observed by Esman and Uphoff may thus be a trompe l'oeil.

To conclude this discussion, not only those environments commonly considered favorable but also those assumed to be difficult may constitute conducive breeding grounds for LOs. In the first case, it is market development, new opportunities, and new rules of the game that induce people to organize to take advantage of new possibilities. In the latter case (for example, under pressure from population growth and/or environmental degradation), if the pressure for change is sufficiently strong, it is the absence of the evil eye of the state that gives local initiatives room to maneuver. It can also be that where governments are more benign (or disinterested), the scarcity and/or ineffectiveness of government projects in remote areas forces people to organize to help themselves, especially in times of impoverishment. This would also confirm the experience that self-help is only taken as a last resort (see, for example, Münkner 1983).

Environment and LO Orientation

In line with this reasoning, Esman and Uphoff suggest that "it would probably be more accurate to regard environments as settings than as influences" since "influences from the environment are not very strong or likely in themselves to present major barriers to LO performance" (1988, 126, 136). But we cannot totally disregard the influence of environments or context. Even if performance or effectiveness, as Esman and Uphoff conclude, does not appear to be very different among LOs operating in different environments, the structures and undertakings of LOs are likely to differ, perhaps greatly, because these environments present different opportunities and constraints. As this study shows, environment exerts a strong influence on organizations' orientation, performance, and effectiveness. Apparently, Esman and

Uphoff do not distinguish between bonding and bridging objectives among the LOs they studied. Since these are strongly associated with environment, they also miss restrictions and options present in different contexts.

Economic theory sees economic self-interest as the driving force behind development and places much hope on the entrepreneur as initiator and carrier of development. Gyllström proposes that "individual economic self-interest is a decisive cross-cultural force in social reproduction processes [and that] efforts aimed at initiating a self-sustained process of [local development] essentially have to build on this recognition" (1991, 12; see also Bates 1981). No doubt, entrepreneurs are often important. It is, however, equally important to recognize the limitations of such theorization. All societies have institutions (custom, tradition, social-control mechanisms) that define what can be done and how, and what cannot. Schumpeter points out that going beyond these restrictions always has a price—and more so in small communities where people are closer to one another and social control is comparatively strong. "Every step outside the boundaries of routine has difficulties and [invokes] . . . the reaction of the social environment against one who wishes to do something new" (Schumpeter 1951, 84ff.). Hence, the successful entrepreneur must be a strong-headed and rather egoistic type of personality.

Bayart, Ellis, and Hibou's (1999) above-mentioned assertion that African societies are characterized by "frenetic individualism" leads to the hypothesis that self-seekers and entrepreneurs are likely to meet with few obstacles in contemporary Africa. The validity of such an assumption must, however, be cast in doubt. There is considerable evidence pointing in the opposite direction. Traditionally, African societies have developed strong institutions militating against individual accumulation of wealth and capital. Platteau underlines that tribal societies have a strong tendency to "opt for radical measures of redistributive taxation, which are potentially hostile to economic change" (2000, 189). Institutions governing people's access to land is a case in point. African land-tenure systems are often mistakenly called communal, which implies that every individual can lay claim to a piece of land or be granted access at will. In most cases it is the other way around. Social organization in sub-Saharan Africa, as pointed out by Mafeje, is based on the principle of lineages or descent groups. Legally, property is held by and transmitted through them. "In sub-Saharan Africa the [land] holder could be any of several things—the territorial authority *(dominium eminens)*, the clan, the lineage, the household or production unit—but never the individual" (Mafeje 2003, 2).

Such arrangements give security to the members of groups. However, they also militate against socially unsanctioned transfers, which "inevitably lead to conflict, if not actual violence" (Mafeje 2003, 2). Pre-modern agrarian societies are also highly vulnerable to climatic and environmental vagaries and therefore institutionalize a wide range of risk-egalitarian and risk-pooling arrangements including wealth-sharing mechanisms and other forms of enforced reciprocity (such as land lending, labor-exchange gangs). "If one individual is lucky enough to have an excess of food this day or this week, then it makes sense for him to share with another individual who is in deficit in the expectation that the latter will be similarly generous when he is lucky in the future" (Mafeje 2003, 192). Sharing practices are thus often seen as a mutual insurance system (see, for example, Hårsmar 2006). There is nothing romantic about this.

"In many African rural communities social differentiation is perceived as a threat to the traditional social structure and to the solidarity system" and "sharing tends to go beyond the practice of mutual insurance." Redistribution "is often imposed on the better-off members, and a kin group [may take] collective action to block exit by some members, even though the group as a whole would gain from their migration" (Bernard, de Janvry, and Sadoulet 2005, 2, 5). From a social security point of view, this is understandable, but from a development perspective it is highly problematic that jealousy is frequently reported to limit people's possibilities of getting ahead (Golooba-Mutebi 2005). Conformism and group pressure are thus seen as particularly strong and inhibiting in pre-modern, agrarian societies. Dynamic individuals and would-be entrepreneurs tend to be forced to opt for distant emigration in order to set up businesses where they cannot be touched by the evil eye of their relatives and fellow villagers (Platteau 2000). At first glance this would seem to confirm Schumpeter's claim about dull village life and aversion toward novelty. However, that would be to miss the point. In localities with little or sporadic integration with the wider society, as in large parts of rural Africa, there are fewer opportunities for would-be entrepreneurs to exploit.

It has also proved to be extremely difficult to introduce "modern" types of organizations built on a different rationality in such environments. Hydén, commenting on the negative experience with inefficiency and misallocation of funds in formal cooperative organizations before SAP, writes: "Nowhere else is it more true than in cooperatives that a person who can serve his local constituency at public expense becomes a hero" (1983, 115). Huizer likewise notes: "Many aspects of this . . . 'economy of affection' are also present in modern type organizations" (1997, 2). The World Bank states: "The more the state is involved . . . the greater is the potential for corruption" (2007, 254). This is probably to miss the point. The previous bad record of state-led organizations and "pseudo-cooperatives . . . imposed from above by official donors and official development agencies or 'charity institutions'" (Huizer 1997, 2) should perhaps be blamed less on governments and top-down management styles and more on the fact that they were of external origin and therefore fair game in local communities.

In highly subsistence-oriented societies—which offer few protective mechanisms beyond family or kin group, and where wealth and status depend on size of household—group norms constrain the possibilities for breaking away in order to realize individual, economic self-interest. Those who do "can be accused of practicing witchcraft." This is no negligible inconvenience. "Those accused of witchcraft may be expelled from the community. Some may be murdered" (Golooba-Mutebi 2005, 940–41). Hospes found that "people are afraid of moving ahead because of jealousy. . . . If you are doing well, you have either 30 relatives in your yard or you are bewitched" (1999, 282–83). Bewitched, that is, by what Yaro calls "parasite households" (2006, 146; see also Hårsmar 2006).

It would be wrong, though, to explain witchcraft as a sign of aversion to change in the first place. Neither do we need to refer to the theory of the limited good, presumed to govern world views in tribal societies (see, for example, Hospes 1999; Platteau 2000). Also, in tribal societies "customs, values and norms . . . adjust as a result of economic changes" (Platteau 2000, 289). At issue is rather a fear that the (poor) family might lose important sources of labor if young men (which seems most often to be the case) break away on their own careers. This is also why most sorcerers are primarily attacking their relatives rather than outsiders (Platteau 2000; Golooba-Mutebi 2005).

It would also be easy to assume that jealousy and witchcraft accusations, which act as a brake on social differentiation, would be stronger and more widespread in remote and "backward" localities. That appears, however, not to be the case. Golooba-Mutebi found that "amongst the contexts in which witchcraft accusations appear to flourish are those where social solidarity and mutual support are *not* essential for survival" (2005, 939, emphasis added). Instead, they are more common in areas where opportunities for capital accumulation and individualistic projects are greater, that is, in more accessible and high potential areas. Although witchcraft accusations tend to be absent or less frequent in remote and "backward" areas—where Gemeinshaft relations are stronger—this merely reflects the lack of opportunities there. These observations indicate that accomplishing development from below by way of erecting (modern) local organizations might be a more complicated undertaking than often assumed. Accordingly, Hospes found it "very hard to convince [the villagers] to organize themselves into . . . groups" (1999, 284).

Be that as it may, livelihood adaptation is widespread in contemporary sub-Saharan Africa. But it is highly variegated and takes many forms and directions. Bryceson states, "SAP and market liberalization policies have triggered a widespread erosion of local peasant economies and social communities" (2002, 737). Also Yaro reports about the "erosion of the structures of the 'good old days of village Africa'" (2006, 149). Hårsmar found that "household structures are under pressure, as more and more economic activities become the realms of individuals rather than of households" (2004a, 138). In contrast, Milligan and Binns talk about an "alleged weakening of customary institutions." They find that "whilst the power and authority of customary leaders on paper has shifted to local government, in practice they remain key organs in the outplaying of customary tenure regimes" (2007, 148, 154). The situation is, therefore, unclear—or, rather, variegated. Consequently, Hårsmar observed varying degrees of "reluctance to change" and made the qualification that "the extent to which such changes have emerged varies between villages" (2004a, 138).

Bernard, de Janvry, and Sadoulet propose that "formal village organizations (VO) can be classified into market-oriented (MO) and community-oriented (CO) organizations, with the former aimed at supporting entrepreneurship and raising members' incomes while the latter are oriented at the provision of public goods for the whole community." They further suggest that "an MO's economic performance . . . is constrained in communities with strong sharing norms. . . . In some cases, the pressure to share are so high that no MO can emerge" (2005, 1). While this is likely to be the case, the location of these villages will have a bearing on the options and constraints encountered. The geographical aspects of this problematic need more consideration than they normally get, not least because they influence which interventions can be successful where.

Based on the above considerations, it can be hypothesized that we will find quite different types of LOs in the two referred to types of environment—perhaps a more externally oriented, bridging, and developmental type of LO catering more for growth oriented and individual goals in favorable areas (however, not without opposition) and a more conservationist, bonding, or communitarian variant in remote areas. If that is so, there are reasons to reconsider the usefulness of the "development from below periphery inward" development theory paradigm that has attracted so many concerned scholars, donors, and NGO activists in recent years.

At the same time, although there are signs of an ongoing—but slow and uneven—market expansion in Africa, which, if the above reasoning holds, provides a seed bed for bridging and "developmental" LOs, it could also be hypothesized that, due to lack of rural infrastructure, undeveloped markets and state withdrawal from the countryside after SAP—and therefore a subsequently enlarged periphery—the latter, bonding or "conservationist" type of rural LO would become increasingly common. Bryceson, for example, writes about villages becoming "increasingly remote" (1999, 22). If that is the case, expectations on LOs as change agents and vehicles for development may well turn out to be unrealistic or at least exaggerated. It would also have far-reaching implications for if and how donors and foreign NGOs should intervene in development in Africa.

It is not only context that matters. Based on the above reasoning it can be hypothesized that whereas cooperatives and other market-oriented organizations will primarily be of interest for a comparatively small group of well-to-do farmers, the poor majority has limited ability (and desire) to organize in unorthodox ways for a common purpose.

A third hypothesis guiding this study is that donors and INGOs, while paying lip service to empowerment and local ownership of development, in reality try to shape Africa to their own liking.

The following chapters present field observations from a large number of empirical studies and aim to shed light on the situation—and possibly to determine which process is the strongest and which type(s) of LOs are the most common in contemporary Africa. Attention is also directed at the involvement of foreign NGOs and their effects on indigenous organization building in sub-Saharan Africa. A comparison is made between Eastern and Southern Africa (henceforth ESA), on the one hand, and West Africa on the other.

In the chapters that follow organizations are grouped into three broad categories: INGO, a Northern or international support organization with projects and operations in one or several developing countries; NGO refers to a domestic intermediary development organization operating on national or sub-national levels; and LO refers to an organization that has a local or near-local (neighborhood) area of operation and that can be more or less communitarian and may be member based or not. Nevertheless, in cases where it does not obscure the presentations, and in order to give justice to the sources I have relied upon, other concepts (such as CBO, CSO, and others) will be used as well.

Part II

THE EASTERN AND SOUTHERN AFRICAN EXPERIENCE

Local organizations in Eastern and Southern Africa (ESA) are of many kinds. They have evolved in different environments and for different reasons, some spontaneously and others due to external initiatives. They thus reflect different histories and display quite varied ownership profiles, ambitions, and capabilities. They also pursue highly diverging ranges of activities, which may be more or less developmental and more or less market or community oriented—activities and orientations that further tend to change over time depending on circumstance and opportunity. They also display quite different degrees of visibility, since many belong to the informal sector and therefore tend to disappear from NGO studies as well as from public records and statistics. As pointed out by Manji and Naidoo (2006), we have only a relatively small amount of information on local organizations (LOs), especially those operating in rural areas. It is therefore a delicate matter to venture to generalize about their presence, constraints, and potential. Despite these disclaimers, local organizations are also bound to share many experiences and to have many characteristics in common.

In an effort to document such commonalities, this section is divided into two chapters and is structured as follows: In order to grasp their space to maneuver, Chapter 2 puts local and community organizations in context within a broad organizational landscape, that is, it highlights the contemporary status of cooperative organizations and investigates decentralization and the impact of local governments on the options, constraints, and performance of LOs and CBOs as development vehicles. Various forms of cooperation and joint ventures among public authorities, NGOs, restructured cooperatives, and newly formed CSOs are highlighted. Within this framework Chapter 3 focuses on the new, indigenous organizations themselves, their linkages to communities, donors, and INGOs—and how the latter affect the development and performance of LOs.

But before engaging with Africa proper, it seems useful to place organizational evolution in sub-Saharan Africa in an even broader perspective. This introductory note therefore glances through some literature on LOs of a more general kind, which includes but goes beyond Africa south of the Sahara.

Implications from Some Comparative Studies

In this section, *comparative* refers to the circumstance that comparisons, to some extent, can be made between continents and parts of continents. It does not, however, mean that comparisons can be made of performance and the like among different kinds of organizations. That comes later. For now, the objective is much more modest. By glancing through a number of more comprehensive publications on LOs' experiences, it limits itself to acquiring a rough idea of how frequently LO activities have been reported about and/or presented as good examples for others to learn from. It could be objected that the sample is too small to have any analytical value. On the other hand, I have searched widely for this kind of literature, and the fact that so few were to be found may in itself indicate that we should lower our expectations about LO activities and success stories in ESA. Apparently, there are few showcases to write about.

Krishna, Uphoff, and Esman in *Reasons for Hope* (1997) report on the evolution of eighteen successful cases of LOs in more or less close cooperation with governments and/or NGOs in developing countries. Of these, ten are from Asia, four from Latin America, and four from Africa. Among the last, one is from West Africa and the other three from ESA. Those in ESA are engaged in activities such as child nutrition (Tanzania), wildlife resource management (Zimbabwe), and water supply (Malawi). None of the LOs in ESA reported about is engaged in business-oriented activities such as farming or processing of farm products. Indicatively, communal projects are more common.

Uphoff, Esman, and Krishna in *Reasons for Success* (1998) draw experiences from thirty success stories with development from below and (assisted) LOs building from developing countries. Of these thirty cases, twelve are not mentioned in Krishna, Uphoff, and Esman's 1997 book and are taken from Asia (eight), Latin America (two), and Africa (two), respectively.

The ILO's *Rediscovering the Cooperative Advantage* (Birchall 2003) lists eleven projects that the ILO deems successful. Of these, only two are African, one each from West Africa and ESA, the latter being an urban shoe-shiners' club.

The World Bank's *Producer Organization-Donor Partnerships in Project Implementation in Africa: Risks and Precautions from a Social Perspective* (Delion 2000) only reports about LO projects that it has supported in

Africa. Of the nineteen cases mentioned, fifteen are from West Africa and only four from ESA.

From this admittedly unsystematic and impressionistic evidence it appears that not only are LOs in ESA few and far between, but they also seem to be less frequent in ESA than in West Africa. Moreover, LOs in Africa also appear to be less common than in Asia and Latin America, an assumption that is confirmed by similar observations in other and somewhat older literature (see, for example, Holmén and Jirström 1996). Also more recent literature finds NGOs and farmers' associations in Africa to be much less powerful than in other regions of the developing world (Michael 2004). Michael, however, based her judgment on findings from Tanzania and Senegal, which seems an insufficient base from which to draw conclusions about the whole region. Whereas there seems to be no shortage of urban NGOs in Zambia, Ngoma (2008) found only few engaged in agriculture. It is perhaps symptomatic that in a recent, comprehensive study of smallholders and agricultural production conducted in relatively high-potential areas and interviewing more than three thousand smallholders in some one hundred villages in nine African countries, no CBOs or local producers' organizations were found, although they were deliberately looked for (Djurfeldt et al. 2005).[1] Nevertheless, there are also other stories told, and the following two chapters aim to give a more solid ground for conclusions.

Two

The ESA Experience—Part 1

Rural NGOs try to work with the government,
whereas urban NGOs try to keep an eye on it.
—FRANK MUHEREZA, 2007

The World They're In

The objective of this chapter is to put LOs, cooperatives, and
NGOs in context. Organizations do not operate in a vacuum and,
moreover, the contexts—physical, cultural, administrative, and
so on—in which organizations find themselves are not only different, but to varying degrees they are also undergoing change.
Moreover, ESA is large—encompassing some twenty-five countries and, in 2006, being the home of almost five hundred million people. For obvious reasons the subcontinent—and the
organizations operating there—cannot be accounted for in its
entirety. Nor would it be meaningful to try to do so. Hence, the
two chapters included in this section are based on observations
and experiences primarily from a limited number of countries:
Ethiopia, Kenya, Malawi, Republic of South Africa, Rwanda, Tanzania, Uganda and Zambia. These countries—and the studies
conducted in them—are sufficiently diverse to allow a deeper
understanding of circumstances affecting organizations as well
as of the pros and cons associated with different approaches to
organization building for development. At the same time, they
also display some important commonalities, which will allow
conclusions of a more general nature.

Contemporary Status of Rural Cooperatives

Today cooperatives in ESA are a kind of NGO; that is, their liberalization from governments is varied and sometimes unstable.
At the same time, they are also part of the context in which other

49

NGOs and local associations operate (or not). Due to their particular history and the special potential and problems they encounter, they are here treated under a separate heading. In most of ESA rural cooperatives have a long history, in most cases dating back to colonial times. Their history since then has invariably been one of state control, top-down management, and for the most part, inefficiency. This inefficiency has had many causes, including excessive bureaucracy, paternalistic management attitudes, and exploitative pricing often resulting in corruption and late payments for marketed produce, but also smuggling and non-payments of debts among the peasantry. Most of all, critique has centered on the circumstance that cooperatives, besides having economic objectives, often were given a range of social, political, and welfare objectives as well. This hampered their economic effectiveness, and one conclusion was that "cooperatives with the least political and social content, being mainly concerned with straightforward economic benefits, may in the end, paradoxically, have a greater [social] impact than those that explicitly but ineffectively seek to transform society" (UNRISD 1975, 13).

This conclusion can, however, be questioned, at least to some degree. Based on the theoretical reasoning in Chapter 1, organizations tend to mirror their environment rather than to reshape it. In such areas where conditions are favorable for market-oriented organizations, it is likely that the pre-SAP type of state-supported cooperatives were hampered because their profitability was reduced by the need to take on social functions. In other areas it may well have been the case that social obligations were a precondition for these state-controlled cooperatives to gain local acceptance. The major problem, however, was that these cooperatives were often built from above according to the one-size-fits-all principle and, in one-party states, were assigned tasks that would otherwise have been the responsibility of local governments. This also made them prone to be captured by local economies of affection (Hydén 1983).

Beside the task of providing inputs, extension, and marketing services to peasants, these state-organized cooperatives offered a comparatively simple means to make the state visible in rural areas. Such political ambitions often led to perverse results from an economic and/or developmental perspective. On the one hand, weak governments, lacking the will and capacity to take the lead in development—especially in rural development—bought legitimacy and accepted both local elite capture of cooperatives and low or nonexistent loan repayments among their members/clients (Holmén 2005). On the other hand, politically well-connected villages could receive much more than they needed of scarce inputs such as seeds and fertilizers while other villages received only a fragment of their requirements (Friis-Hansen 1994).

With the introduction of SAP in the 1980s the then-prevailing cooperative systems virtually collapsed. Many organizations were liquidated, while efforts were made to reconstruct others. The World Bank is quite optimistic about the impact of SAPs on associational life in Africa and recently found that political liberalization opened opportunities for producers to become active players through organizations of their own. Contrary to before SAP—when cooperatives had often been assigned a multitude of non-business objectives—it has since frequently been underlined that cooperatives are actually "business organizations" (Birchall 2003, 69) and "private sector entities" (ICA 2003, 5). This change in orientation is not clear-cut, however. For one thing, opportunities are not evenly spread, either geographically or socially. And voices are still aired that cooperatives should resume a broader set of roles than "just" safeguarding their members' economic interests. At a cooperative workshop in Dar es Salaam in 2003 it was suggested that "cooperatives should increasingly assume social responsibility for community (including nonmembers) in terms of development and provision of basic services as a means of providing 'safety nets' for the poor" (ILO/ICA 2003, 5). With such diverging views about the purpose of cooperation, it is no surprise that in some cases restructuring came about only after intense conflicts between governments, "rebel groups," and new leaderships (Otim 2003; IFAP 2005).

Since about 1990, cooperative structures all over Africa have officially been liberated from government patronage, and today they mostly constitute (rather) independent organizations. In reconstructed cooperative organizations it has often been difficult for staff and management to function for new purposes and with new rules of the game. In the 1990s officials were found not to know what to do with their newly won autonomy and their performances were frequently reported to be "weak" or "shaky" (see Holmén and Jirström 1999; Isinika et al. 2005). Many cooperatives still suffer from a "dependency syndrome" that delays their adoption of a fully commercial orientation (COPAC 2000). Financial starvation added to the difficulties. With the "de-officialization" of cooperatives came a "collapse of government support to the co-operative sector in most countries" (ICA 2003, 4) and "several donors . . . found it more effective to assist self-help organizations other than co-operatives" (Braverman et al. 1991, 35).

For such reasons, allegedly because "cooperative" has acquired a bad reputation, but more likely because at present cooperatives only rarely provide subsidized inputs, the number of members has diminished now that membership has become voluntary.[2] Figures about the present size of the cooperative sector are inconsistent. This is so in part because cooperatives are sometimes promoted under different labels (such as farmers' organizations or common-interest organizations), and then often in competition with restructured formal cooperatives, and in part because some primary societies are dormant or moribund but nevertheless reported about. In 2003 the ILO/ICA reported that membership was four million in Ethiopia, almost five million in Kenya and that in Lesotho 42 percent of the population were members of cooperatives. With the possible exception of Ethiopia, these figures seem highly inflated and of dubious reliability. Most likely they contain double registrations and also include urban societies.

For the rural cooperatives, sources give much lower numbers. In Kenya in 1983, just before SAP, membership in agricultural service cooperatives reached 945,000 (Gyllström 1991) but in "farmers' organizations" was down to 23,000 in 2002 (Odhiambo 2003). This in itself is not a problem, because it seems reasonable to assume that those who now join cooperatives or remain members do so because they have a genuine interest in strengthening and developing these organizations. Also, whereas membership in old cooperatives has declined, other self-help organizations are expanding their activities. In Kenya, for example, whereas "cooperatives are dissolving" (COPAC 2000), "the number of self-help organizations is high" (BTI 2006i, 8). In Tanzania "groups involved in village trading . . . grew from 350 in 1982 to 1300 in 1992" (Cracknell 1995). Available figures on local cooperatives vary greatly between countries, partly due to differences in definition; in Malawi, Mloza-Banda et al. (2003) reported twenty cooperatives comprising 10,900 farmer clubs, whereas Kenyan coops numbered 212 in the same year (Odhiambo 2003) and primary farmers' cooperatives were reportedly 3,800 in Ethiopia (RELMA 2003). In Uganda "there are some difficulties in establishing how many active cooperative societies there are" (Flygare 2006).

A regional cooperative workshop lists the main functions of the new cooperatives:

- Lobby, negotiate and push agendas of the importance of membership
- Facilitate or provide linkages to governments, donors and the private sector
- Provide relevant information on policies, markets, existing or potential opportunities, etc.
- Provide market information and effective marketing of farm produce
- Assist farmers to participate in deciding their destiny. (RELMA 2003, 1)

RELMA is not clear about it, but if this list is read as an order of priority, there is reason for concern. Marketing, market integration, and empowerment of peasants appear to have low priority, whereas more concern is directed at the top end of the organizational structure, that is, lobbying and providing linkages to governments.[3] If this is the correct interpretation, it indicates that there is still an aspiration to build cooperative structures from above. It also shows that the newborn cooperative organizations in ESA still find it difficult—and perhaps lack the confidence—to stand on their own legs. On the other hand, they have not always been empowered to do so. It is not only the case that official support to cooperatives collapsed with liberalization, but "undue political influence has also hindered the formation and operation of farmers' organizations" (RELMA 2003). On many occasions farmers' organizations in ESA do not yet seem to operate in an enabling environment.

In Ethiopia the situation is a bit ambiguous. Most cooperatives were created during the military government era and constituted an extension of the government's political machinery. With the new government a reorientation from policy executer to voluntariness and market orientation began. In 1998 the proclamation on cooperatives emphasized their voluntary character. This has led some authors to proclaim unlimited success. Assefa thus states: "Ethiopia serves as an excellent example to other countries that socialist cooperative societies designed to serve solely the interests of the government can be successfully rehabilitated and revitalized as market-oriented and private business organizations" (2005, 4). This might be a premature conclusion, however, and is likely to reflect donor (USAID) wishes more than Ethiopian reality. Mulat and Teketel found that, although the cooperatives are being reorganized, the present government is "unwilling to tolerate independent unions or associations" (2003, 29). This seems to reflect the government's ambivalence toward administrative decentralization, which, despite a discourse of popular participation and empowerment, remains "essentially top-down, authoritarian, coercive and arbitrary in nature" (Amha, Adebe, and Demeke 2008a, 15). Vaughan and Tronvoll explain this ambivalence not by referring to the State's selfishness or corrupt nature but by stressing that "the change can be expected to have a convulsive effect on local development processes, either galvanizing them into new life, or potentially effecting a paralysis" (2003, 93).

This is not to deny that the Ethiopian government is moving in the proclaimed direction, but the process is slower and more cumbersome than sometimes assumed. The five-year development plan (2006–10) aims to "provide services to 70% of the population through the presence of at least one cooperative in each Kebele [district] by the end of 2010" (Amha, Abebe, and Deneke 2008b, 24). While this is an ambitious target, in 2005 cooperatives existed in only 35 percent of the districts, mostly in accessible areas, and served only 9 percent of the farmers with poorer households less likely to participate in cooperatives (ibid.).

In Rwanda, where in 2002 some 300,000 peasants were organized in 250 local cooperatives, rather than setting their own agenda they "usually rally around specific crops when government identifies such crops as a priority" (Sebastian 2003). In Uganda, the president urged the farmers' associations to form an umbrella organization with which he could negotiate (Otim 2003). Not surprisingly, one of the reported strengths of the Ugandan cooperatives is that they enjoy strong support from the government (ILO/ICA 2003). This may be a double-edged sword, however.

Uganda's decentralization policy is commonly considered "one of the most important agriculture-related initiatives undertaken" (Diaz 2003, 3). The country's Plan for Modernisation of Agriculture presented in the year 2000, emphasizes capacity building for "private sector institutions, commodity associations, farmer organizations and co-operatives" (ibid., 52). According to Diaz, "Cooperatives have become one of the major participants in factor and product markets in rural areas, reaching most of the villages" (ibid., 8). In contrast with Otim's statement above, Diaz further claims that the National Agricultural Advisory Service (NAADS) has "privileged the strengthening of organizational and participatory capacities at local level, giving a lesser priority to national-coverage producers' organizations, with the argument that their links with base communities are rather weak" (ibid.).

The Ugandan government's contemporary policy of cooperative rehabilitation is interesting for many reason, not least because it illustrates the "cooperative dilemma" facing many governments and recently liberated cooperative organizations in the region.[4]

The old cooperative system (it would not be correct to call it a movement) of agricultural cooperatives met with the same adversities as so many other cooperative organizations in ESA have done: political control, overloading with non-economic tasks, top-down management, and inefficiency. The old cooperatives did not pay much attention to their customers and the market; instead, they lobbied the government for different kinds of concessions. These were often denied because many politicians feared an autonomous peasant movement. Under this "regime" the cooperatives didn't fare well, and the SAP-induced economic cutbacks further undermined the cooperatives, which had more or less collapsed by the beginning of the 1990s, when most of the primary societies were dormant. The new political direction under President Museveni emphasizes market reforms and development of the private sector. Under this paradigm small-holder agriculture must become more productive and thereby function as an engine for the whole economy. Hence, a policy for strengthening the role of cooperatives has been launched, but this time the government's strategy is to let cooperatives function as private business enterprises. A possible indication that this policy is successful is the recent strong growth in the number of savings and credit cooperatives (SACCOs).

Apparently, the new role of cooperatives for national development will be as great as such roles were in the 1970s (in theory at least). The political drive to revive the cooperatives was presented in 2002 with the report "Building a Uganda Middle Class to Generate Wealth through the Cooperative Approach," and the official hope is that farmers' cooperatives will link small-scale or subsistence farmers to markets. The minister of finance, who took office in 2005, has strongly emphasized what he calls the "cooperative society model" and has called for "the formation of cooperative societies in every parish in Uganda." The Uganda Cooperative Alliance represents the entire cooperative movement. It has a mandate to advise the government on issues concerning cooperatives, and it has been invited as a stakeholder in the process of initiating and implementing the Plan for Modernisation of Agriculture (PMA).

This is an interesting initiative, not least because the NAADS is aware that it may not be so easy to get people to organize themselves in groups or cooperatives, and that the enthusiasm for entering into cooperatives may vary in different parts of the country—not because people "understand" the need for organizing differently, but because in different milieus people perceive the need to organize differently. This indicates that the contemporary national agricultural administration might be more sensitive to management and initiatives from below.

However, there are also reasons to be worried. Despite the strong emphasis on market orientation, and the need to strengthen financial services and farmers' organizations, there are indications that control might still be high on the government's agenda. After decades of civil strife Uganda is again in the midst of a delicate process of nation building. President Museveni has opted for a populist strategy where until 2005 political parties were not allowed and everyone was assumed to be part of the same revolutionary "movement." Seen in this light, it is revealing that the principal secretary to the vice president in 2003 declared: Cooperatives are "a critical entity for organizing all these people and making a critical mass. . . . *You cannot . . . transform these people individually, you need them to be organized"* (quoted in Flygare 2006, 69, emphasis added). Even more telling is a declaration in the same year by the minister of tourism, trade, and industry that "the co-operative movement has the capacity to *deliver Government programs"* (ibid., 73, emphasis added). This may explain why, at the sub-national level, "in some districts the political leadership is looking at the farmers' organizations as rival institutions" (ibid., 65). It remains to be seen whether Uganda's effort toward cooperative revival represents something new or will turn out to be a late variant of state-run cooperatives resembling those common in the 1960s and 1970s.

Leaving Uganda and returning to the regional level, it is clear that even though cooperatives have been officially liberated and restructured all over the region, the extent of de-linking is sometimes less than declared; at least some governments still appear to have difficulties "letting go" of cooperatives as tools for central policy. In Zambia, for example, it has been found that a major weakness is that cooperatives are still "government-led rather than member driven" (ILO/ICA 2003, 13; see also *Times of Zambia* 2005). To the extent that governments remain suspicious of independent organizations, it is understandable if cooperatives and farmers' organizations devote a lot of effort to negotiating with and lobbying governments. But this also results in a comparatively large amount of energy being directed at the top end of the cooperative structures, that is, on establishing apex organizations, while there is a risk that the important work on the ground directly with and by members might be neglected.

It has been found that generally after SAP "agricultural cooperatives in many countries of the region are not performing well. A considerable proportion of their market share has been lost to private traders" (ICA 2000b, 3). That was to be expected, since many cooperative organizations lost their previous monopolies on trade in agricultural inputs and produce. However, to refer current problems solely to loss of market shares serves to hide other, and perhaps more severe, weaknesses of restructured cooperatives in the region. A report investigating the "health" of cooperatives in eight countries in ESA lists a range of other problems currently hampering their performance.[5] Generally they suffer from lack of financial resources, shortages of experienced and trained manpower, lack of management skills and entrepreneurship, and lack of or inadequate training for members, leaders, and employees (ILO/ICA 2003).

Consequently, in Zambia after liberalization, for example, cooperatives have been virtually incapable of competing with private merchants in the maize trade (Cracknell 1995). In other cases activities are maintained but on a much reduced scale. In Tanzania primary cooperative societies for cashew nuts and cotton are still active on a limited scale, whereas in both cases unions have been crippled. In 2000 cashew cooperatives reached some 280,000 peasant families but featured primarily as agents for merchants. Recently, some local cooperatives—especially those in easily accessible areas—have started to accumulate funds of their own to buy and distribute inputs. Also, in some districts small-scale processing groups of five to twenty members have been organized. Activities, however, are mostly small scale, with small amounts sold and narrow profit margins. There is a need to increase production capacity, to improve quality, and to learn marketing techniques (ICA 2000a). Cotton cooperatives, likewise, face financial constraints at the local level, and their supply of inputs is limited. Member participation is very low, and credit provision to members has been canceled because those indebted were reported to sell their produce to private traders in order to avoid debt repayments (ICA 2000b).

Rural banks are virtually nonexistent in ESA, and when they exist the interest rates are so high that they are prohibitive for smallholder peasants (Holmén 2005). To compensate for this, SACCOs have been established. Their present number is unknown, but some years ago there were reportedly seventy in Malawi (ILO/ICA 2003), about one hundred in Kenya (ICA 1998), and some four hundred in Tanzania (ICA 2000c). Also, here geography matters since almost all SACCOs were situated in the more affluent and favorable areas (ICA 1998; 2000c). In Tanzania, they provided only saving, they had no marketing strategy, their technical capacity was failing, and they did not reinvest member savings in nonfinancial business (ICA 2000c). The picture in Kenyan SACCOs was somewhat different. While much of the rest of the cooperatives reportedly were dissolving, the most rapid increase in cooperative development was the formation of SACCOs (COPAC 2000). Having originally served only small farmers, a trend was observed toward a more diversified membership by extension of services to small and micro-entrepreneurs in the off-farm sector. More recently, a new type of SACCO is emerging, one which is community based rather than crop based with membership drawn from a broad range of occupations.[6] While this could be interpreted as a sign of positive development and economic diversification, that could be an unwarranted conclusion. In Kenya, SACCO lending is "increasingly directed to welfare aims and cash-flow management. . . . Lending for investment appears to have diminished" (ICA 1998, 8).

Many local cooperatives are small and dispersed and lack resources, information, and management skills (Mloza-Banda et al. 2003). They therefore could benefit from networking and mutual learning. However, so far networking has been poorly developed (ILO/ICA 2003; RELMA 2003). To develop networking seems crucial because whereas markets in most areas remain poorly developed, "the real problem may not necessarily be the absence of markets, but rather the flow of information on market opportunities" (ICA 2003, 26). As a remedy, agricultural commodity exchanges have been established in, for example, Zimbabwe, Zambia, South Africa, Kenya, and Uganda (ICA 2003), and recently also in Ethiopia (Kurata 2008). The purposes of these commodity exchanges, which work hand in hand with cooperatives, are to facilitate trade; to serve as a source of marketing service, information, and intelligence; and to function as a meeting place for peasants and traders. The rate of uptake is still low, and more efforts need to be directed toward building trust, improving communication and quality-control measures, and developing infrastructure for information dissemination (ICA 2003). Nevertheless, even if the process is both slow and uneven, it appears to be under way.

There are other encouraging stories told about cooperative restructuring. Hopkins, Neven, and Reardon (2005) show how an informal group of smallholder commercial farmers in the Lusaka province of Zambia succeeded in becoming a fresh produce supplier to a major exporting firm and in the process transformed itself from being a part in an outgrower scheme into an independent, formal union of cooperatives. In 1999 one of Zambia's largest fresh fruit and vegetable exporters initiated the outgrower scheme in order to increase production of snap peas and baby corn for export. Ten cooperatives within a fifty kilometer radius from Lusaka, comprising about 250 farmers, were selected as suitable smallholder organizations to be included in the scheme. Over the first four years of operation the relationship between the peasants and the company soured (the peasants complained over unfair pricing and pack rates), and in 2004 the company went out of business. Just before that event, the peasants formed the Lubulima Agriculture and Commercial Cooperative Union (LACCU), which since then has successfully built business relations with two major input suppliers, sought out replacement markets (both domestic and export), and in 2005, was developing future expansion plans. In the same year the executive committee stated that the organization's production capacity comprised approximately five hundred trained farmers (although not all were active participants). It was estimated that the average income from marketed produce had increased tenfold since the initiation of the scheme, with the major improvement coming after restructuring (ibid.). In 2006 LACCU achieved EurepGAP certification, which is necessary to reach European export markets, but applies it to all its produce in order to attract other buyers (Graffham 2007; New Agriculturalist 2006). Efforts are also being made to spread the Zambian system of farmer-owned horticulture-exporting coops to Uganda, which has a "less well developed export sector and institutional framework" (DFID 2005, 14).

In Kenya, the National Federation of Agricultural Producers (KENFAP) was formed in 2002 when the Kenya National Farmers' Union was merged with various national agricultural commodity associations. As elsewhere in Africa, Kenyan peasants (and cooperatives) faced mounting difficulties after implementation of SAP—no private sector to replace a retreating government and collapsing extension services. KENFAP members, who had nowhere else to turn, demanded that the federation offer extension services. KENFAP, however, did not have the resources necessary to engage extension staff and therefore, with help from the FAO, adopted the latter's farmer schools concept, which means that members themselves have to function as trainers and leaders in this pursuit. In other words, what is being practiced is farmer-to-farmer extension. Reportedly, this has proved successful and "some schools have become full fledged community groups" engaging not only in extension but able to "influence the market and do collective bargaining . . . achieving the right quantity to allow for collection by the export companies" (IFAP 2005).

Restructuring and rebuilding cooperative systems in ESA after SAP has been a slow and difficult process. Still, these initiatives show that some cooperatives find new ways and do not wait to be dragged along. Instead, while emerging markets induce peasants to organize, cooperatives can fill important roles in the development and integration of these markets. At the same time, there still appears to be uncertainty about whether cooperatives should pursue "business" or "community" objectives. Meanwhile, the impression is that reconstructed cooperatives tend to cater primarily to a small and better-off group of farmers.

The above-mentioned success of LACCU was due to several exceptional circumstances. Whereas in Zambia many cooperatives are remotely located and tend to lie "dormant and only become active during the subsidized fertilizer distribution period" (Xinhua 2007, 1; see also Hopkins, Neven, and Reardon 2005), the preconditions for LACCU were quite different. From its initiation the organization has received assistance integral to its formation and growth from an array of government and non-government agencies. The nearness to the capital and the comparatively well-developed road and transport infrastructure are part of the explanation. Besides that, "the composition of the members is distinctly different than that which is found farther into the interior of Zambia. Specifically, there is a trend for middle/younger-aged people from the city, as well as a strong contingent of retired civil service servants, beginning to farm in the area" (ibid., 5). LACCU members are thus "more highly educated and enter farming with a broader array of experiences. For example, LACCU's executive committee is composed of a retired banker, a retired human resources manager and a certified accountant who specialized in giving credit to farmers" (ibid.).

The successful activities reported by KENFAP mention banana production for the market, fresh produce for the export market, and leafy vegetables for supermarkets (IFAP 2005). Other success stories are about marketing and processing cash crops, nuts, and soybeans in Zambia and Mozambique (NCBA 2004) and coffee in Tanzania (ADF 2005). Similarly, the (limited) success stories reported by ICA (1998; 2000a; 2000c) all concern cash crops such as cotton and cashew nuts. Apparently, although food shortages are recurring problems in SSA, the new or restructured cooperatives do not engage in production or marketing of staple food crops, which are relatively more important for the smallholder peasants. The possible exception could be Zambia where, under the Fertiliser Support Programme, purchasing of maize from the farmers was supposed to be done by cooperatives. However, whereas distribution of inputs has been somewhat problematic, marketing and post-harvest handling has faltered grossly. Due to erratic funding from the Food Reserve Agency and choked storage capacity, "huge amounts of maize have gone to waste" (Chimangeni 2007).[7]

Considering, the fact that (so far) cooperative membership has dwindled, that only a small minority of African peasants produce for the market,[8] and that the poor majority of smallholders are "stuck with maize" while the better-off minority are both more market oriented and more diversified in their production strategies (Larsson 2005), present developments seem to confirm the hypothesis that cooperatives tend to serve the needs and interests of a middle layer of agricultural producers, most of whom are in easily accessible high-potential areas.

Public Decentralization, Development, and Collective Action

During the last twenty years, and parallel to the dismantling or reorganization of formerly state-owned cooperatives, various other strategies have been followed to promote group-based initiatives at the local level in rural Africa. Among these are, for example, devolution of administrative authority and a supposedly more permissive attitude toward NGOs at the local level. Administrative decentralization and devolution of power to local governments and district assemblies are, of course, not the same as devolution of functions and responsibilities to independent associations and common interest groups outside of government. However, local and district governments are local organizations as well. Moreover, they are part of the overall framework in which other LOs find themselves, and to varying degrees they determine the conditions for common-interest groups, cooperatives, and peasant associations. Local governments often also collaborate with NGOs and common interest organizations and to varying degrees they pursue group approaches themselves. The implications of politico-administrative reform for innovative group formation is briefly touched upon in this section.

Decentralization and Development from Below

Too much effort may have been devoted to analyzing the effects of SAPs at the macro level (currency reforms, tariff reductions, and quantification of privatization of state enterprises), that is, to whether governments comply with external demands or not, while paying less attention to the effects of administrative decentralization on communities, local authorities and smallholders' group formation. A few studies are available, though, which are used here to shed additional light on the circumstances and environments in which farmers' organizations may or may not evolve in response to macro-level changes. Observations from South Africa reveal:

> Despite a legal mandate in South Africa for civil society participation in the local governance process, civil society engagement with local government is ineffective, inconsistent or lacking all together. Since the establishment of democracy in South Africa in 1994, the civil society sector, including NGOs and community-based organizations (CBOs), has found it difficult to make the transition from anti-apartheid activism of engagement and partnership with government in promoting development.
>
> Many CBOs are unaware of how local government functions and how they can influence local governance in a way that will benefit their communities. They also have little understanding of how participatory democracy complements politically legitimate and legally responsible structures. At the same time local government authorities have

shown a limited capacity to embrace and exercise the principles of participatory governance. Community participation structures (i.e. ward committees) are often absent or
ineffective. (Pact 2003, 1)

It could be assumed that South Africa, because the apartheid
system was only recently abandoned, is a special case, too atypical to illustrate a more general situation in southern and eastern
Africa. That appears, however, not to be the case. With only minor modifications the above quotation would apply to many countries and localities in the region (see, for example, Larsen 2003;
Hoon 2004; Conyers 2007; Diaz 2003). In Malawi, for example,
decentralized local governance has enhanced corruption and elite
capture of resources among the local assemblies (Tambulasi and
Kayuni 2007).

One example is the new National Irrigation Policy and Development Strategy, inaugurated in 2000, which transfers management responsibility for sixteen irrigation schemes from the state
to newly created smallholder-based water-user associations
(WUAs). Investigating this turnover, Ferguson and Mulwafu found
the new structures to be "highly ineffective, often laden by problems of corruption, poor governance and lack of direction" (2007,
216). The success of such transfer depends on the existence of
well-functioning WUAs. In Malawi there are no such strong traditions, "in part due to the discouragement of public associations during the previous [Hastings Banda] political regime"
(Goodman 2001, 13). Donor pressure not only led to this "innovation," but it also contributed to its hasty implementation—sometimes at "breakneck speed" (Ferguson and Mulwafu 2007,
221)—with disastrous results. Lines of authority are unclear to
farmers and officials alike. Although an INGO was called upon
to provide training to peasants, only 13 percent of the peasants
said they had received training on transition issues, and the WUAs
have played an insignificant role in decision making. In one investigated scheme, "most decisions . . . were made by a small
group of newly elected WUA Executive Committee members and
government scheme officials [mostly made up of] . . . members
of the previous scheme Management Committee, composed primarily of a small group of wealthier plot-holders, their relatives
and friends" (ibid., 220). Not surprisingly, Ferguson and Mulwafu

point out, the majority of the peasants did not understand that the WUA was their membership organization. Instead, most of them thought the WUA was a new name for the Scheme Management Committee. The real paradox, however, is that "the very people who have been given authority to enforce the new regulations are the ones known in the past for violating them" (ibid., 222).

Even in Uganda, where, according to Dauda decentralization has made "significant progress" (2006, 292), the process suffers from competition, rivalry, and overlap of functions between local and central governments (Kabumba 2007; Wadala 2007). Patronage has been found to be perfectly compatible with processes of political and economic liberalization, resulting inter alia in elite capture and private monopolies replacing state monopolies (see Bayart, Ellis, and Hibou 1999; Tangri 1999). This, arguably, is not necessarily—as is today frequently argued—because African political elites are particularly corrupt, but rather because "social organization in SSA is based on the principle of *lineages* or unilineal decent groups" (Mafeje 2003, 3). This, as previously argued, does not militate against domination or exploitation. In Africa, only a small minority of land users—often politicians, higher-level civil servants, or their kin—have acquired formal land titles. They are often absentee farmers and

it is common practice among them to use their land titles to secure loans to finance business ventures outside agriculture. A fair amount of their accumulation often goes into social investment within their decent groups, home community and other potential allies—not an unusual way of augmenting one's social capital in traditional societies. In the long run this guarantees them access to more resources, services and labour in the form of poor relatives and clients. In other words, they get richer not so much by direct exploitation of the land but rather through its direct control. This does not make them landlords but "big men" whom kinsmen and free peasants in African villages do not mind having in their midst. (Mafeje 2003, 9)

In fact, people at the grassroots may even prefer it. One consequence, says Crook is that "in most of the African cases, 'elite capture' of local power structures has been facilitated by the desire of ruling elites to create and sustain power bases in the countryside" (2003, 86). Hence, despite decentralization, there is "hardly any country where communities have the right to govern their own affairs" (Saltzer 2003, 5). Decentralization has therefore not altered the "expectation that elected councillors will act as patrons to bring projects to their home village, such that planning allocations are matters of horse-trading amongst elected councillors" (Crook 2003, 83). Whereas administrative reform has to some extent devolved tasks and responsibilities to local and regional councils, inter alia resulting in "predatory taxation by decentralized district councils" (Ellis and Freeman 2004a, 1; Ellis and Bahiigwa 2003; Ellis, Kutengule, and Nyasulu 2003; Isinika, Ashimogo, and Mlangwa 2005), the "revenue collected is almost wholly used on sitting allowances for councillors rather than providing locally specific services to rural citizens" (Ellis and Freeman 2004b, 19; see also Ferguson and Mulwafu 2004). In many cases reforms have not been able to alter the "persistent influence and power of traditional elites" (Kaarhus and Nyirenda 2006, 11).

Again, Uganda is a case in point. Uganda under President Museveni has often been called the darling of the donors due to its apparent embracing of liberal reforms. The reform program initiated in the 1990s was initially successful but was gradually undermined by overwhelming forces. With the legitimacy gained as liberator after the disastrous years of the Amin and Obote regimes, Museveni's new administration initially managed to ride above local power cliques. Reform initiatives, however, turned out to be short lived. Over time, they were captured by the "imperative of preserving the institutional foundations of neopatrimonial policies" (Robinson 2006, 8). In order to preserve an independent power base, the new national leadership gave power to a group of people with personal or family ties to the President, a measure that represented no less than a resurgence of patrimonial policies. The seemingly autonomous no-party movement was captured by "the dominant political constituencies within the movement . . . [which] offered few checks and balances [to] large-scale corruption by senior political figures connected to the Movement" (ibid., 33f.).

But the National Resistance Movement was not only over-whelmed from within. President Museveni, caught between the old and the new, and in dire need to secure political power once the liberation war ended, also needed to please external but lower order power centers.

> Museveni has been adept at manoeuvring within the terrain of institutional multiplicity and even turning it to his government's political advantage. Since taking office, the government has encouraged people to coalesce around various institutional arrangements associated with chiefdoms, kingdoms, NGOs and churches. However, these institutions have been subordinated to the rules of the NRM regime and the organizations co-opted by the state. . . . These organisations provide local political entrepreneurs with avenues for accessing resources from the centre and thus incorporate them into the president's patronage network. (Hesselbein, Golooba-Mutebi, and Putzel 2006, 3)

Robinson points out that this can be interpreted or explained in several ways. For example, it can be seen as a failed "response to the expectations of aid donors who increasingly demanded evidence of regime commitment to governance reforms, . . . having provided funding for many of the reform initiatives." Or it could be seen as an "outcome of a shrewd political calculus in which political self-preservation was a dominant consideration" (2006, 32). Whatever the case, whether showing the shrewdness or the weakness of the government—or the weakness of the civil society—the Ugandan experience perfectly illustrates the hazards involved when trying to impose certain "modern" administrative principles in a country based on a completely different set of institutions. It also illustrates the fallacy of rolling back the state in a situation when nation building, and hence the strengthening of the state, ought to be a priority.

This not only has implications for the degree of poverty alleviation impact of recent administrative reforms, where "local elites [often are] resistant or indifferent to pro-poor policies" (Crook 2003, 77) and use their positions to privatize public resources (Tambulasi and Kayuni 2007). Based on a large number of micro-level interviews, Ellis and Freeman found that "village leaders and councils play a significant, and often effective, role in matters of social cohesion and conflict resolution; but are rarely mentioned in a developmental capacity" (2004b, 17). Nevertheless, when villagers were asked to rank different institutions concerning their degree of helpfulness when it comes to enabling or hindering people from gaining a better living, clan chiefs and village elders ranked highest, followed by traditional community groups (such as rotating saving clubs and burial societies), and NGOs, which, in turn, were followed in descending order by unhelpful institutions such as decentralized government and other government agencies (Ellis and Bahiigwa 2003; see also Ellis, Kutengule, and Nyasulu 2003; Snyder 2008). Also KDDP found that more often than not "communities were not very satisfied with Government service provision [and that] . . . administrative and political leaders were mentioned for not being very supportive" (2004, 56). Sometimes they even sabotaged agreed undertakings. This does not sound like a particularly enabling environment. However, the picture is mixed and contradictory and other (but fewer) local authorities were found to be both active and supportive of grassroots' and community projects (ibid., 62).

NGO Participation in Poverty Reduction Strategies

With the turn of the millennium a new type of donor conditionality was introduced: the requirement that aid-receiving governments should prepare comprehensive poverty reduction strategy papers (PRSPs). The double goal of enhancing transparency and involving civil society in the process was to be achieved by holding public consultations about the strategy and involving CSOs in the preparation of the PRSPs. This kind of public–civil society cooperation is a rather new phenomenon, and the outcome of the process is, as could be expected, mixed. Driscoll and Evans assert: "The PRS approach has resulted in *unprecedented engagement by civil society organisations* in poverty policy debates" (2005, 4, emphasis added). It thus seems this conditionality has been extremely effective in leveling the playing field and providing a significantly enlarged room for policy debate and participation in Africa. It would, however, be premature to draw such a conclusion. Booth, for example, found that "PRSPs have been associated with *some* worthwhile improvements in policy processes, especially in countries that were already moving in the direction of greater results' orientation and accountability [and that] these improvements are *modest* in character even in the best cases" (2005, 3, emphasis added). How can such diverging interpretations be explained?

The immediate answer would, of course, be that it is too early to generalize. But apart from that it needs to be underlined that sub-Saharan Africa is diverse—and so are its governments and its CSOs and their relations to each other. Depending on their "nature," governments can be more or less open to civil society involvement. But this openness is also influenced by the nature of the CSOs knocking on governments' doors and by the kind of influence they strive to exert. Sometimes, it seems that African CSOs have misinterpreted the ideas of empowerment and stakeholder involvement and actually contribute to undermining an evolving but shaky democratic political system.

From Malawi, Kachele reports that "one of the ultimate goals of the Farmers Union . . . is to see an active participation of farmer Organisations in the actual process of policy formulation and not just in lobbying for policy changes" (2004, 20). For the same reason Buhere (2007) criticizes many Kenyan CSOs for not being content with trying to influence policy and instead try to take a shortcut and claim the "right" to be part of decision making without having been properly elected and having no mandate to decide for others. This critique should be seen against the background that "in Kenyan civil society there is 'a serious credibility deficit.' . . . The general perception is that NGO leaders are in it to make money or as a steppingstone to politics. The high-profile, elitist lifestyle fits many an NGO leader into the class of the so-called 'Lords of Poverty'" (James et al. 2005, 53). It is therefore quite understandable if governments sometimes are suspicious of so-called CSOs when it comes to their aspiration to influence policy. But apart from this somewhat anarchistic attitude toward political participation, many would-be representatives of the grassroots face other obstacles to involvement.

In South Africa, for example, Hassim (2004) found serious gaps between advocacy groups and their "constituencies." It is also a common experience in sub-Saharan Africa that civil society is weak (Larsen 2003; Hassim 2004; Hoon 2004; Driscoll and Evans 2005) but not only because governments are (or have been) oppressive. African CSOs often also lack the skills and resources to make independent analysis and to communicate standpoints (James et al. 2005).

The possibilities for CSOs to influence PRSPs thus vary greatly. In Zambia "civil society is free to monitor the implementation of the budget and to conduct independent research" (Chowdhury, Finlay-Notman, and Hovland 2006, 7). In contrast, it is commonly the case that CSOs in sub-Saharan Africa complain that "in order for policymakers to be seen as fair and open, a CSO is invited to join the agenda-setting 'debate,' but only once the government has made up its mind, and made a decision irrespective of the outcome of the debate with the CSOs" (ibid., 5; see also Diaz 2003). There is no doubt that this is sometimes the case, but it would be misleading to claim that it is always so. On some occasions such critique appears to be merely an excuse for some CSOs to carve out a bigger role for themselves. It may also reflect a misunderstanding of the role that CSOs should play. Reportedly, there is a widespread feeling of discontent among CSOs because they are "treated as 'subcontractors' and not as equals" (Chowdhury, Finlay-Notman, and Hovland 2006, 5; see also Igoe 2006).

A much more realistic assessment of the roles of CSOs in PRS consultations is presented by Braathen (2006). According to him, both the roles of CSOs and the relations between CSOs and governments are much more diverse than the above-mentioned complaints would make us believe. Hence, "the government in Malawi to a large extent seemed to accommodate non-state participation. The civil society in Zambia showed how to mobilise itself and tap into the policy dialogue during early formulation as well as final evaluation of the policy. Uganda had a participatory set up for monitoring the policy implementation" (Braathen 2006, 4). In Tanzania, "CSO involvement and their impact on outcome of the process [was] very limited" (ibid., 75). From this one can conclude that governments in SSA are not all bad and that civil society is not all good. From this it follows that one should not take for granted that CSOs everywhere have such a strong desire to influence policy. James et al. found that in

Uganda (and most likely all over SSA) CSOs are "being pressured by donors to take on the task of holding governments to account through advocacy" (2005, 51). It seems to be a widespread experience that "politically oriented NGOs tend to be donor driven" (Kelsall 2001, 136; see also Duhu 2005). There is obviously reason for African governments to be skeptical about whose visions are actually being aired by CSOs/NGOs.

The combination of the weak capacity of many CSOs, donor dependency among CSOs, and this emphasis on transparency and participation—highly valued buzz-words among donors and INGOs—may also have contributed to the low quality of many PRSPs. Driscoll and Evans found, for example, that "macro-frameworks have been characterised by a lack of realism and flexibility, including little analysis of policy trade-offs and how these relate to broader poverty goals" (2005, 7). Paradoxically, in a context characterized not only by widespread poverty but also by low levels of productivity, they also found a "relative neglect of the productive sectors" in most PRSPs and that "donors have . . . been the key drivers of this social sector bias in PRSs" (ibid., 8). It appears that donors and INGOs have had naive and exaggerated expectations about the potential contributions of CSOs to PRSs. Moreover, whereas there generally is a "clear demand for capacity development activities for policymakers" (James et al. 2005, 7)—a problem that CSO involvement might help solve—it is also the case that "in order to improve their interaction with policymakers, CSOs need to improve their own capacity" (ibid., 16). Most of all, CSOs need to "realize when they are asking too much" (Chowdhury, Finlay-Notman, and Hovland 2006, 9).

Group Approaches

Advocacy and policy negotiation are only two ways to create a more prominent role for civil society in development. In an effort to render development aid more effective and bring it closer to the people (which, ideally, should be the same thing), group-based approaches have been initiated by contract farming schemes, governments, and donors with varying degrees of success.[9] A few examples, from Malawi, Uganda, Tanzania, and Kenya, illustrate possibilities and constraints.

Community-based Natural Resource Management in Malawi

In 1998 a new and potentially far-reaching local government act was enacted in Malawi. Ferguson and Mulwafu argue that it "paved the way for the devolution of management powers to individuals, communities, user associations and other entities" (2004, 8). Problems with drought, land degradation, and declining agricultural productivity are common in Malawi's rural areas. According to contemporary development orthodoxy, they have to be dealt with locally by organizing those directly affected in user groups. In a relatively short time, community-based natural resource management (CBNRM) has become "a major development model" in the country (ibid., 8). This has turned out to be problematic in several ways, not least because "many of the most acute . . . problems experienced by [the] communities were not local in origin and cannot be solved by community-based participatory strategies alone" (ibid., 21). Moreover, among those supporting CBNRM, "little is actually known about local social, economic or cultural organization, capacities and needs, thus making [this] strategy difficult to implement" (ibid., 10).

This could perhaps have been overcome if the various entities involved had communicated and cooperated with one another. However, mutual distrust seems to override other considerations. Hence, collaboration among user groups, CBOs, NGOs, and district assemblies fell short of expectations. On the one hand, there has been a reluctance at higher administrative levels to devolve power to local and district assemblies (Kaarhus and Nyirenda 2006). On the other hand, the emancipatory ambitions of district assemblies appear to be hampered by the persistent influence and power of traditional elites, who mainly seem to use them for personal gain (ibid; Ferguson and Mulwafu 2004). For such reasons, at least in part, many NGOs and donors were found to prefer to work directly with communities rather than through local government structures, which they "regard [as] . . . another bureaucratic obstacle." Sometimes, however, the reason was that "many of the NGOs and donor[s] . . . are reluctant to have their autonomy reduced" and therefore compete with local governments rather than working jointly with them (Kaarhus and Nyirenda 2006, 15, 24).

At the same time, donors and NGOs do not appear to have much faith in grassroots either. This allegedly participatory approach appears not to be in response to an expressed desire among grassroots to form CBNRM groups. On the contrary, they have been forced upon (commonly resource-poor) local groups and "communities" by outside agents—donors and NGOs—leaving little room for local influence. Whereas "the degree to which these policy reforms reflect the will or voice of the people is difficult to ascertain" they have been "developed in a top-down fashion informed by the developmental and academic discourses of donors rather than input from, or knowledge of, local communities" (Kaarhus and Nyirenda 2006, 6, 10).

The situation is aggravated because NGOs and donors compete not only with grassroots and local governments but also among themselves. Whereas "numerous NGOs and donors are now active in rural water supply," "little coordination exists among ministries, NGOs, CBOs, donors and other promoters of CBNRM." Many such group-based approaches are untenable as they involve "creating, participating in and contributing work and funds to a plethora of village-level committees." In many cases this also creates confusion at the community level where the formation of user groups is being promoted following different guidelines and implementation procedures. This has strained village capacity for collective undertakings when several projects, "sponsored by different organizations and requiring different forms of 'participation,' co-exist in the same locale. . . . [and] most of these village-level committees are non-functional and exist only on paper" (Kaarhus and Nyirenda 2006, 3, 9, 23, 9, 23).

Farmers' Forums and Reformed Agricultural Extension in Uganda

Uganda's often praised PMA, adopted in 2000, meant a complete overhaul of principles for extension provision in the country. As part of both the government's decentralization and poverty reduction policies, responsibility for the organization of extension was transferred from central to district and local governments. The national extension service, NAADS, is no longer to be used as a mechanism for disseminating centrally decided plans and campaigns. Instead, it has been given the mandate to develop a demand-driven and farmer-led advisory system especially emphasizing women, youth, and people with disabilities (PMA 2000). The vision, says Bingen, is "to reach all of the country's districts and sub-counties by 2010 with a decentralized, farmer-owned and private sector serviced extension system" (2004, 11). In order to realize this goal, local governments have to "design systems for financing and delivery of agricultural sector services in partnership with a wide range of local and external stakeholders including NGOs, CBOs, the private sector and the donor community" (PMA 2000, xi). And farmers are called upon to organize themselves into Farmers' Forums at the sub-county level. The Farmers' Forum is responsible for contracting the extension services required by the groups. It is also represented at the district Farmers' Forum, which works directly with NGOs and the district NAADS coordinator (Bingen 2004).

A precondition for such a system to function satisfactorily is the (pre)existence of viable and articulate farmers' groups and associations. In Uganda "there exists a great diversity of civil society organisations . . . mostly related to agriculture and rural activities with varying life-cycles and a wide-ranging set of objectives and roles, but mainly characterised by their small size and scope, their limited impact, their reduced managerial capacity and their vulnerable financial sustainability" (Diaz 2003, 9). Hence, farmers' organizational capacity was found to be less than expected, leading local governments to appoint interim Farmers' Forums. Whereas this is meant to be a temporary solution, it may prove to be the Achilles' heel of the new system.

Bingen found "a significant knowledge and power gap" between these base groups and the appointed interim forums, which is why most members "still regard the FF as a government program" (2004, 21, 29). Lack of organizational capacity at the base level is only one side of the coin. Changing the approach and attitude of formerly supply-led extension workers in order to adhere to the principles of demand-led operations is not accomplished overnight. Hence, because of the still weak institutional framework and despite the participatory language permeating official documents, stakeholders complain that most events organized to facilitate consultation at the local level were instead information meetings to explain the governments' program, thus reviving a top-down communication pattern (Diaz 2003). Even if this policy shift aims at empowering farmers and enhancing their influence over research and extension—and therefore is applauded by a great many donors and NGOs—it appears so far to be a shaky construction that would have benefited from being erected on a more solid foundation.

Community-based District Development in Kenya

In 1997 the multi-sector Killifi District Development Programme (KDDP) was initiated by a foreign aid agency as a follow-up on an earlier mono-sector program. The Killifi district is a remote and dry area in a low potential agri-ecological zone with widespread poverty. The aim was to create participatory, democratically controlled development where local inhabitants initiate, manage, and own the development process. This was to be done in collaboration with official authorities. However, the central government has been rather passive, whereas local authorities have been more diverse in their attitudes, some of them supportive, others obstructive.

After an initial awareness-raising campaign, village development committees, which are registered as legal entities, were elected to be in charge for the development of their respective village communities. Immediately, they initiated small start-up projects that could be implemented quickly without financial assistance from external sources. Otherwise, village development committees were not to run projects but rather to support and supervise projects run by various other committees. Projects were to varying degrees co-financed by donors. On average, 31 percent of finance contributed came from the villagers themselves.

All in all, 111 village communities (with a population of 180,000 inhabitants) took part in the program, and by the year 2004 a total of 840 projects had been dealt with, an average of eight projects per community. The evaluators were quite happy with the results, stating that the program had "made it possible to bring people together who have hardly worked together before" (KDDP 2004, 11). They further found that "many communities have taken full charge of their development, have implemented or are in the process of implementing numerous projects to a great extent on their own" (ibid.). The majority, 61 percent, of these projects were community based, that is, they provided some kind of public good such as classrooms, local roads, a bridge, wells, water pans and pipelines, and village pharmacies, and taught improved NRM (for crops, livestock, fisheries, and so forth). Income-generating projects represented only 29 percent of the total. Among these, projects related to production and NRM were, however, not so numerous. Of the 342 projects completed by 2004, only 88 were in NRM, fewer than a project per village in eight years' time. Market-oriented projects were even less frequent, with only eight projects in trade.

This is in line with the theoretical assumptions about bonding scope and character of LOs in remote areas. However, an effort was made to enhance the bridging role of these LOs. A savings and credit component was added in the year 2000 in order to accelerate income-generating activities. Also, promotion of the Killifi District Farmers Association was another trade-related activity undertaken. Various farmer groups were persuaded to found an association in order to market cashew nuts and other farm products. For a short time the association thrived—artificially—on externally supplied credit. Yet, members, not too keen on repaying loans, were seduced into selling their products to other middlemen. This deprived the association of its core function, and it soon came to a standstill (KDDP 2004).

The above recounts both successes and failures. The local people in Killifi district have proven themselves both willing to and capable of designing and managing projects. Communal projects were many, diverse, and apparently well administered. On the other hand, projects aiming at personal gain, such as improved productivity or marketing produce, were not only much fewer, but they also came much later than community undertakings and the marketing association failed. The KDDP blames this partly on the fact that they worked close to the Kenyan government and partly on subsidies and credits. "Hardly any loan taker had the sincere intention to pay them back." Instead, the peasants "started to wrangle as to who is next in receiving a share for doing their own business" (2004, 41 32).

This should have been expected since it is common knowledge that "loans coming from a project which is close to the Government [are] widely considered as grants" (KDDP 2004, 41). In any case, the high level of subsidization may militate against the goal of self-reliance, and it is an open question whether the projects will be sustainable when the external partner withdraws. Remoteness, in combination with adverse climatic conditions, is likely to have played a role too. With undeveloped and unreliable markets as well as high prices for purchased inputs it may not be considered worth the risk to opt for productivity-enhancing investments. If, for example, failed rains lead to a low harvest, peasants may be unable to recover production costs. If, on the other hand, good weather brings a bumper harvest, the local market will be saturated and prices will drop, with the same disastrous result for the smallholder. It seems that a precondition for trade- and production-oriented projects to be successful in this kind of environment is enhanced accessibility; without heavy investment in transport and communication infrastructure peasants will prioritize bonding types of association and risk-aversive but low-yielding subsistence-oriented strategies, and "modern" types of associations will have difficulty developing.

Group-based Public Extension Services in Kenya

In 2000, as part of the government's overall decentralization policy, the Kenyan ministry of agriculture launched a new, participatory and demand-led extension program—NALEP (National Agricultural and Livestock Extension Programme). It centered on selected focal areas, each consisting of around four hundred farmers.[10] In each focal area, a development committee was elected to implement community action plans and enhance rural development initiatives. Simultaneously, farmers were encouraged to form common-interest groups in order to access extension services more easily and to handle production and marketing of individual commodities of interest for income generation. By 2003, roughly 800 focal area development committees and at least two thousand common-interest groups (each with fifteen to twenty members) had been formed in forty-two districts (Agrisystems 2003).

An initial PRA-based awareness raising campaign and election of focal area development committees was followed by a three-day training on the roles of focal area development committees. Similar training for common-interest groups—which were to form the basis of the structure—was, however, overlooked. Also, for other reasons this experiment must be deemed a failure. The system was hampered not only by inadequate training and poor management skills, but also by lack of transparency, gender bias, undemocratic election methods, over reliance on Ministry of Agriculture staff and "apathetic extension personnel." Hence, "no good example had been found that could maintain . . . FADC sustainability without external support." On the other hand, "CIGs had fared better because of their income-generating component arising from involvement in the commercial supply of inputs . . . and value-adding in products for marketing" (Agrisystems 2003, xi). The program was launched in 2000, and in 2003 the supporting donor, Sida, found that it was "regarded as the most efficient rural development programme of the MoA" (Sida 2003, 2).

It is quite possible that it was. However, in contrast to the previously reported case, the outcome of the program primarily reflects the different opportunities that exist in more favored areas. However, not even in favored areas were benefits evenly distributed. It is questionable whether common-interest groups have any relevance for poor farmers. Sida found that the activities had mainly benefited the "better off farmers but had been less relevant to poor and vulnerable families" (2003, 2). Also an external evaluation team found that

> the resource-poor, though they could be attracted to FADCs and CIGs, even where knowledgeable, had few or no means to participate and be accepted as group members in the long term. . . . [They] were either temporarily represented before they dropped out or were not represented at all. . . . [At the same time] the relatively rich community members could have been represented but chose not to join FADCs and CIGs due to their feeling self-sufficient status. (Agrisystems 2003, 18)

Again, this confirms the hypothesis that commercial organizations tend mainly to cater to the middle layer of producers. Moreover, the fate of focal area development committees has been quite diverse; some survived, whereas others were closed down or transformed into common-interest groups or CBOs. Some of the survivors ceased working with the government and instead joined an umbrella organization initiated by an NGO (Agrisystems 2003, 22).

Nevertheless, by 2006 it was estimated that more than seven thousand common-interest groups had been created with an approximate membership of 150,000 individual farmers (Cuellar et al. 2006, 3). This—together with reports that more that 80 percent of interviewed farmers stated that the program had offered them new opportunities, and that more than 70 percent of the interviewees claimed that "NALEP had led them to regard farming as a business rather than a way of surviving" (ibid.)—implies a high degree of success. However, doubts arise because NALEP's monitoring and evaluation approach has been "poorly developed" (ibid.). Actually, demand-driven extension service was only emerging in *some* of the focal areas, and the difficulty about including or benefiting the poor remains. The external evaluators found that many common-interest groups have tended to carry out too many activities and have met with a very limited degree of commercial sustainability. Hence, "the overall success rate of the CIGs, related to their original plans, is [only] somewhere between 30 and 50 percent" (ibid., 3).

This is due to both internal and external circumstances. The common-interest groups have not only focused on commercial activities but have also sought to incorporate widows and female-headed households as well as to cater to orphans and HIV/AIDS-infected households, which all have special needs and constraints. The program has also focused on advocacy and promotion of human rights. This care-taking of community responsibility no doubt has hampered commercial effectiveness. When it comes to external factors, NALEP is facing unfair competition from other donor-assisted projects and NGOs.

> NALEP does not practice free hand-outs to farmers and groups, [but] a number of major projects provide free or highly subsidized inputs and special allowances to farmers and staff. The latter practice tends to hamper the work of NALEP staff and neutralize the ability of the farming communities to mobilize on a self-help basis for long term sustainability. (Cuellar et al. 2006, 5)

It is thus likely to be correct that "*in comparison with other rural development approaches,* it appears that NALEP is highly efficient" (ibid., emphasis added). However, the above observations show

(1) that we should perhaps better lower our expectations, and (2) that donor and NGO activities are sometimes detrimental to local mobilization for development.

Community-based Water Management in Tanzania

Similar observations (to some degree) were reported in a study of a local water use association in northern Tanzania (Cleaver and Toner 2005). The Uchira Water Users' Association was established in the late 1990s as a local, community-initiated project under the village council. Funding was sought from a foreign donor, which also provided technical assistance. This turned out to be a mixed blessing. On the one hand, while water provision was rendered more effective, the project became victim to elite capture and the poor were marginalized or excluded. External support for group formation, "conscientization," and so forth did not lead to a more democratic mode of organization. Instead, those individuals with good links to external agencies were able to use these links to enhance their control over resources. At the same time, "local community ownership was heavily contested and the Water User Association showed a shift away from community control towards professsionalism," that is, much of the evolution of the Uchira Water Users' Association was guided by what was viewed as appropriate by the outside agency, [which] had the effect of marginalizing the democratically elected village government" (ibid., 14).

The same experiences are reported in a recent study of community-based water management in central Tanzania (Mtinda 2006). The water supply systems were all initiated by foreign NGOs and were initially based on a participatory approach, which has since largely been abandoned. In the older schemes village water management committees were formed and supervised by the donors. "Participation" was at the forefront of the supporting NGOs' agendas but local people were not involved in planning or in the choice of technology. On the other hand, they did participate in implementation once the plans were made, for example, choosing location for water taps and contributing cash and labor (such as procuring construction materials and digging trenches). The systems did not work well, for several reasons: participation in village meetings was low; members of the water management committees didn't have the necessary skills and training; and because their work was voluntary, they could only devote a limited time to a task that demanded more.

Also, the village water committees were not independent but suffered interference from politicians and village government leaders who sometimes diverted funds for other uses. Committees were not free to decide the price of water, and it was impossible to build funds for maintenance. Hence, the schemes were not financially viable; lacking both funds and skills, they were changed when pumps and engines broke down. In 2007, in old rehabilitated schemes, donors decided either to replace management committees by a private entrepreneur or to transfer responsibilities to a board of directors of newly formed water companies. In newer schemes the idea of community management appears to have been abandoned and the supporting NGOs have decided to instead have the companies operated by hired professionals.

Public–Private NGO in Tanzania

A quite different type of public sector–civil society cooperation occurs when public employees create "their own" NGO, which, at least in part, does the same thing as those public servants would do anyway. In Tanzania I came across such an organization where a group of public employees in a ministry for rural development had established an NGO to encourage rural community-based microenterprises, especially among women. Women were encouraged to form groups and saving clubs to invest in small-scale business projects (at the time of my visit, commercial crab-breeding and carpet production). The projects were very small, and both profitability and product quality were highly questionable. This could improve over time, however.

The NGO had been established virtually without funding but with the hope of being able to attract donor support at some later stage. A short consultancy job had provided a meager financial platform to get the NGO started. Most NGO work, including field visits, was done during normal working hours; the ministry's vehicles (and petrol) were used—with silent permission from higher administrative levels—thus providing an unofficial subsidy. If the projects were successful, this would boost the good will of the ministry (or at least the department involved), especially if foreign funding could be obtained. If not, it would not do much harm. The probability of success did not appear great, however. Lack of solid financial grounding and appropriate skills, as well as irregularity of contacts with groups involved, all illustrate a common tendency to set up groups and associations in a hasty and ill-prepared way. The above-mentioned projects had been preceded by other projects (for example, apiculture), which had failed.

What the above example tells us is that the border between the public sector, on the one hand, and the private sector/civil society, on the other, is not impenetrable. Many hybrid forms exist. It also illustrates that in many cases public officials are not as lethargic or unconcerned as sometimes suggested. On the contrary, they can be quite innovative and even if the main driver may be the possibility to obtain consultancy jobs and/or foreign project funding, some public servants also have a genuine desire to improve the lot of the less fortunate. Hence, this "irregular" behavior may be seen as enlightened self-interest just as well as viewing it as corrupt. Apart from this, it also perfectly illustrates how many NGOs, community organizations, and local groups are set up on a very shaky basis and hence with little likelihood of being sustainable.

Concluding Remarks

The above paragraphs show mixed experiences of newly reformed governments' and public employees' efforts to promote development by way of group-based undertakings. Formal government institutions (central as well as local) generally lack the necessary resources (financial, managerial, and so on) to design and implement projects. They often have not yet had time to acquire broad-based legitimacy, and public engagement and participation in elections are often low. It is no wonder that their records in project implementation often leave a lot to be desired or, for that matter, that grassroots sometimes abandon governments' projects to start their own organizations—or that public servants in a rather unorthodox manner create NGOs on a "part-time" basis. The last cases can be a sign of health and entrepreneurship.

On the other hand, the tendency among (some) donors and NGOs—even when officially collaborating—to bypass local governments, to follow their own agendas, and to do things for local councils rather than with them, can be disastrous in the long run. It undermines (emerging) formal democracy, prolongs dependency, and most likely delays development. The same disastrous effects result from donor and INGO competition, where subsidized "aid" unfairly undermines both local initiative and public development programs. In a situation where Africa is in the midst of a process of nation building, it is imperative that donors (in particular) and INGOs contribute to strengthening the legitimacy as well as the managerial capacities of local political institutions. Great efforts need to be made to ensure that donor-government joint undertakings do not lead to a situation where "the NGOs take the credit for good results, while the Government remains with the blame for the failures" (Kaarhus and Nyirenda 2006, 28).

It is thus not self-evident that nongovernmental is always better, or that "community" exists in any progressive meaning. Two examples of assisted village-based development illustrate the point: Havnevik explains the successful outcome of a village-based NRM project in Tanzania—"a gradual accumulation of benefits . . . and continuous incentives for villagers to respect the management plan and the associated by-laws"—not as a result of village ownership of the resource per se. Rather, it resulted from "the building of mutual trust between district and external personnel and villagers" (2003, 38). In contrast, a study of a village-development project in Zimbabwe found that the sustainability of the scheme was open to question. Partly, this was due to "extreme vulnerability of investments to drought, and poor leadership of the credit scheme." What appears to have been a more serious problem, however, was that committee functioning was "far from satisfactory, and the elite (largely traditional leaders and their families) dominate resource management and use. The complexity of local organisations and power struggles are likely to defy any attempts by development projects to facilitate change" (Campbell, Luckert, and Mutamba 2003, 5, 6).

This must be seen against a background where half the population lives below the poverty line, where the economy of affection remains strong, and where both state and civil society are weak. Hence, liberalization has been halfhearted and has in many cases led to increased corruption and elite capture of publicly provided assets and opportunities. Consequently, many local governments have limited capacity—or even desire—to spearhead development. The status of cooperatives is often unclear and contradictory, and central governments still find it difficult to relinquish control. Local and community organizations, on the other hand, have limited capacities and often do not know how to work with local governments. Nevertheless, there are positive signs of local and joint organization building. Success stories can be found. However, they so far seem to be exceptions rather than the rule, and they mostly describe a small group of better-off farmers in high-potential and/or easily accessible areas.

In many respects this does not appear to be an enabling environment—especially not for grassroots. Not surprisingly, donors and INGOs, who are supposed to work jointly with local authorities, often try to bypass them (and grassroots) and implement projects and policies according to their own interpretations of need. This not only undermines nation building, but it is also likely to delay development—at least it does not seem to provide much space for development from below. At this stage, this remains a hypothesis. The next chapter focuses more directly on NGOs and LOs along with their respective capabilities, aspirations, linkages, and relations, which all have a bearing on their contributions to development.

Three

The ESA Experience—Part 2

> Some NGOs only exist to go round the world looking for funding.
>
> —Walter O. Oyugi, 2004

NGOs and Peasants' Associations in ESA

This chapter deals more directly with LOs and NGOs without so much focus on the context wherein they operate. Organizations do not, of course, live a life of their own without influences from the surrounding society. The intention of this chapter is not to give such an impression. But it separates LOs and NGOs, as far as this can be done, from the formal structures and authorities discussed in the previous chapter. This is motivated partly by analytical considerations and partly by the nature of the sources referred to. Some highlight the organizational landscape in a broader sense; others instead place their searchlight elsewhere. I have perceived this as an advantage because it allows a more explicit focus on certain aspects of organization building, constraints, accomplishments, and inter-organizational relations—between NGOs and donors/INGOs, among LOs and NGOs themselves, and between NGOs/INGOs and the grassroots.

The first section below addresses the fast growth of NGOs and the consequences for organization building and performance; the next section focuses on the question "organizations for whom?" where beneficiaries are often not those assumed or intended; the third section provides glimpses of organizations at the grassroots; and the final section highlights the often destructive role of donors and INGOs for domestic organizational development in ESA.

The Sudden Growth of NGOs

Compared to other major regions in the developing world, NGOs in sub-Saharan Africa are of rather recent origin, at least on a grand scale (Holmén and Jirström 1996). An NGO boom came with SAP and the reductions of state involvement in service provision in the 1980s and onward. Since then, ESA has been flooded by NGOs, both foreign and domestic. Looking at pure numbers, the NGO explosion of the two latest decades looks impressive indeed. In Uganda registered NGOs grew from 160 in 1986 to 4,700 in 2003, a thirtyfold increase (James et al. 2005). This figure, sensationally, is "much bigger than the number of registered private sector establishments" (Nkwake 2007, 282). In Kenya (which has a longer history of CSOs) there were 90,000 CSOs registered in 1995 and as many as 220,000 in 2002 (James et al. 2005). These figures, however, appear to be seriously inflated. Barr and Fafchamps (2005) commented that, in Uganda, not all registered NGOs are operational. James et al. found that behind these figures were a "high infant mortality and . . . thin roots to communities" (2005, 51). Likewise, in Kenya there were 2,300 registered *development* NGOs in 2003.[1] This is an impressive figure in itself (a growth from 120 in 1978), but it nevertheless represents only 1 percent of the total number of registered CSOs in the same year (ibid.). In Tanzania, only seventeen new NGOs were registered between 1961 and 1978 (Kelsall 2001). The number of registered NGOs then grew to 224 in 1993 and to 8,499 in 2000 (Duhu 2005). And recently, NGO formation has escalated even further. In Tanzania there were 1,764 new NGOs registered between January 2005 and June 2007—or an average of fifty-seven new NGOs per month (*Daily News,* August 9, 2007). However, allegations abound that many are "bogus" NGOs (ibid.).

It is, however, not only the organizational birthrate that is high. So is the extinction rate. Farmers' organizations in ESA are frequently reported to be weak (see, for example, Rusike and Dimes 2004) and their average lifetime appears to be short. Kumwenda and Mingu (2005) report that out of thirty-four farmer organizations in Malawi that had been investigated in 1995, only ten could be traced ten years later, and of those only seven were still functioning (to different degrees), while three had been disbanded. Similarly, in May 2008 the Malawi's Ministry of Agriculture and

Food Security database on farmer organizations listed 2,175 organizations. Of these, only twenty-two (1 percent) were classified as clearly "sustainable," whereas 1,032 were classified as "non-sustainable." For the remaining 52 percent the status was less clear (MAFS 2008). All over ESA, farmers' organizations face serious problems trying to survive, and it is my firm belief that the above figures are fairly representative for the whole region.

This exceptional growth of organizations is, however, only partly a spontaneous phenomenon. Many, perhaps most, NGOs/CSOs have been created by donors and foreign NGOs or in response to external demands. A very strong stimulus was also the changed aid flows as donors increasingly circumvented governments and redirected their financial contributions to work with or through NGOs. This not only invoked a sense of jealousy and suspicion from governments (see, for example, Oakley 1999; Oyugi 2004), but it also spurred a wave of opportunistic behavior and many NGOs (often urban-based middle-class creations) turned out to be "briefcase" NGOs (Barya 2000; Munene 2005) owned by "crooks and swindlers" (Barr, Fafchamps, and Owens 2005, 658) and in many cases set up with the sole purpose of tapping this newfound external resource (CBR 1994; Dieklich 1998; Bayart, Ellis, and Hibou 1999; Oyugi 2004; Fafchamps and Owens 2006). Even when that is not obviously the case, many organizations have been set up without clear guidelines (Kachule 2004) and "one often wonders what is the purpose of this or that NGO" (John Kadzandira, personal communication).

Consequently, most LOs and NGOs in ESA are rather young. Only in a few cases do they date back to earlier times, sometimes to the colonial period. Many of these older NGOs were charitable organizations linked to churches. After SAP they often faced a problematic situation as they found it necessary to reorient themselves from (apolitical) missionary and relief objectives to instead engage with development (an unavoidably political task).

Whereas there are examples of early successful cases of LO and NGO activities in ESA (Esman and Uphoff 1988; Krishna, Uphoff, and Esman 1997), in many ways the SAP-induced policy shifts turned out to be problematic. On the one hand, both already existing INGOs and NGOs and a fast-growing number of newly established NGOs ventured to fill the gap after retreating states, which often viewed them with suspicion (Dieklich 1998), especially when they aimed at influencing policy (Oyugi 2004). In Kenya, former president Arap Moi threatened to re-register NGOs since they "lacked the mandate to lobby—who were they actually speaking for?" (Ruth Onyang'o, personal information).[2]

This appears to be a persistent problem. In Kenya the independent NGO Council was dissolved in 2005 due to allegations of corruption (Munene 2005), but political motives cannot be totally disregarded. In Uganda the government strives to increase control over independent NGOs (Human Rights Watch 2001; Flygare 2006). In Malawi, likewise, "the political climate continues to threaten the existence of [NGOs], especially those working in the areas of human rights and good governance" (CONGOMA 2002). In Lesotho, "associations which are close to the 'grassroots' . . . [have] little influence in the policy-making process" (Bird, Booth, and Pratt 2003, 17). In Tanzania, "despite the government's post-liberalisation willingness to allow local NGOs to exist, its fear of political opposition has constrained the space available to local NGOs in the country" (Michael 2004, 83; BTI 2006g; TANGO 2007). In Zambia in 2004, an NGO that had advocated for transparency and broader participation in the ongoing constitutional review process was de-registered on the accusation that it "engaged in activities compromising State security" (IJCSL 2004). For similar reasons NGOs in Ethiopia tend to shy away from political issues and instead display "an excessive focus on 'relief'" (ID21 2006, 1). In Zimbabwe there have been "deepening attacks on all autonomous institutions with no close links to the ruling party or the state [and] . . . true national civic organizations . . . can no longer be identified" (Larsson-Lidén 2006, 151).

Governments' attitudes toward NGOs are not totally negative, however. They rather tend to have "a love-hate relationship with NGOs" (Amutabi 2006, 194). Whereas they often would prefer to "make NGOs an arm of the government rather than an alternative to it" (ibid.), they also benefit from NGOs providing services the governments can no longer provide post-SAP and from NGO activities in regions where government is hardly present. In rural areas NGOs often tend to be less critical of governments, and sometimes they cooperate on various issues. The governmental ambivalence is also reflected in the fact that governments and senior politicians (and, as we have seen, public employees at the middle level) sometimes have ventured to take over NGOs and/or to establish their own quasi-NGOs both in order to siphon off aid money channeled to and through NGOs and to control this emerging "sector." This has led to a "privatisation of development" in ways completely opposite to those assumed by donors and IFIs. The result, according to Bayart, Ellis, and Hibou, was "a reinforcement of the power of elites, particularly at the local level, or of certain factions, and sometimes a stronger ethnic character in the destination of flows of finance from abroad" (1999, 99). Different NGOs, therefore, enjoy different degrees of freedom from state control. Whereas some appear to be rather tightly monitored and constrained, others are much less so. The latter tend to be "the well-connected NGOs, who have powerful patrons capable of shielding them off from any harassment by state agents" (Oyugi 2004, 40).

This mushrooming of NGOs often turned out to be problematic in other ways. The sudden growth of African NGOs was seldom a spontaneous process but rather a "forced birth" (Abdillahi 1998). Many were set up hastily, often by or in collaboration with foreign organizations. Not uncommonly, LOs and NGOs lacked experience as well as management skills, technical competence, and financial resources (CBR 1994; Wiggins and Cromwell 1995; Gyimah-Boadi 1996). A study of more than one hundred NGOs in East Africa found that "the principal problem confronting NGOs, particularly those community-based, [was] that of technical training. . . . [They] lack[ed] the capacity to analyse their problems [as well as] the skill to design and run projects" (CBR 1994, 7). This lack of capacity still seems to be a widespread phenomenon (Rusike and Dimes 2004; James et al. 2005; Fafchamps and Owens 2006). Contrary to expectations, many local and intermediary organizations also lack vision (Aloo 2000; Kachule 2004) and innovative capacity (Livernash 1992; Sinclair 1995). Instead, they tend to "ape other formal sector methods" rather than offering clear operational alternatives (Wiggins and Cromwell 1995, 413; see also Agrisystems 2003). More often than not, indigenous rural organizations are small, fragmented, and isolated from each other (CBR 1994; Dieklich 1998; Offenheiser 1999; Barr, Fafchamps, and Owens 2005). Particularly constraining is an apparently widespread "lack of a sense of ownership amongst most of the members. This results from the fact that most of the RPOs [rural producers' organizations] are initiated by external agents" (Kachule 2004, 21).

The picture is not all that homogenous, however. Whereas in Botswana there is a relatively high density of urban NGOs, civil society is weak (Hoon 2004) and rural interests are under-represented (BTI 2006j); and whereas in both Tanzania and Malawi independent civic groups are weak or very weak "even by African standards" (BTI 2006g; BTI 2006k); in Zambia there is reportedly a "robust but heterogeneous web of autonomous, self-organized groups, associations and organizations" (BTI 2006h, 7). In Kenya, "the numbers of self-help organizations is high. There are 3,000 self-help groups operating in the agricultural sector alone . . . trying to organize better marketing for their products and assist their members, mostly without any government funding" (BTI 2006i, 8). As mentioned, one should read such numbers with a fair amount of caution.

Various factors contributed to the sudden growth of NGOs, as well as to their problems. One was the—although limited—widened political space in the aftermath of SAPs, which made it possible to engage more in advocacy and lobbying.[3] However, many NGOs are not that keen on advocacy and engagement with the government but are being pressured by donors to hold governments to account through advocacy (Hearn 1999; James et al. 2005). Actually, INGOs' favored strategies emphasize "policy influence and advocacy" (Bornstein 2003, 400) and "most donors . . . express commitment to a political role for NGOs" (Kelsall 2001, 134). This puts both governments and many NGOs in a rather awkward situation. NGOs are pressured to assume roles they might not want to perform. If they don't, they are likely to lose access to external funding. Governments, for their part, must ask whose interests—African or foreign—it is that advocating NGOs represent. Since some NGOs have displayed a rather confrontational attitude toward officials, governments often responded with suspicion and hostility. Hence, these organizations were "to a significant extent, marginalized from policy reform activities" (Swartzendruber and Njovens 1993, 6; Bird, Booth, and Pratt 2003).

From that perspective it seems as if external ambitions with NGOs have backfired. It has also been found that rural organizations are more practically oriented and less keen on influencing policy (see, for example, Hassim 2004), and that whereas rural areas are dominated by (sometimes few) development NGOs, urban areas tend to be dominated by political NGOs (Frank Muhereza, personal communication). Not surprisingly, when campaigning NGOs venture to spread their gospel in the countryside, they have sometimes met "lack of community participation, or resistance by the community to the campaign" (Manji and Naidoo 2006, 6). Hence, it appears that donor/INGO pressures have sometimes had the effect of alienating NGOs, not only from the state but also from the grassroots.

Another factor behind the sudden growth of NGOs in ESA is the perceived weakness of civil society—poor, fragmented, and patrimonial (Gyimah-Boadi 1996; Tangri 1999; James et al. 2005)—in the hands of which NGOs were expected to place initiative and control of development. Financial constraints, however, have often made LOs and domestic NGOs dependent on foreign financing (Gyimah-Boadi 1996; Abdillahi 1998; CONGOMA 2002; Fafchamps and Owens 2006). In Uganda, for example, around 80 percent of total NGO sector funds come from international grants, while contributions from members and local private donors make up less than 3 percent (ID21 2007). Since money is seldom provided without strings attached, this invites external agenda setting, and NGO activities tend to reflect the priorities of international actors. Hence this kind of "support" has often limited the scope for empowerment and development from below. In fact, *empowerment,* while serving as a strong legitimizing buzzword for most INGOs and NGOs, "is a term more often invoked than made real" (Winter 2001, 37). Instead, leaders of indigenous NGOs and LOs "have become less and less accountable to their communities. . . . [Their] energies have been diverted into activities to please donors" (Igoe 2004, 1; see also Michael 2004; Duhu 2005; Fafchamps and Owens 2006; Amutabi 2006; Shivji 2006).

Organization for Whom?

These circumstances partly explain why many indigenous NGOs, while running projects in rural areas, often do not display any true grassroots contacts (Abdillahi 1998; Dieklich 1998; Arnesen, Kapelrud, and Øygard 2002; James et al. 2005). Quite a few NGOs are "one-powerful-man" organizations (Barya 2000; *Daily News*, August 9, 2007), and top-down management appears to be almost as common in NGOs as in government structures. Many LOs and NGOs, domestic as well as foreign, have turned out not to be the democratic institutions that donors assumed them to be (Holmén and Jirström 1996; Holmén and Jirström 2009; Hassim 2004; Fahamu 2006). Instead, competition and mistrust have been common both between indigenous NGOs and their external linkages and between indigenous NGOs themselves (Abdillahi 1998; Onyando 1999; ANC 2002). In some instances "NGOs, mostly local ones, took an 'easy ride' on the successes of [others]. . . . Competing organisations caused confusion among communities by altering proceedings and names, and by talking badly about the other organisations' performance and approaches" (KDDP 2004, 63). Not only that, the ICA (1998) found that externally supported NGOs, strengthened by foreign funding, "compete aggressively" with indigenous cooperatives. Amutabi contends that

> each NGO is preoccupied with its own agenda and it tends to pursue it in blissful isolation from others, even where their programs match. Inevitably, there is plenty of duplication and overlapping. This arises because of the selfish and very fierce competition for donor funding, pride and prestige among NGOs. (2006, 192)

Aggressive competition may take many forms.[4] For example, whereas remote communities tend to be neglected by NGOs, attractive areas suffer from "extensive duplication of NGO effort at the local level" (Barr and Fafchamps 2005, 29; Michael 2004). Also, subsidized NGO undertakings, such as provision of agricultural inputs (see Kelly, Adesina, and Gordon 2003) may put local entrepreneurs out of business. In Kenya, NGOs, heavily dependent on foreign subsidies, provide microfinance—but not for agriculture—to smallholder peasants (ICA 1998). The cooperatives, which put priority on saving associations, opine that there does not seem to be a need for NGOs' microcredit institutions because the savings propensity among smallholders is high (ibid.). It is investment opportunities that are missing. Rather than fostering self-reliance, such credit provision runs the risk of enhancing external dependencies, especially in areas where markets are volatile and rudimentarily developed. Not uncommonly, both NGOs and LOs have proved instrumental in providing patronage rather than empowerment (Bayart, Ellis, and Hibou 1999; Offenheiser 1999; Lockwood 2005). Consequently, Zaidi (1999), among others, does not hesitate to call this "NGO-approach to development" a failure (see also Offenheiser 1999; Aloo 2000; Amutabi 2006; Shivji 2006).

There is much to support this conclusion. Although in recent years a verbal consensus has been established among donors, IFIs, governments and INGOs on development priorities (privatization, democratization, good governance, poverty focus, and so on), and although "some progress has been noted through policy declarations . . . this has had little or no impact on the ground [where] farmers' organisations . . . [remain] weak" (IFAP 2004). Hence, they also have limited impact (Ellis and Freeman 2004a; Barr, Fafchamps, and Owens 2005).

Limited impact has many causes. One is that, despite the participatory rhetoric and capacity-building zeal supposedly characterizing NGO activities, in practice capacity building often seems to have a low priority (Practical Action 2005). Even though NGOs speak loudly about empowerment, they do not always accept what they see when their clients are empowered to find their own solutions. Garland, analyzing the work of an INGO in SSA, found an underlying assumption that Western ideals need to be transferred and rebuilt locally. The NGO worked with "bushmen" who readily set out to build "civil society" with external help. However, their priorities differed from the NGO's "modernization" objectives, and they were criticized by the expatriate staff for creating the wrong kinds of civil society institutions based on clan and kin (Garland 1999).

Oyugi, in a study of Kenyan NGOs, found that only *some* NGOs "establish an operational relationship with community based organisations (CBOs) that are supposed to know the nature and character of the need existing in a given area" (2004, 33). Instead of allowing projects to be truly participatory or demand driven, "what projects actually are implemented in a given area by NGOs is influenced both by the mandate and perception of the NGO and only occasionally by the demonstrated need on the ground" (ibid., 34). Rather than empowering rural grassroots and CBOs, "many NGOs [are] preferring instead to do what *they* believe is good for the people" (ibid., emphasis added). Also Amutabi stresses that many INGOs and supported NGOs "short-change the participatory process and reduce it to a façade. They . . . [have] walked into communities . . . with fixed notions of what a community needs and reproduce centralized development at community level" (2006, 196).

Consequently, in a real sense "most agricultural services projects still do not directly support PO [producers' organization] development" (Delion 2000, 3). When they do, it is often the case that, whereas group support should be a long-term commitment,[5] NGOs working with peasant groups sometimes stay only a short period and often have not "established a means for assuring . . . continuity beyond the life of their projects" (Bingen and Munyankusi 2002, 3). It is a widespread experience that groups or CBOs seldom survive the project period of INGOs and NGO. It is commonplace for NGOs

> not to safeguard existing capacities, such as already existing local groups and committees. When new projects are initiated, new committees are created, one for each new project. The reason, apparently, is that NGOs get funded based on the number of groups/committees they have established. Community members may therefore end up as "members" in an indefinite number of (single-purpose/short-duration) groups. (Roger Kirkby, personal communication)

Hence, one cannot but wonder "whether the NGOs have left any sustainable development structures or demand driven characteristics amongst the communities they have worked in" (Agrisystems 2003, 24).[6] Moreover, NGOs "are not think tanks" (Lockwood 2005, vii), and they sometimes make serious mistakes such as "introducing inappropriate breed of cattle, or uninformed efforts at land management" (Bingen and Munyankusi 2002, 4). Not surprisingly, foreign NGOs or externally supported organizations have sometimes not only met with "lack of community participation, [but also] resistance by the community" in their areas of operation (Fahamu 2006, 6).

Organizations and Vulnerable Groups

Partly, and contrary to expectations, impact is limited also because it has often proved difficult to include the poor in organizations or to make them benefit from organizations' activities (Weinberger and Jütting 2001; Mansuri and Rao 2004). Whereas, for example, the externally initiated NASFAM in Malawi is "focussing on motivated farmers and good business opportunities . . . [it] does not work directly with food crops nor does it directly serve the interests of the poorest and most marginal sections of the rural population" (Chirwa et al. 2005, 5). Similarly, the Cotton Growers' Association in Zambia, "appears to be composed primarily of large commercial growers" (Tschirley, Zulu, and Shaffer 2004, 10; see also deGrassi and Rosset 2003, 58). Overall, viable associations among smallholder peasants still seem to be rare (Tschirley, Zulu, and Shaffer 2004; Michael 2004; Larsson 2005; Coughlin 2006). A lack of collective action has been observed also among other categories such as, for example, traders (Nkonya 2002) and women's groups (Hassim 2004). Not surprisingly, Cleaver (2005) found that the poor (many of whom are women) hardly benefit from contemporary rural organizations. Since almost half the population in sub-Saharan Africa ekes out a living below the poverty line, this is serious indeed. Often the entry fees for formal associations are too high to attract the poor. On other occasions the poor were initially allowed to join, "having managed to scrape together the entry fee (or at least an instalment of this). However, their inability to make regular contributions, or even to turn up to meetings reliably, ensured that they were soon excluded" (ibid., 902; see also Agrisystems 2003). To a significant degree the poor, therefore, still seem stuck with whatever material gains and protections they can get from informal sharing institutions and patronage structures.

When it comes to women (and other marginalized groups) the contemporary situation is quite unclear, however. Not only are women's organizations very heterogeneous, but they are also frequently informal (Karega 2002b) and, albeit being the most numerous associations at the base level,[7] they are the least visible organizations (Hassim 2004)—a reflection of women's often subordinate position in society. In fact, women face enormous obstacles in organizations (Manuh 1998; Meinzen-Dick et al.

2005). Rural women have "limited productive associational ties, and less time to participate in local social networks" (Havnevik et al. 2007, 47). Despite women's excellent loan repayment records and great trustworthiness as treasurers (Wonani 2004; Pandolfelli, Dohrn, and Meinzen-Dick 2007; see also Holmén 1994), they are often not recognized as members in formal organizations (Pandolfelli, Dohrn, and Meinzen-Dick 2007). When they are, "addressing gender issues is done on an ad-hoc basis and often based on the conditionality that is given by funding agencies" (Wonani 2004, 5). In mixed organizations women's participation tends to be minimal, and, hence, in various locations women have formed their own independent organizations.

The information available about women's organizations is not only scant, but it is also extremely varied. Whereas Hassim (2004) firmly states that African women's organizations are weak, others declare that, despite disadvantages, they are strong. Manuh, for example, asserts, "While many of these associations receive external funding, a number seek to stress internal responsibility, African agenda-setting, and the development of organizational potential" (1998, 16). Karega likewise found that, in Kenya, women's associations entering the new (emerging) market economy assume new opportunities and roles and have transformed into entrepreneurs. Kenyan women, she says, "neither retreat into the economy of affection, nor permit elite-exclusive access to the benefits of public and private resources" (2002b, 2). Also Tripp contends that women's organizations are strong. In Tanzania, they have "challenged clientelistic practices tied to the state" (A. M. Tripp 2001b, 33; 2001a).

However, organizational strength and participation appears to be rather selective. Since women constitute the majority of the poor and the illiterate in rural Africa (Manuh 1998), it is of no small significance that Weinberger and Jütting (2001) found a "middle-class" effect of participation. The opportunity costs for the poor to join organizations are often high. And even when local organizations include the poor, "community level women's organizations often do not have the time, expertise or resources to address decision-makers" (Hassim 2004, 15). Hence, while making less noise, they tend to concentrate on practical issues and immediate needs, leaving lobbying, advocacy, and other civil society–undertakings to the (urban) middle-class organizations.

It is, however, not only urban organizations that have been able to lobby successfully. Indigenous peoples represent another category that is widely seen as either being threatened by globalization or bypassed by development. In whichever case, indigenous peoples are frequently seen to deserve special attention. Igoe points out that "although the term 'indigenous' implies a state preceding that which is foreign or acquired, indigenous movements in Africa are a recent phenomenon" (2006, 399). Often perceived by outsiders (sometimes correctly so) as being denied their cultural identity and the land they claim ancestral right to, various indigenous movements have managed to mobilize external support for their plight. The East African Maasai movement has been particularly successful in this regard. Although a large proportion of Tanzania's population could probably be labeled indigenous (notwithstanding dislocations during colonialism and the Ujamaa period), the "Tanzanian indigenous peoples' movement represents only about half a million rural Tanzanians, and it is unlikely that more than a few hundred of them actually self-identify as indigenous through participation in NGOs and international fora" (ibid., 404). Through intensive networking, this small group has gained international support for its struggle (for example, over land rights) a networking that over time "has come to represent a strategy of extraversion. A small group of NGO leaders has converted access to funding and other material resources into local political influence" (Igoe 2006, 405).[8]

Being self-selected, these representatives of Tanzania's indigenous peoples are, however, not representative in the conventional meaning of that word. Cleverly displaying a Janus-face toward outsiders, they (unlike indigenous movements in other parts of the world, who demand special treatment for their minorities) seek equal treatment for their people when dealing with the Tanzanian government. In contrast, at the international level they do receive special treatment due to their cultural distinctiveness. In 1994, a forum for indigenous peoples—PINGO, a loose coalition of pastoralists and hunter/gatherers—was formed, including and dominated by the Maasai. Enthusiastically, donors funded the construction of a PINGO advocacy center in the city of Arusha.

As they gained recognition from Western donors, however, indigenous NGOs in Tanzania began to change. Urban workshops and international activism moved NGO leaders away from their communities. More and more of their time was taken up with grant writing, accounting, and managing increasingly large, bureaucratic NGOs. Local people complained that they were no longer connected to the NGOs that were ostensibly working on their behalf. (Igoe 2006, 415)

This, however, is not just another example of conflicting aspirations within an organization, separating "us down here" from "those up there." It has a wider significance since non-Maasais "complain that Maasai NGO leaders made a superficial show of interethnic harmony and participation, while dominating PINGO and its activities." Ironically, by skilfully playing donors and foreign NGOs, they were able to "expropriate the marginalization of other groups to their own ends" (Igoe 2006, 416).

This is not the only example of its kind. Quite a few organizations in ESA have "an almost monochrome ethnic homogeneity" (Murunga 2000). Also, in the competition for donor funding and external support, visibility is imperative. At the turn of the millennium a South African NGO—SANGOCO—was asked to prepare the NGO forum at the World Conference against Racism (WCAR), held in Durban in 2001, so that the forum would become inclusive and "the voice of civil society [would be] heard on a range of issues" (ANC 2002, 1). This NGO, however, opted not to pursue these objectives. Instead, "the WCAR was . . . largely taken over by SANGOCO [and some foreign NGOs] (ICARE 2001). "'Civil Society' was reduced to a narrow network of . . . organizations affiliated to SANGOCO, who were themselves inadequately consulted" (ANC 2002).

Success Stories

One should be careful, though, not to stretch generalizations too far. Whereas exclusiveness and opportunism no doubt have been prominent, there are also examples of inclusiveness and altruism in African organization building. A case from Uganda will illustrate the point. The CBR reports that a certain NGO development center was the result of an initiative from an individual who ha[d] devoted most of his resources for the benefit of would-be destitute youths in the community. He ha[d] donated his own land and personal savings as seed money for the establishment of construction, black-smithing and tailoring courses— free of charge. [The investigators] came across a total of 8 such grassroots-based but middle class-initiated NGOs in Uganda and Tanzania. (1994, 4)

Hence, while the impact of organizations has been mixed, and often not on a par with expectations, not everything is a failure. The literature also presents examples of more successful rural associations. Krishna, Uphoff, and Esman (1997) and Metcalfe (1997) report a few cases of successful LO projects dealing with child nutrition, water supply, and wildlife resource management, respectively. Onyando points out that NGOs sometimes are "providing relief and risking life and limb delivering services . . . in places the government does not even know exist" (1999, 2). Michael, reporting from Tanzania, found that

the majority of local groups which call themselves NGOs are involved in caring for the sick, disabled and elderly, with varying degrees of professionalism and success. However, these local welfare organizations commonly lack any engagement with the wider issues of underdevelopment . . . [and] the credit and business sector . . . is . . . very small. (2004, 72–73)

Similarly, Oyugi (2004), in a study of Kenyan NGOs, found that the role of NGOs as service providers rather than as capacity builders is well established. What is noteworthy is, on the one hand, that these organizations all depended on external support, and, on the other hand, that they were all community oriented (providing public goods) rather than business oriented. Although they provided important services in the villages where they operated, they have been less effective as development instruments or change agents.

More recently, although information is scant, Tibblin (2006) reports about an apparently successful local, peasant-initiated marketing association in Kisumu, Kenya. And the African Development Foundation does the same about a peasant-owned coffee-marketing association in Tanzania (ADF 2005). In Rwanda, the Abahuzamugambi Coffee Cooperative was started in 1999. In 2005 it had more than two thousand members, the majority women, and economic turnover had increased from about US$40,000 in 1999 to almost US$3 million in 2005. This reportedly has not only benefited coffee growers directly but also enhanced school enrollment, investments in roads and piped water, and the emergence of a differentiated local economy (Göteborgs Posten 2005). Seward and Okello (2000) likewise report about a successful project in Kenya to extend the use of fertilizers to smallholders who, in most cases, had never used them before. Normally, fertilizers were sold in fifty kilogram (110 pound) bags, which the majority of poor smallholder peasants could not afford. In 1995 the Sustainable Community Oriented Development Programme (SCODP) was established to set up an infrastructure for the supply of fertilizer to the poor. Combined with farmer-participatory research programs, so-called mini-packs of fertilizer—usually one hundred gram and two hundred gram bags (three and a half to seven ounces)—were sold at market price. The project led to a dramatic increase in fertilizer use in the area. Moreover, the vast majority of the new users were women, who used the fertilizer on food crops, leading to improved food security among the poor. In Madagascar, a local NGO successfully engaged in developing and disseminating new techniques for rice cultivation that resulted in doubling or tripling of yields (Moser and Barrett 2005).

It is quite possible that many of the negative or at least questionable experiences of NGO and LO building in ESA reflect "growing pains" and therefore constitute temporary rather than lasting deficiencies. Abdillahi reports about the "emergence of a small number of 'quality' NGOs . . . [which] has been accompanied by a withering away of many 'artificial' NGOs" (1998, 5). Similarly, Aloo opined that "a new breed of NGO has begun to emerge" in sub-Saharan Africa a kind of organization that has "begun to become more professional" (2000, 58). The cases referred to above indicate that they might judge the contemporary situation correctly. Another such case could be the above-mentioned peasants in Kenya who, disappointed with the ineffectiveness of a government's program to establish farmers' groups from above, transformed themselves into CBOs, joined an umbrella organization initiated by an NGO, and assumed the role of entry point for service providers coming into the area (Agrisystems 2003). A further indication is that the more recent examples referred to have more bridging and less bonding orientation than did earlier success stories. However, such examples remain few and scattered, and they have not yet altered the general picture of powerlessness, opportunism, and dependence among NGOs.

Nevertheless, these examples show that, at least in some cases, members of local groups and organizations can empower themselves and find their own way to solve problems. Similarly, IFAP (2005) explains the cooperative success story referred to above as resulting from KENFAP reorienting its focus "from being entirely a lobby network to an organization providing services to the members." If more organizations were to reorient themselves from demanding services from governments and donors and instead relied more on themselves, that would further underscore Aloo's and Abdillahi's claims.

Group Activities at the Grassroots

Besides NGOs there are smaller, LOs of various kinds and with a multitude of purposes. Without providing any figures, Ellis and Freeman note that "the last decade has seen a multiplication of community-based organisations in rural communities" (2004a, 19). Dieklich mentions that apart from the seven hundred officially registered NGOs in Uganda in the early 1990s, there were "hundreds if not thousands of indigenous grassroots associations that [were] not registered" (1998, 148). In Tanzania, when in 1991 membership in cooperatives ceased to be compulsory, "groups involved in village trading reportedly grew from 350 in 1982 to 1,300 in 1992" (Cracknell 1995). Delion counted eleven thousand small farmer groups in Chad alone, "the vast majority formed without any outside influence" (2000, 4).

As mentioned, little information is available about these grassroots-based and often community-oriented organizations. Also, as indicated above, many have been created for purposes other than development. Some are "real" organizations whereas others are loose associations or temporary groupings formed by others for practical reasons. For example, many donors, NGOs,

American River College Library

and extension services have increasingly come to use the group approach for dissemination of credit, technology, and so forth because it is more "practical." Sometimes such small, informal groups can act independently and innovatively. In other cases they are merely links in a delivery chain. The literature is obscure about such particularities at this level. An example of how difficult it can be to assess both the activities and the degree of success or development orientation among these grassroots groups is taken from Ellis and Freeman: "The most prevalent groups are burial groups (present nowadays in most villages), women's groups, and credit groups created for particular purposes" (2004a). This indicates that most collective activities are community oriented, perhaps with some developmental purpose, depending on what credits are used for. However, in an earlier version of the same paper the authors found that "the most prevalent groups are burial groups (present in most villages), women's groups, and drinking groups (male membership)" (Ellis and Freeman 2004b, 17).[9] The difference may not seem great (in a personal communication Ellis said the drink was obtained by means of a savings and credit group), but it does indicate that such groups may not have any development orientation whatsoever. The issue here is not to determine which of the two writings is the "correct" one, but rather to illustrate how difficult it is to obtain reliable information about peasants' own associations at the micro level.

Also at this level, geography matters, and accessibility and market development represent strong motivating forces for establishing "modern" bridging and developmental organizations. In a study of rural organizations in Kenya, Cleaver reports:

> The type of organization predominating varied from village to village; the more marketized southern agricultural villages displayed greater individualization of social life, labour was hired rather than collective, membership of clubs and associations was largely for productive purposes such as livestock rearing or managing irrigation water. In the pioneer villages to the north of the district, where people settled in order to pursue mixed agricultural and pastoralist livelihoods; associational life revolved much more around reconstructed versions of "traditional" collective labour

arrangements, singing and dancing groups, and public events such as rainmaking. (2005, 901)

Atieno likewise reports about the successful development of the largely smallholder-based dairy sector in Kenya that managed to integrate smallholders with the private sector in a way that has "wide pro-poor benefits." It was, however, not an autonomous project but benefited from "substantial investment and government support." But this is only part of the story. The success was also due to "effective farmer unions and groups," but primarily they came about because the effort had "a focus on high potential areas with sound market infrastructure" (Atieno 2006, 1–2). Attempts to replicate it in other areas have not been as successful.

Also Schreiber found that in more accessible and "favoured" areas, "market-oriented actors—cooperatives and private companies—are the farmers' most important sources of innovation [and] marketing channels, [whereas in more remote locations] . . . self-help groups emerge as the most important sources of innovation . . . but their role in terms of providing access to services is often limited" (2002, 5).

NGOs and the Weakening of Civil Society

Against this background it is hardly surprising that donors and INGOs, when engaging in development in ESA on a grand scale, find few, if any, suitable partners to cooperate with and, therefore, often choose to "do development" themselves—at least for the time being. LOs and domestic NGOs were often seen to need capacity building, that is, a weaning period,, before they could be entrusted with "taking charge" of development. Somehow, such weaning periods never seem to end. Kelsall noted: "Donors and INGOs have a real problem in that at the same time as wanting to see NGOs getting their hands dirty at the grass roots, they also want sophisticated accounting and reporting systems in place, systems which one assumes would be facilitated by a well-equipped office. They are rarely willing to fund both" (2001, 142–43). In fact, INGOs and donors prefer to finance projects, but they are not funding the popular sectors of society (Hearn 1999), only the depending intermediaries. And even that appears to be

halfhearted, as they generally do not provide funds for "core functions" and "institutional capacity building" of the NGOs with
which they work (Onyando 1999; Bornstein 2003).

Donors' and INGOs' funding of NGOs is highly selective (ID21
2007) and "directed at a very particular section of civil society"
(Hearn 1999, 1), namely, at those NGOs that are willing to work
as subcontractors and accept foreign priorities and interpretations of need. Not only are African NGOs often reduced to subcontractors, but some "complain that grants or contracts
presented by Northern NGOs have been one-sided arrangements,
offered on a 'take it or leave it basis'" (McMahon 2007, 8). Over
time this has created a spiral of cumulative causation (some
would say a vicious circle), since the lion's part of funding goes
to the already well connected (Fafchamps and Owens 2006).
Because external funding represents such a large amount of
NGOs' resources, this is no minor inconvenience. Most NGOs
receive no or very little external funding and those that are funded
from abroad (and have their agendas decided from abroad) are
able to increase their market share. The effect is that externally
supported NGOs replace CBOs and grassroot initiatives (Roger
Kirkby, personal communication). Both Fafchamps and Owens
(2006) and Aipira et al. (2008) find that donors and INGOs actively (but perhaps not intentionally) are complicit in "crowding
out" unsupported domestic NGOs. In ESA there is much to support Duhu's conclusion that practices and conditions imposed
by donors "weaken civil society" (2005, 52).

Preliminary Assessment

While this chapter paints a rather disappointing picture of experiences with rural organizations after implementation of SAP in
ESA, it does not say that such organizations cannot fulfill important roles in development. Disappointment is always related to
expectations, and in many cases expectations have been both
naive and exaggerated. Organizations cannot create the preconditions for their own success. In an environment where poverty is
widespread, government often is nearly absent, markets are undeveloped, transport infrastructure leaves a lot to be desired, and
family, clan, and the economy of affection affect social as well as

economic interaction, there are no quick and easy solutions—especially not if these are based on foreign rationalities and misguided assumptions about the nature of aid-receiving societies.

True development from below is a slow process, but many of those who support this approach in theory appear to be in too much of a hurry to accept it in practice. Hence, the abovementioned "forced birth" of many LOs. This, in combination with external pressures to quickly scale up size and activities (Cracknell 2000) turned out to be particularly constraining, often exhausting African NGOs and LOs and stretching them beyond their capacity.

Nevertheless, for all the criticism of NGOs and farmers' associations in ESA, Ellis and Freeman underline that "it is plain that more useful things are accomplished and left behind to the future benefit of village citizens by NGOs, than by governments. In some instances, for example agricultural advice, . . . it is often only NGOs that have provided this type of service to villages" (2004a, 19). Similarly, Barr and Fafchamps found that "in general, client-community satisfaction with NGO interventions is high, even though some NGO staff are viewed as unresponsive, under-skilled, or self-serving" (2005, i). In some of the abovementioned cases the NGO "sector" obviously was preferable. Also Amutabi found that

Apart from paying salaries to civil servants, it seems that the government does not do anything else. It is not surprising to hear rural dwellers contending that . . . to them only NGOs are meaningful to their lives as they have always gone to their rescue, and provided them with "development." (2006, 193–94)

This positive record of NGOs—while sometimes well deserved—must, in all fairness, be seen in comparison with government agencies and programs, which have often been accused of inactivity and/or have had difficulties in reaching out in rural areas.[10] It can't be too difficult to leave a more positive imprint on the ground. However, the last part of the quotation indicates a (perhaps severe) dependency syndrome among beneficiaries where NGOs apparently are seen as providers of development rather than as mobilizers for development.

Hence, it is difficult to generalize about the character, status, and impact of peasants' associations in contemporary ESA. The examples of organizational efforts and experiences referred to above are by no means statistically representative. Nor were they meant to be. Rather, they underline the great diversity of organizational experiences that exists in contemporary ESA. Besides diversity, they also highlight some dubious aspects of externally supported organization-building policies, aspects supporting agencies often seem to overlook. Moreover, the most interesting kind of organization, the smallholders' own associations at the grassroots level, is the one we know the least about. Besides these, there are numerous organizations as well as types of organizations, and their records point in very different directions. Some are run by swindlers; others by philanthropists or business-oriented entrepreneurs; and yet others are "communal" with weak or nonexistent ambitions to function as change agents. Whereas the developmental potential of many organizations is hampered by lack of financial means and competence as well as by patronage and/or external dominance, others, albeit fewer, have shown a capacity to act independently and progressively and appear to be more self-reliant and confident than previously was the case. While these observations are indications of a new and promising development, one needs to keep in mind that there are few such stories told.

On the whole, governments are not all that comfortable with an organized but uncontrolled citizenry. Formal cooperatives, in most cases, suffer from benign neglect, while in some cases, notably Uganda, the government has made renewed attempts to strengthen (and likely also to control) the cooperatives. In Zambia the government has, in a manner reminiscent of failed policies of the 1960s and 1970s, made renewed attempts to use cooperatives as an outlet for subsidized inputs (but neglects the post-harvest side of the equation). Among associations outside governments, dependence on foreign donors and NGOs is usually strong, and there is often reason to wonder whose agenda is being implemented. A particularly problematic effect of donor-INGO-NGO "cooperation" is the tendency that real, domestic development associations and independent NGOs risk being crowded out and that Africans will be bereft of initiative and ownership of development. Crowding out takes many forms and occurs for many reasons, sometimes by default but sometimes also by design. Indigenous organizations are forced out not only because externally supported organizations have a more solid financial basis and can afford to hire professional staff, but also because they tend to pursue a foreign agenda. Externally supported organizations sometimes also compete unfairly with domestic organizations by distributing subsidized inputs (Cuellar et al. 2006; Aipira et al. 2008). It is also not all that uncommon for them to "pay farmers to attend meetings" (Utviklingsfondet n.d., 4). This process has not come equally far everywhere, and it is unevenly spread geographically. Nevertheless, it poses a real threat to development from below in ESA.

As for so-called indigenous development, we found several examples of viable, bridging, innovative, and market-oriented associations. These, however, are also not evenly distributed over different environments. Instead, the hypothesis that geography matters for organization building was confirmed. Not all of these were externally funded. In fact, some were reactions to external penetration. These "progressive" associations are found in areas already comparatively well connected to the outside world, whereas the bonding or "conservationist" type of organization dominates in the much larger but more peripheral areas. One needs to be careful indeed before venturing to generalize about the developmental capacity of NGOs, farmers' associations and other collective arrangements in ESA. In order to arrive at a more solid base for conclusions, we now turn our attention to experiences with organizations in West Africa.

Part III

THE WEST AFRICAN EXPERIENCE

As indicated in Chapter 1, the situation in West Africa in regard to peasant organizations, cooperatives and other forms of rural associations appears to differ in important ways from that in ESA. Growth in the number of organizations has been exceptional. The *World Development Report 2008* states that in the relatively short period "between 1982 and 2002 the percentage of villages with producer organizations rose from 8 to 65 percent in Senegal and from 21 to 91 percent in Burkina Faso" (World Bank 2007, 14). But it isn't only numbers that attract attention. Several contemporary writings refer to "the rich organizational landscape of [West] African villages" (de Janvry & Sadoulet 2004, 1; see also Toulmin & Guèye 2003; *IK Notes* 2005) and some West African countries have even been labeled "NGO-paradises" (Bierschenk and de Sardan 2003).

Remarkable features in West Africa, which have received widespread attention, are, for example, the frequently reported successes of the Naam movement in Burkina Faso, the acquisition of a British chocolate factory by a Ghanaian cocoa growers cooperative, the presence in several countries of autonomous farmers' associations and producers' organizations strong enough to challenge governments and influence agrarian policies (Bingen 1998; McKeon 1999) and progressive regional cooperation among national farmers' associations (McKeon, Watts, and Wolford 2004). A conclusion about which there presently seems to be widespread agreement is that "in many ways, the region leads the developing world in the blossoming of civil society that has occurred over the last decade . . . reflected in the rapid growth of local NGOs, farmers' associations, producer federations, . . . [and] grass-roots organizations" (IFAD 2001, 34).

This calls for special attention directed at West African organizations and the milieu in which they apparently thrive. One should be careful with generalizations, however. It has also been noted that in Francophone West Africa "the associative movement is stronger than in the region's Anglophone countries" (SWAC 2005, 24; see also Bierschenk and de Sardan 2003; Spore 2005). On a more general level attention has also been drawn to the "poorly developed organization of smallholder producers" (Toulmin and Guèye 2003, 9). Hence, and in sharp contrast to many other claims, it has also been concluded that West African farmers' associations are "ill-equipped to fulfil the expectations of governments and donors" (Spore 2005, 2). The situation thus appears to be considerably more complex than much contemporary literature declares. Hence, before a comparison can be made with ESA, we must try to solve this puzzle concerning the status, limitations, and potential of rural organizations in West Africa.

West Africa is large—sixteen countries with a population in 2006 of 280 million people, most of whom are poor rural dwellers with agriculture as their main livelihood source. It is neither possible nor meaningful to include all these countries in the present study. Hence, this section concentrates on a smaller range of countries, namely, Benin, Burkina Faso, Cote d'Ivoire, Ghana, Mali, Niger, Nigeria, and Senegal. This group includes both anglophone and francophone West Africa and, as in the previous section, allows highlighting both diversity and commonalities.

This part on West Africa is structured differently from the previous two chapters on ESA in the sense that more attention is directed at national experiences. Within the topical framework of each chapter differences and similarities between countries are highlighted. Chapter 4 presents various governments' control strategies, decentralization, and how these have affected organizations more generally. Chapter 5 focuses on cooperatives and rural producers' organizations more directly and pays special attention to a number of success stories. Chapter 6, finally, summarizes the West African experience, (re)interprets success stories, and makes an assessment of whether (and how) organizations in West Africa differ in any significant way from those elsewhere on the subcontinent.

Four

Decentralization and Organizations in West Africa

> Decentralization is a Pandora's box rather than a panacea for curing the evils of a distant state.
> —Carola Lentz, 2006

Economic and political-administrative decentralization is expected not only to enhance growth and democracy, but also— and even more—to facilitate the emergence of a variety of development organizations at different levels of society. As can be expected, the enabling character of the political environment differs among countries, and decentralization has been pursued with varying degrees of success in West Africa (Materu 2002). The region has had its fair share of centralized states, urban bias, and top-down policy implementation—one-party states in most countries; post-colonial "socialist" governments in, for example, Ghana, Guinea-Bissau, and Benin; and military regimes in, for example, Cote d'Ivoire, Ghana, Mali, and Nigeria. During most of the post-colonial era there was, thus, widespread government suspicion of autonomous organizations—and a similar distrust among peasants of government and state officials (Holmén 1990). However, central governments' effective control of rural areas was often weaker than assumed, and in many places there has for quite some time been room for establishing independent associations. Hence, the SAPs initiated in the 1980s and 1990s may have been less dramatic than has often been assumed. For instance, the cotton producers' strike and formation of the politically influential producers' union SYCOV in Mali in 1991 (Bingen 1998), as well as the riots in Senegal in 1988 and 1989 protesting against agricultural policy (Oya 2006) and subsequently leading to the establishment of a farmers' platform to redirect Senegalese agricultural policies (McKeon 1999), all have a preceding history of rural self-mobilization.

One major impetus for accepting (sometimes reluctantly) more decentralized political and administrative structures and the increasing tolerance of more or less autonomous organizations was the Sahel drought that hit West Africa in the 1970s. Millions of people were starving and many became eco-refugees in their own or neighboring countries. The event also exposed the limited capacity of governments, not only to develop agriculture but also to reach out and implement effective relief programs in affected areas. On the one hand, this spurred self-help initiatives in some locations. On the other hand, West Africa was flooded by NGOs coming to assist with relief and trying to organize development from below.

A further, closely linked circumstance was uneven geographical influence of governments in territories they supposedly governed. It has thus been suggested that, in West Africa, SAP-imposed decentralization has mostly taken the form of officially off-loading obligations governments neither would nor could fulfill anyway (Bierschenk and de Sardan 2003; Onibon, Dabiré, and Ferroukhi 1999). It has also been suggested that decentralization may have had mainly negative consequences because it is often locally interpreted as the return of traditional chieftaincy (Hagberg 2004; Le Meur 2006) and has reinforced patron-client hierarchies (Hårsmar 2004b; Juul 2006; Lentz 2006). Hence, a not uncommon opinion is that "the objectives of decentralisation policies can not be achieved because neo-traditional elites may exploit decentralisation measures to reinforce their power at the expense of desired rural development outcomes" (Onibon, Dabiré, and Ferroukhi, 1999, 5). The situation is, however, ambiguous, and the effects of decentralization vary from one locality to another, perhaps more so within countries than between them.

Decentralization in West Africa has followed different paths and has reached different "stages" depending on the historical situation during which it was to be implemented. Focusing on Francophone West Africa, Hagberg (2004) points out that whereas rural communes have been in place in Senegal for thirty years, they are relatively recent in Mali. In Niger, decentralization remains a project, and in Burkina Faso decentralization "in small steps" has been under way for a decade but, to date, communalization remains only partial. On the one hand, this reflects the circumstance that governments have implemented decentralization with varying degrees of enthusiasm—however, not necessarily because they are bad governors. On the other hand, this reflects the fact that decentralization has been forced upon governments by foreign institutions adopting a "blueprint" solution to perceived adversities. As such, it neglects the historical and cultural contexts in which it is to be realized. West African states, like their counterparts elsewhere on the continent, are in a process of nation building, and, therefore, decentralization may in many ways seem an odd or at least counterproductive endeavor. As noted by Hagberg, "The transfer of power from a centre to a periphery involves the construction of such a periphery in the first place!" (2004, 4).

Boone highlights that West African governments often have used quite different policies within their respective territories in regard to governance. These strategies, ranging from "usurpation" and "administrative occupation" (referring to a rather autonomous state with the ability to micro-manage local political processes) in certain areas, to "power-sharing" and "non-incorporation" in other areas (where "power-sharing" refers to "devolution of control over state resources and state prerogatives to rural elites" and non-incorporation to a situation where "state agents do *not* seek to exercise authority in the local arenas" (2003, 360, emphsis in original). The latter two appear to resemble such situations, where neither states nor "higher" classes have been able to "capture the peasantry," that Hydén (1983) has reported about from ESA. Boone found that "non-incorporation has been the state-building strategy in many zones that are occupied primarily by nomadic groups" (2003, 366), that is, in, for example, the Sahel area.

There is also a high risk that contemporary reforms—since they are accompanied by a large influx of foreign NGOs and donors who come with money to facilitate the process—will result not in decentralization but in prolonged or widened non-incorporation—not as a (domestic) strategy but as a perhaps unintended byproduct. "Donors that have been supporting decentralization processes often undermine local governments by channelling public aid through NGOs, leaving district assemblies with scarce resources" (Hagberg 2004, 7). If that is the case, one could expect a certain degree of reluctance toward peasants' and other organizations at both national and local levels of government. This chapter investigates decentralization in some West African countries in order to determine whether or not it has contributed to establishing an enabling environment for independent organizations.

Mali

Hillhorst and Toulmin, reporting from Mali, found that whereas traditional leadership normally remains strong there are also villages where "the traditional leadership structure or *chefferie* has lost much prestige so that the most important internal organisation identified by the villagers is now the *Association Villageoise*" (2000, 14). It is noteworthy that village associations date back to the 1970s, when their creation was encouraged by a parastatal, the Malian Company for Textile Development (Compagnie Malienne pour le Développement des Textiles), in order to provide an institution to handle the relations between cotton farmers and extension agents (ibid.). These village associations soon found it necessary to expand and coordinate activities and ultimately developed into a union, SYCOV, in 1991. Bingen suggested that "the industrial-type discipline imposed on smallholder producers has a catalytic mobilization effect. Cotton is a crop that has to be really 'tamed' from A to Z to achieve its optimum production potential. As such, it fosters the development of a consciousness among peasants roughly comparable to that more commonly found among factory workers" (1998, 275).

This is in stark contrast with formal institutions. Military government in Mali ended in 1991 after heavy popular protests, which also led to the formation of SYCOV. Decentralization manifested itself in 1999, when municipal elections transferred responsibilities from centrally appointed administrators to elected councils (ID21 2005; Hillhorst et al. 2005). Economic and administrative reforms have, however, been hampered by the weakness of the government at both central and local levels. Economically, the state retains control over the two major export commodities: gold and cotton. Administratively, "state ministries are weak and . . . the administration of the recently created communes is unable to provide anything but basic services" (BTI 2006b, 4). Decentralization in Mali is still young, and the local level lacks both an independent tax base and experience working with local groups (ID21 2005). Actually, "the transfer of powers in Mali from central to decentralised structures has become one of the major challenges of the decentralisation process today, and sometimes even restricts it to declarations of intent rather than concrete actions" (Hillhorst et al. 2005, 14). At least in part, this is because local governments, especially in remote parts of the country, sometimes face problems with recruiting personnel, particularly those with the needed skills. Hence, "not all communes . . . have succeeded in employing general secretaries or an administrator" (ibid., 13). More or less by default, this has opened up space for civic organizations, which, however, to a high degree, depend on foreign support.

Mali has a high number of NGOs and other groups (BTI 2006b), but this high number of organizations to a great extent reflects the availability of funding from foreign governments and nongovernmental donors (ibid.; Bingen 1998). Whereas in some other countries relations between NGOs and governments have been strained, in Mali "there is no clear separation of state and civil society; many members of the government also run their own NGOs" (BTI 2006b, 13). Worth emphasizing, however, is that whereas in the wealthier cotton-producing southern regions a new kind of professional (bridging) leadership is emerging (Bingen 1998), in other parts of the country traditional leaders remain strong, especially in the north, which "has remained largely beyond the control of the central state" (BTI 2006b, 1). According to our hypothesis, local organizations in such peripheral areas would be primarily of the bonding type.

Senegal

A common opinion is that "since independence from France in 1960, Senegal has been a showcase of political development in West Africa" (BTI 2006a, 2). This is somewhat surprising because the weak post-independence Senegalese government, like so many others, found it more urgent to secure cheap food for the urban population (by way of exploitative state-run cooperatives and marketing boards) than to meet the demands of a dispersed rural population (McKeon, Watts, and Wolford 2004). By the 1970s, when the country was hit by the Sahel drought, this system was already in crisis. Both farmers and government faced progressive indebtedness, and "the first autonomous peasant associations began to spring up in various regions of Senegal" (ibid., 11). Actually, the Senegalese government encouraged local NGOs to work with people affected by the drought (Michael 2004). In 1976, "12 associations formed a national federation which obtained legal status in 1978 as the Federation des ONG Sénégalaises (FONGS), a title imposed by the government to distinguish them from the official cooperatives" (McKeon, Watts, and Wolford 2004, 11). The "newly emerging Senegalese NGO sector was initially involved in relief activities until the scaling back of the state propelled NGOs into the diverse range of development sectors in which they now work" (Michael 2004, 92). With this broadened room to maneuver for independent associations, Senegal has (together with Burkina Faso) been labeled a "veritable NGO paradise" (Bierschenk and de Sardan 2003, 162).

For example, McKeon, Watts, and Wolford point out that "Senegal was one of the very few sub-Saharan African countries in which farmers' organizations were seriously involved in determining the content of ASIP" (the World Bank-promoted Agricultural Structural Investment Program) in the 1990s (2004, 16). This is despite the fact that "Senegal has a highly centralised political system," which "is present throughout the country, albeit less so in remote areas" (BTI 2006a, 10, 3). It appears to be the same thing with NGOs. Whereas "self-organized associations such as savings groups *(tontines)*, hometown associations or religious groups of a religious leader *(marabout)* are relatively common (2006a, 5), . . . most local NGOs are constantly challenged by the lack of funding . . . resulting [in] high dependence on donor funding and concentration of activity in the capital" (ibid., 5, 9). Outside the capital, for example, in Senegal's groundnut basin, the country's main export-producing region, "the central government [has] allowed and encouraged indigenous rural authorities to capture and colonize nearly all outposts of the state" (Boone 2003, 367; see also Juul 2006). This, however, need not be detrimental to development. In Senegal it has enabled farmers, at least in high-potential areas, to form their own, and as it seems, more progressive organizations, which on some occasions have been able to challenge the government's agricultural policies. For example, Oya reports that "on 26 Jan. 2003, more than 20 000 farmers gathered in Dakar football stadium to demonstrate against the government's inaction vis-à-vis agriculture and pronounced a manifesto with their claims" (2006, 224n39).[1]

The possibly strong position of Senegalese NGOs and farmers' organizations must be seen in relation to the decentralization policies implemented during the last decades. Apparently, government inactivity has not been limited to agriculture. Since 1996 tax collection has been transferred from the state agent to locally elected councils, with the result that tax recovery is now close to nil. Senegal is a formal democracy, and for fear of not being reelected, local politicians do not collect taxes. Taxes "are no longer considered to be an obligation, but rather as a 'contribution' to local development" (Juul 2006, 835). Hence, "by 2001 the rural councils found themselves paralysed by lack of development funds" (ibid., 823). Consequently, "none of the anticipated development projects are being carried out and no investments [are] made. . . . Instead, politicians concentrate on trying to mobilize donor agencies to provide the missing funding" (ibid., 835). Clearly, there is room for a wide spectrum of domestic as well as foreign nongovernmental associations in rural Senegal.

While the above circumstances have led many writers to conclude that Senegalese NGOs and associations are strong and independent, Michael (2004) gives a much less optimistic picture of Senegalese NGOs than do most other authors. Although not denying their comparatively prominent position in society, she finds them generally to be both weak and dependent. Unlike in, for example, Tanzania, where domestic NGOs are highly specialized, Senegalese NGOs lack focus and specialization. An overwhelming majority are generalists working across a variety of fields, and there is a high degree of duplication of activities. In contrast, there is an outspoken geographical specialization, and domestic NGOs are never in direct competition with each other. Senegalese NGOs differ from similar organizations elsewhere in Africa also in the sense that they have acquired a certain financial independence from donors and INGOs. Even with a low ability to self-finance, they have—and make use of—the power to turn down external funding.

With their generalist approach and geographic monopolies, if one donor does not suit them they will likely obtain funding from another who is eager to register projects. Hence, Senegalese NGOs have been able to respond to the ever-changing funding priorities of donor agencies and find themselves a niche regardless of the development trend of the moment. It is, however, a limited freedom. Lack of specialization is also a weakness because all that these domestic NGOs have to offer is a role as a go-between. The result, says Michael, is that donor agencies have used the same strategy and have "balkanized the country" with different donors taking different regions as areas of focus. It is, however, questionable whether this should be blamed entirely on the external agencies. It may just as well be a sign of their ability to adjust to local circumstances. In any case, even though Senegalese NGOs to some degree can play one donor off against another, they do remain dependent on outside funding. The focus of domestic NGOs—as is also often the case with local governments—is decided, or at least heavily influenced, by donors. The situation of Senegalese NGOs appears to be quite ambiguous. According to Michael, they "sacrifice their potential to develop power in the long run. Financial security and an ability to turn down donor funds are important manifestations of power, but they are likely to be meaningless if an NGO has lost sight of its objectives and is following someone else's priorities" (Michael 2004, 106).[2]

Burkina Faso

The former French colony Upper Volta (renamed Burkina Faso—the land of the honest people—in 1983) is one of the world's poorest countries and almost completely located within the Sahel region. Since independence the country has been plagued by corruption, political instability, military rule, and a series of attempted or accomplished coups d'état. Burkinabé governments appear to have followed what Boone (2003) calls a "non-incorporation" strategy with little presence of state institutions in the rural areas. State resources seldom reach the countryside, instead being usurped by a small elite through patronage (BTI 2006f). Authoritarian rule has been constantly challenged and, following strong pressures from below in the late 1980s (ibid.), a course of democratization and decentralization was begun in 1991 (NSSD 2003) and a law on decentralization was passed in 1998 (World Bank 2001).

However, due to the state's limited presence—and hence authority—in rural areas, democratization and decentralization have resulted in the emergence of parallel structures of authority (Thiéba 2004). Worse, "lack of clarity regarding certain issues, such as the role of elected local officials" (ibid., 29), has led to fragmentation of political arenas and informalization of political authority and to complicated political games at the local level rendering the political process increasingly unpredictable (Hagberg 2006). Consequently, "democratic reforms have been partial and short-sighted, reaching only as far as needed to appease looming social unrest and intense popular pressure" (BTI 2006f, 14). Implementation of decentralization "essentially concerns urban settings and small towns in rural areas. . . . The current legal framework is supportive of community-based organisations at the village level, yet does not assign responsibility to rural districts to provide services to villages outside their own town boundaries" (UNCDF 2004, 2). Reportedly, a new period of authoritarianism set in in the late 1990s (BTI 2006f; Soulama 2003; Enrico Luzzati, personal communication). New regulations reduced the levels of local government to two (region and municipality) and, paradoxically, "made it more complicated for villages . . . to become involved in the decentralisation process. . . . Placing villages under regional rather than provincial control will distance villagers from the authorities that are supposed to represent them—the regional councils scheduled to be put in place in 2011" (Bagré et al. 2004, 13).

At the same time, natural resources in Burkina Faso are sometimes managed by

> legitimately constituted local users' associations. . . . There are several types of users' association: for example those centred around natural resources with high economic value, such as the co-operatives in irrigated areas . . . or fishermen's

associations; and associations in sylvo-pastoral areas. [However], . . . representatives of these associations or cooperatives are worried on several accounts. . . . They are particularly concerned that local governments in rural areas will strip them of the powers they already exercise over natural resource management. . . . They also worry that local government does not delegate the rights prescribed in the TOD [Textes d'Orientation de la Décentralisation—legal framework for decentralization]." (Thiéba 2004, 27–28).

Freedom of association is guaranteed in the constitution, and Burkina Faso is the home of a great number of active NGOs and associations (Thiéba 2004; BTI 2006f), the number of which has grown considerably since the big drought in the 1970s (NSSD 2003). Whereas "several NGOs play an important role in expressing needs and goals and employ all legal and/or tolerated means of doing so" (BTI 2006f, 4), their de facto autonomy from the ruling elite can, however, sometimes be doubted. Although Burkina Faso is formally a parliamentary democracy, behind the scenes the military remains strong and "retired army members often play an important role in NGOs" as do several members of parliament (ibid., 5). Nevertheless, a culture of self-help is said to permeate society, and elite capture of NGOs may be limited. As others have emphasized, "The Sankara era (Captain Sankara ruled Burkina from 1983 to 1987) continues to define Burkina Faso" (ibid.).

The former president's revolutionary reform policies, which aimed for an African socialist society based on communities and self-reliance, are said to live on in the memory of many Burkinabé. Burkina Faso is also the birthplace of the Naam movement that, beginning in the 1970s and emphasizing community-driven development, has spread to a large number of countries in West Africa. (The Naam movement will be discussed in more detail in Chapter 5.) Even during the latest drive toward increased authoritarianism (since 1997), "civil society gained in power as hundreds of NGOs, one of Africa's strongest human rights movements, trade unions, students and women's associations used their remaining liberties to express their dissatisfaction with the government . . . [eventually forcing the regime to] implement political, constitutional and electoral reforms" (BTI 2006f, 3). But it is not only at this level that organized civil society has become influential. "Peasant organizations . . . have [also] come to occupy an important political space at the local level" (Hårsmar 2004b, 3). Hence, political power is, in an informal way, shared with presumably nonpolitical institutions. Whereas local governments are constrained and central government has limited outreach, local authority is fragmented and unpredictable—a situation reminiscent of many other countries in the region (such as Benin, Nigeria, and Senegal). Burkina Faso represents an interesting case where corrupt and repressive rule apparently goes hand in hand with strong and flourishing CSOs.

Benin

Since independence in 1960 the political development of Benin has been characterized by "regime instability and a series of military interventions" (BTI 2006e, 2). After Lieutenant Kérékou's coup d'état in 1972, a Marxist-Leninist regime was installed and remained in power for eighteen years. This regime was, however, not as omnipresent as the label Marxist-Leninist might imply (IFAD 2005). Gazibo characterized it as "soft authoritarianism" (2005, 74). In 1990, after popular protests and mass uprisings eventually leading to a Conference Nationale, the regime was replaced by a multi-party system (ibid.). Having avoided political violence and extremism and sustained "an exceptional level of democracy," it has been stated that "Benin's process of transformation defies conventional wisdom" (BTI 2006e, 1).[3] Despite the fact that decentralization has not been completed (Bierschenk and de Sardan 2003, 146), Benin has been called "a showcase of democracy in West Africa" (BTI 2006e) and is widely regarded as a model of democratic transition (Gazibo 2005). One circumstance that contributed to this success was the atypical treatment by foreign donors. In 1989 an agreement was signed with the IMF and the World Bank, and Benin was one of the first countries to have a substantial part of its debt canceled. At the same time, Benin enjoyed a comparatively benign reduction in bilateral aid while multilateral aid tripled between 1988 and 1990 (ibid.).

The above-mentioned enthusiasm from donors and international institutions may seem somewhat premature since these favorable debt and aid agreements were not provided in appreciation of liberal reforms undertaken. On the contrary, they predated democratization and may be interpreted as a bribe. In any case, the transition has not been as smooth as suggested. Politically, decentralization has been delayed, in part due to hesitations and maneuvers fueled by political and religious conflicts in parts of the country (Le Meur 2006). Economically, privatization has stagnated (IFAD 2005), and it is prohibitively expensive to register an enterprise (Bierschenk, Brüntrup-Seidemann, and Hoffmann 1999). In the cotton sector, privatization "was managed so inefficiently that most growers prefer a return to a fully public and centralized marketing board system" (BTI 2006e, 8). Administratively, the reform measures have also stagnated (IFAD 2005)—or failed. Formally, devolution has been directed only at one level of local government, the communes (UNCDF 2003). However, the institutional context remains weak (BTI 2006e), with the state unable to deliver (Bierschenk, Brüntrup-Seidemann, and Hoffmann 1999) or to impose its rules (Bierschenk and de Sardan 2003).

The result is not only weak local government and "frictions between appointed district governors and elected councils and mayors" (BTI 2006e, 6), but, in fact, democratization has "heightened the existing fragmentation of local arenas and the informalisation of political practices . . . thus reducing the predictability of political processes and the accountability of local political institutions" (Bierschenk and de Sardan 2003, 146–47). The outcome is a situation where "political power is exercised not solely by official political authorities (such as community councils), or by officious ones (such as the traditional chiefs), but also through institutions which at first sight do not seem to be political (for example . . . peasant associations)" (ibid., 159). The challenge for decentralization in today's Benin, says Le Meur "concerns the integration of village governmentality into a decentralized state design" (2006, 895).

Freedom of association is legally guaranteed and Benin is the home of a multitude of social and political associations (BTI 2006e). The country has seen an "explosive growth of NGO-activities since the early 1990s" (Bierschenk, Brüntrup-Seidemann, and Hoffmann 1999, 413), with more than one thousand NGOs officially registered in January 2000 (IFAD 2000). Most have a rural orientation, and rural organizations exist in all parts of the country (ibid.). They tend to be of the "bonded rather than bridged" kind (BTI 2006e, 7). Most national level associations have been recently established and have encountered a number of difficulties—financial, technical, and managerial—and their performance is frequently deemed mediocre (ibid.). Their dependence on outside finance is often strong (IFAD 2000; BTI 2006e; Bierschenk, Brüntrup-Seidemann, and Hoffmann 1999). At the national level there is no significant state intervention in the activities of associations (BTI 2006e), which is most likely explained by the fact that "the majority of NGOs do not have political agendas" (Bierschenk, Brüntrup-Seidemann, and Hoffmann 1999, 429). Instead, they are, according to Platteau and Gaspart, often merely "empty shells established with the sole purpose of capturing aid" (2003a, n6). In contrast, on the local level "government services do make efforts to control and co-ordinate NGO activities. . . . The only problem is that NGOs are often not interested in being co-ordinated" (ibid.).

Cote d'Ivoire

In Cote d'Ivoire the post-independence regime of Houphouet Boigny ignored indigenous rural authorities, which had few points of access to state power and resources. Whereas in the interior the government's strategy appears to have been "non-incorporation," in the southern part of the country

> indigenous rural authorities were extremely weak, both politically and economically . . . colonial rule [and] . . . land pioneering across the entire south created rural communities that were new, ethnically heterogeneous, and marked by low levels of social cohesion. The Ivorian government's administrative presence at the local level has been minimal and its strategy in the south has been "administrative colonisation," a strategy that *avoided* the creation of local-level points of access to state power and resources. (Boone 2003, 368)

This has remained the pattern also post-Boigny and post-SAP. Consequently, says Boone, not only the rural elites but also peasant society in general have remained weak in Cote d'Ivoire. Local governments have "neither the capacity nor the legal powers to take action." Crook notes that "Cote d'Ivoire's system of *communes* . . . should in principle have encouraged a popular community-based development. . . . [However], communes have been dominated by Mayors, mainly elite politicians who often continue to reside in Abidjan" (Crook 2003, 80).

"Cote d'Ivoire has been in profound economic and social crisis since the 1990s" (Bosc et al. 2002, 69), which may explain why there is comparatively little published, especially in English, about NGOs or farmers' associations in the country. The civil strife of the early 2000s has not created a more enabling environment. What is known is that organizational structures tend to be weak and that both the union and the newly liberated rural producers' organizations lack the "organizational, administrative and negotiating capacities that would enable them to collectively manage marketing [and so on] . . . within a context that has suddenly become [violent], competitive and uncertain" (ibid., 34).

Ghana

In Ghana the situation has been quite different. Whereas state presence and control has been comparatively light in the interior, in the southern parts of the country

> Nkrumah faced a direct challenge to his rule from a politically and economically powerful rural elite . . . [that] contested directly the regime's attempt to intensify the taxation of export-crop producers. In response, the Nkrumah regime built institutions to link state and countryside that were designed to destroy the political power of the rural elite and to usurp their economic power. (Boone 2003, 368)

Later, the coup d'état by Jerry Rawlings in 1981 "ushered in one of the most ambitious and profound reform programs in African history (BTI 2006c, 3). The Rawlings regime undertook to rebuild the "local state" (Boone 2003) and introduced district assemblies, which were "initially successful in enhancing electoral participation and giving access to representation to normally excluded groups" (Crook 2003, 79). By the late 1980s, however, their influence was fading (ibid.).

In the end, governance structures have remained largely intact. "The politics of institutional choice have been remarkably similar to what was observed during the Nkrumah period" (Boone 2003, 372). In other words, a strong presence in the south, whereas in the northern, "less populated, rural areas . . . the visibility of the state is not as prominent" (BTI 2006c, 4). The Ghanaian government's reform policies have aimed at economic reform but have given much less attention to administrative reform. Hence, devolution of power remains limited, and local governments in Ghana remain weak and without the legal power to take many initiatives (Crook 2003). For example, local councils are highly dependent on allocation of resources from Accra, and 30 percent of the members of the elected district assemblies are appointed by the president, as is the district chief executive (Public Agenda 2006; Jütting et al. 2005; BTI 2006c). Nevertheless, decentralization has reinforced clientelism and neo-patrimonial rule (Lentz 2006).

While this may not sound like an enabling environment, civil society in Ghana is and has been stronger than in Cote d'Ivoire (see, for example, Boone 2003; Young, Sherman, and Rose 1981) and is now said to be "asserting itself and is increasingly visible in the urban areas" (BTI 2006c, 7). However, it has also been found that NGOs in Ghana are "of a top-down nature. They are urban-based and have little or no contact with grassroot farmers" (Seini and Nyanteng 2003, 21). Also, "in the rural areas, social self-organization has increased modestly" (BTI 2006c, 7). Crook opines many peasants' associations, "in spite of their 'community based' character, . . . are run by local elites and attempt to raise funds through encouraging patronage. . . . They would rarely challenge existing social hierarchies" (2003, 80). Nevertheless, as will be shown below, some rural, independent, but nonpolitical peasants' associations have recently made some remarkable achievements.

Nigeria

Contemporary Nigeria is complicated. Information about decentralization, NGOs, and farmers' associations is scarce and contradictory. Nigeria, West Africa's largest and most populous country, became an independent nation in 1960. From 1966 to

1999 the country was ruled (except during the short-lived Second Republic, 1979–83) by military regimes, which seized power in coup d'états and counter coups. Economic SAP was implemented between 1986 and 1993, and in 1999 democracy was reachieved and a civilian administration installed. It has been stated that, since then, "Nigeria is one of the few countries in the developing world to have significantly decentralized both resources and responsibilities . . . to locally elected governments" (Khemani 2004, 2). Others, however, are of the completely opposite opinion, saying that it is rather a question of "decentralization by default" (Andrae 2004, 2) and that the government has "failed to pursue policies aimed at political transformation. . . . Overall, Nigeria has made modest progress toward democracy and a market economy, but there have been serious setbacks as well" (BTI 2006d, 1).

With the return to democracy the role of states (Nigeria is a federation made up of thirty-six states and the federal territory of Abuja) and local governments has been accentuated. The 1999 constitution provides for the establishment of local governments, which, however, have been made "creatures of the state government" (Akindele, Olaopa, and Obiyan 2002). The African Development Fund found that there is still "a heavy, top-down orientation to the role of government and civil society" (2005, 12). In particular, the economic dependence of local governments remains strong. Nigerian local governments have shown an "inability to raise substantial portions of their total recurrent revenue requirements from local sources" (Akindele, Olaopa, and Obiyan 2002, 565), instead being "overwhelmingly dependent on federal revenue transfers for the discharge of their responsibilities" (Khemani 2004, 3). Since "the current constitution (1999) . . . is ambiguous with regard to the authority and autonomy of local governments in providing basic services" (ibid.), there is "overlap of responsibilities among the three tiers of governments" (African Development Fund 2005, 13). Despite reforms, local governments suffer "continuous infringements of their revenue rights by state governments" (Akindele, Olaopa, and Obiyan 2002, 565).

Nigeria is unique among sub-Saharan countries in that it has enjoyed large incomes from oil exports. This has been a mixed blessing, however, and the sharply climbing oil prices in the 1970s and 1980s turned the country into "an institutionalized kleptocracy" (BTI 2006d, 3), where "oil revenues have tended to disappear into many deep pockets, while the pockets of the poor remain as empty as ever" (Djurfeldt 2006, vii). Also, after democratization "politics is still basically warfare" (Ibeanu and Nzei 1998, 30), and the military lurks behind the scene. Nigeria is still "ranked among the most corrupt countries in the world." One major reason obviously is that "the government lacks a monopoly on the use of force, political will and a judicial control." Hence, at all levels of society, the Nigerian government has "limited *de facto* power to govern." Consequently, the presidential elections in 2003 were "marred with widespread fraud, violence and open ballot rigging." The result was "a wave of previously unknown political violence, organized crime, and ethnic and religious conflicts [which] hit most of the 36 federal states and Abuja." Similarly, in 2004 the local government elections were "stage-managed by the ruling party" (BTI 2006d, 13, 5, 11, 3, 1, 4). Not only are there tensions between central government and state governments, there is also competition between state governments, and local governments on the one hand, and between modern and traditional sources of power on the other. Milligan and Binns found "little evidence that customary institutions had broken down or were malfunctioning." At the grassroots level "the emergence of the police and local government, as a parallel form of conflict management . . . enable people to 'forum shop', selecting the fora that are likely to find in their favour" (2007, 149).

One could assume that, under these circumstances, there would be little room for people to organize. It has, however, been claimed that Nigeria has a long history of associational groups and organizations that "challenge the state and critique its response to political and economic problems. . . . They are not political parties but associations whose social and economic agenda compel them to make claims on the state" (Okome 1999, 1). Hudock likewise states: "Nigeria's NGO sector has been particularly powerful in terms of challenging the establishment" (2000, 3). Even if unlikely, it may of course be true that autonomous groups thrive under situations of extreme repression, as claimed by Okome (1999). The present situation is ambiguous. Whereas it has been suggested that there are now a multitude of strong and influential farmers' associations in Nigeria (Patrick

Kormawa, personal communication), others claim that "outside the state system and state sector only a few influential interest groups exist" (BTI 2006d, 6).

The Department of Rural Development encourages farmers to work collectively and supports "enclave projects," which, however, "tend to be showcase projects . . . attractive to retired high-ranking civil servants and other privileged members of society" (Bingen 2003, 18). Hence, a plausible assessment of the scope for independent organizations to thrive in contemporary Nigeria is that "the country's rather limited experience with civil society, democracy and the rule of law has hindered the stabilization and expansion of democratic transformation" (BTI 2006d, 10).[4] Presently, therefore, "self-organization . . . encounters political and socio-economic barriers that include violence and lack of funds . . . [and] there is relatively little trust among the population that cuts across different segments of society" (2006d, 7). The space available for autonomous organization building among grassroots appears to be severely constrained, and Nigeria is hardly attractive for NGOs either.

From the examples above it appears that donors and foreign NGOs may have a heyday in contemporary West Africa. It is, however, equally clear that the playing field for domestic NGOs, independent associations, and grassroots organizations in contemporary West Africa is not as level and clear-cut as has often been suggested. This is highlighted by the contrasting interpretations of the status and potentials of organizations that are often presented in the reviewed literature. Although much has been written about West African organizations, to a large extent they remain in a "black box." The above summary indicates that, despite some exceptional successes, West African civic organizations still face a mass of hurdles. Administrative and economic reforms have to some extent provided wider room for maneuvering for some organizations. In other cases control attempts and bureaucratic obstacles limit the field of action. Whereas, in most countries, the number of NGOs and other organizations has grown rapidly during the last decades, progressive (that is, professional, bridging) organizations seem to be confined to rather limited high-potential areas, while the much larger peripheries primarily are the home of more conservative, bonding organizations. Bearing in mind that bridging functions also provide ample room for patronage to leaders of associations, this is not to say that the former type of organization necessarily is more democratic or inclusive.

Moreover, while a few organizations may be well endowed, most domestic NGOs and other organizations (including local governments) lack financial resources as well as technical and managerial skills, and their dependence on external support is generally high—as is sometimes their dependence on close links to governments and established elites. At the same time, the existence of parallel power structures—not only between traditional and modern authority, but also between political and presumably nonpolitical entities—makes the whole situation obscure and unpredictable, allowing "forum shopping," which further undermines formal authority. Moreover, not only in Ghana but all over West Africa, "decentralization projects [have] become arenas of debate over the boundaries of community and the relationship between 'local' and national citizenship . . . [as well as] the relevance of ethnic versus territorial criteria in defining local citizenship" (Lentz 2006, 901).

Furthermore, and contrary to expectations, it has been concluded that "devolution does not motivate more local 'self-help' . . . but rather intensifies special-interest politics and political mobilization which is aimed at securing a 'larger share of the national cake,' in the form of more state funds, infrastructure and posts for the locality" (Lentz 2006, 901–2). Thus, the economy of affection reasserts itself and often seems more capable of capturing the state than vice versa. This is also likely to have far-reaching effects on the character, activities, and ambitions of organizations in West Africa. Before a final assessment can be made of the characters, potentials, and limitations of West African associations—and their operational environment—a closer look at cooperatives, producers' organizations, and other rural associations at the grassroots level is warranted. This is the topic of the next two chapters.

Five

Farmers' Associations in West Africa

Show me the high public official that doesn't on some occasion create his own NGO.
—J-P OLIVIER DE SARDAN, 2007

Against the background of decentralization policies adopted (more or less), and broadly given account for above, this chapter focuses directly on rural organizations. It highlights the fate of cooperatives and gives special attention to some remarkable experiences of organization building from below, which seem to make West Africa quite exceptional. Apart from presenting similarities and differences in national experiences with organizations, it also pays attention to recent efforts of organizational cooperation at the regional (that is, supra-national) level—a feature that, likewise, appears to be unique in an African context.

Cooperatives, Producers' Organizations, and Farmers' Associations

Cooperative organizations in West Africa have in large degree experienced the same history of colonial control and post-colonial state capture, subordination and inefficiency as did their counterparts in ESA (Holmén 1990). Hence, Akande declares that formal cooperatives "have not been universally successful" (2006, 121), and McKeon, Watts, and Wolford point to the "failure of state-sponsored agricultural policies and rural cooperatives" (2004, iv) in West Africa. Mistrust of formal cooperatives was widespread, and in many areas a largely uncaptured peasantry managed to take the exit option and either retreat into subsistence production or form their own associations, or both. For example, in Senegal "during the 1970s, autonomous village-based associations began to spring up alongside of the State-promoted cooperatives, stimulated by the drought and the food crisis" (McKeon 1999, 335). In Ghana "the majority of farmers has long since abandoned the government-run coops" (Taylor 2003, 2). In that sense, it may be justified to speak of a cooperative crisis. However, West Africa is also the scene for innovative and decentralized approaches to development and has seen the birth of large numbers of autonomous associations of various kinds. Hence, while "the traditional [state-led] model of cooperative is passing through a crisis, . . . a lot of other groups or associations, which may be considered as informal cooperatives, are arising" (Kibora 1999, 171).

Many factors have contributed to this development. SAP and withdrawal of the state from many of its previous functions are, of course, part of the story. However, this doesn't set West Africa apart from eastern Africa except that SAP came later to West Africa (Friis-Hansen 2000). One circumstance that distinguishes West Africa is the Sahel drought in the 1970s, which forced people to be innovative and find new ways to cooperate for mutual benefit. Another, linked, reason was that many foreign donors and NGOs came to rescue the victims of the drought by way of strengthening or introducing cooperative and other forms of group-based undertakings. Thus, large parts of West Africa (for example, Tchad, Niger, Mali, Burkina Faso, and Senegal) have a longer history of (massive) promotion of associations than most other parts of Africa. This is likely to have contributed to the apparently greater contemporary presence of associations and organized self-help initiatives in the region. Many cooperatives are independent, "spontaneous" creations, but sometimes the state—as part of decentralization policy—actively contributes to their formation. For example, in 1998 the government of Burkina Faso adopted a national policy to promote cooperatives (SWAC 2005). So, perhaps, did the Nigerian government (see below). As the following sections show, attempts to reform and restructure cooperatives as well as to create an enabling environment for other associations have been made with varying objectives, seriousness, and ambitions—and with different degrees of success.

Nigeria

At the time of writing, the fate of cooperatives in Nigeria is unclear. When military rule was about to end, Ibeanu and Nzei frankly declared that Nigerian cooperatives were "in a poor financial state" (1998, 51). Haskell has reported that farmer associations, frequently called cooperatives, "do not have a history as viable business entities. Rather, they have served as vehicles for distribution of governmental programmes [and] . . . farmers have rarely made use of cooperatives for marketing purposes" (2004, 1). Hence, the FAO (2005) found a "lack of effective farmer organizations and cooperatives" in the country, and Bello noted a "low capacity of the organized farmer groups in service delivery" (2007, 46). One reason could be that "the word 'co-operative' is hardly used anymore, yet farmers' associations thrive" (Patrick Kormawa, personal communication). The ambiguity of the matter is extensive. Whereas Ogunbayo states that "the contribution of various farmers' cooperative societies in the country is high" (2003, 39), and Haskell contends that the Nigerian government presently places "increased emphasis on the development of successful cooperative businesses" (2004, 1; see also Akande 2005; Adeyemo and Bamire 2005), Bingen found that "recent policy documents addressing agricultural and integrated rural development policy do not address producer organizations" (2003, 18).

This may be playing with words. However, in the prevailing (previous?) system, "individuals or cliques often co-opt the primary cooperatives for political gains. Similarly, the apex cooperatives often do not have the national authority, expertise or information that their names suggest. Furthermore, some commodities . . . have more than one 'national' producer organization vying for producer loyalty and policy support" (Bingen 2003, 18). This could, perhaps, explain why Nigeria's erstwhile cooperative system is now being replaced by farmers' groups organized and managed by NGOs, which, according to Akande, "have proved extremely efficient and effective in their operations [but have] . . . very limited effect in terms of coverage" (2006, 122; for the latter aspect, see also Ogunbayo 2003). As with everything else in contemporary Nigeria, the present status and potential of cooperatives and other rural association remains clouded and highly uncertain.

An indication of how cumbersome it can be to organize, even for harmless purposes, is taken from Adeyeye (2001). The Family Economic Advancement Programme (FEAP) was introduced in 1997 to make credit available to the poor for investment in income-generating projects. FEAP was designed to provide loans on a cooperative basis.

> FEAP credit guidelines stipulates [*sic*] that prospective beneficiaries must submit application for loan to their ward head through the ward secretary; have their application screened by the ward, local government and state co-ordinating committees respectively; and have their integrity vouched for by their ward head and verified by the local government and state co-ordinating committees. . . . All applications for FEAP loan [*sic*] must be submitted with the following documents: copy of cooperative society registration certificate, copy of group registration certificate issued by FEAP secretariat, evidence of account with participating bank; two recent passport photograph [*sic*] of group leader and the Secretary or Treasurer who shall be signatories to the account and bearing attestation as guarantors. Also, recommendations and endorsement of loan application by the ward committee, local government committee, and the state co-ordinating committee are to be submitted while participating banks are to approve and disburse the loan based on their assessment of the loan application with respect to project's technical, financial and economic viability as evidenced in a duly prepared feasibility report. (Adeyeye 2001, 24–25)

This, the author says, reflects a more general situation where the Nigerian economy is "full of attempts at alleviating poverty especially among vulnerable groups based on cooperative ideals [however] with large degrees of failure" (Adeyeye 2001, 1).

Niger

In Niger, "decentralisation . . . is still a project" (de Sardan 2004, 2). This is not because the state is overly centralized, but rather because it is weak, with limited geographical influence. Whereas urban-based NGOs are "extremely tied to politicians" (de Sardan

2007, 12), "in the rural milieu, the chieftaincy is still the administrative power base" (de Sardan 2004). Since the liberalization in the early 1990s, Niger has seen an "associational boom" (Mohamadou 2004). Nevertheless, there is a general lack of effective farmer organizations and cooperatives in the country (ibid.; Souley and Hahonou 2004; FAO 2005; de Sardan 2005; de Sardan 2007), and many of those groups and associations that do exist are "fakes, created just to get money from foreign aid" (Astrig Tasgian 2006, personal communication; see also de Sardan 2004). External pressures for decentralization are strong, and the government has, reportedly, "gone further than most other governments" in order to turn a previously highly centralized irrigation system into a decentralized system based on cooperatives (Abernethy et al. 2000, 1). A brief summary follows.

> Modern methods of irrigation were introduced in Niger in the 1960s. The purpose was twofold: to produce rice for (mainly) a growing urban population and to settle peasants in a country where good farmland is scarce. Water is pumped from the Niger River and distributed to the fields through a network of canals. In the year 2000 there were forty-two of these systems, covering an irrigated area of almost ten thousand hectares (approximately 24,650 acres) with an average size of 230 ha (568 acres) per system. Since 1982 the governments' policy has been to promote irrigator organizations at each of the irrigation system, and to transfer the responsibility for operating and maintaining the facilities to these organizations. Two levels of organizations have been promoted, production groups and cooperatives. Both are hydraulically defined. The mutual production groups (Groupement Mutualiste des Producteurs, GMP) compose the lowest formal level of organization with on average 150 members farming an area that usually ranges from 40 to 60 ha (approximately 100 to 150 acres). GMPs typically exist for the command of a specific secondary canal and all tertiary canals dependent on it.
>
> The cooperative is the unit responsible for an entire irrigation system, including the main pumping station on the river. It controls most of the collection and spending of financial resources and handles agricultural inputs and crop

outputs. The sizes of some of these cooperatives are on the order of one thousand households. Beside these two types of organizations, the government has established an agency called ONAHA, the National Office for Irrigation Systems (Office National des Aménagements Hydro-Agricoles), for constructing irrigation facilities and delivering operational support services after construction. ONAHA provides a system director to each irrigation system, but apart from repairing pumping equipment, its role is advisory.

The cooperatives finance their activities by collecting irrigation service fees and charges for other services provided, for example, supply of inputs (especially fertilizer). There is no profit element in the fee computation, and all cooperatives have struggled financially. Some have not been able to make timely payments for the services they receive, mainly due to late payments of fees and charges by the irrigators. Whereas irrigation service fees are very high, the rewards to irrigator families are only moderately good, hence, there is a growing need for working capital. It has not been possible to build up a reserve fund to enable the cooperatives to deal with future needs. Instead, resources intended for building such funds are used to finance current operational needs.

Besides financial difficulties, ownership rights on the irrigated lands remain unclear, administration is far from adequate, and maintenance of the irrigation systems suffers from neglect due to lack of clarity about responsibilities. Not surprisingly, many farmers expressed alienation from the system of management. Niger has some of the lowest levels of literacy and basic schooling in the world. It is not surprising, therefore, that management skills among the rural population are very limited. Unfamiliarity with formal processes of record keeping and other transparency mechanisms are aggravated by the large size of the cooperatives. Size however, is dictated by the capacity of the pumping stations. Moreover, the irrigator households generally have other economic activities (such as unirrigated agriculture), and irrigated agriculture is the primary activity for relatively few of them. Considering the short wet season (limited time for planting) and the small size of irrigated land per household (approximately one-third ha, or less than one acre), one cannot expect that households will automatically allocate their labor to their irrigated land at the agronomically optimal time or in some agronomically optimal intensity. There is thus an inbuilt conflict between farmers' needs and the scheme's needs.

Officially, the purpose of the system is to enhance food production and to reclaim land from the desert in order to settle more peasants. It appears, however, that the real purpose has been to transfer costs from government to peasants. The Republic of Niger is one of the poorest countries in the world. The government's financial weakness poses great difficulties for the sustainability of irrigation systems. Capital for construction of irrigation schemes can be obtained from external donors or lenders. Operational costs are a totally different matter. The method that the government of Niger has chosen to solve this issue has been the formation of cooperatives. These are, thus, government-sponsored organizations, established according to a paradigm laid down from above. The policy objective is thus not primarily to empower peasants but to minimize (and if possible, eliminate) the financial burden on the treasury. Thus it endeavors to ensure that the irrigation users repay a significant share of capital costs as well as operational costs. However, this objective has not been fulfilled, the system under-performs, and in its present form, it is hardly sustainable. (Abernethy et al. 2000)

Several factors contribute to this outcome. The state need not be hostile to decentralization per se but needs to balance carefully between traditional and modern contenders for power (de Sardan 2004). Apparently, impatient foreign institutions have been pushing for a too rapid dismantling of central authority and transfer of tasks to groups and "communities" that do not (yet) have the capacity to assume these new responsibilities.

Mali

A similar—but to some extent more encouraging—experience of decentralization and group-based irrigation management is the story of how the Office du Niger irrigation scheme in Mali, after nearly twenty years of reconstruction, was transformed from "a technical and financial failure [into] . . . a success story" (Couture, Lavigne Delville, and Spinat 2002, 1). A résumé follows.

Created in 1932, the Office du Niger is the oldest colonial irrigation scheme in West Africa. The water-management system is based on gravity irrigation from the Markala dam through a main supply canal that bifurcates into two branches. Constructed in order to meet the needs of the French textile industry, the scheme was planned to irrigate one million ha (2.5 million acres), but only 68,000 ha (approximately 168,000 acres) were actually developed. Originally planned for the production of cotton, the scheme was later extended to include paddy and sugar cane. The Office du Niger was the most important enterprise, the heart of the state, and also a "state within the state" in the French Sudan colony as well as in the young Republic of Mali. Through the control of labor and water, the aim of the Office du Niger was always to contribute to the state budget through rational optimization of the area's high agricultural potential. Hence, authoritarian colonial paternalism was the predominant ideology even after independence in 1960, and for a long time settlers were acting more as workers than as autonomous farmers. Exploitation, corruption, nepotism and neglect of infrastructures led to low productivity, alienation, and desertions by settlers. Having continuously been dependent on subsidies, at the end of the 1970s the scheme was bankrupt, and one-third of the developed area was no longer cultivated.

Restructuring was carried out over a long period of time (1979–96) and reached a turning point in 1994 when the Office du Niger's status was changed and a performance contract was established that redistributed tasks and responsibilities among the state, the Office du Niger, and farmers, who were progressively getting organized first in village associations and later in unions. The Office du Niger was cleared of all that dealt with agricultural product sectors, credit, and organization of farmers, and its budget was cut by two-thirds. Instead, it could concentrate on central functions such as water services and networks maintenance. Other functions have been suppressed, transferred to farmer organizations, or privatized. Water services are now provided through shared responsibilities by way of "representation committees" bringing together farmers and Office du Niger agents. This has resulted in physical upgrading and improved water management, increased yields, a more diversified production system, and improved incomes for settlers.

Another result has been strengthened farmers' organizations. Village-based farmers' organizations, modeled on the Associations Villageoise (informal organizations with no legal status, supposed to be pre-cooperatives) were created in 1984 and numbered 146 in 1999. The failure of some village associations and the need for legal status for contracting with merchants led to the creation of 221 economic interest groups and 101 women's economic interest groups by the same year. The first farmer trade union was created in 1997, and another in 1998. Credit has been reorganized and decentralized, threshing and milling are done almost exclusively by village associations, which also are responsible for extension and, together with economic interest groups, deal with traders.

It should be noted, though, that these evolutions were (originally) made with few peasant representatives. Peasants will need time to be able to play their new roles inside the new structures. Trade unions are still young, and, at the local level, many peasant organizations are weak, and most have financial or organizational problems (Couture, Lavigne Delville, and Spinat 2002).

Couture, Lavigne Delville, and Spinat are not the only ones who find this a remarkable success story (see, for example, Bélières et al. 2002). A more cautious statement, however, would be that the above story is a tale of both success and failure. While many farmers have abandoned the old approach of self-sufficiency, they have now gone onto the offensive, take more risks, spend more on productive capital, and have increased productivity (Couture, Lavigne Delville, and Spinat 2002). But while farmers' organizations have been able to assume new roles and progressively engage in economic and other activities, they remain small and vulnerable. Moreover, the area has experienced a veritable population explosion, with population doubling between 1995 and 2003, along with a dramatically shrinking average size of farms (from 11 ha [27 acres] in 1974 to 2.5 ha [6 acres] in 2003), which, however, has to some extent been compensated for by increased yields. A more serious problem is the effect on extension services, which have been reduced from three hundred agents to sixty, or from one agent for each village to one agent for eight villages. At the same time, private support services remain limited and "the producers' commitment to help fund agricultural advisory services remains a problem" (SWAC 2005, 70). The reform of the Office du Niger, for all its virtues, was (as in Niger) a reform from above that was, perhaps, too hastily implemented. As such, it resembles a general trend in Mali.

Looking outside the irrigation scheme, the contemporary Malian development model "depends heavily on some form of farmer organization" (Tefft 2004, 2). Before 1980, there were only two national NGOs and one main trade union in the country. By 2000 there were "1,836 NGOs and more than 5,000 associations, a hundred networks / co-ordinations / alliances / federations / collectives" (Touré 2004, 16). This growth and, particularly, the rise of the farmers' union SYCOV in the 1990s has been seen as a sign that farmers' organizations presently are strong in Mali (R. J. Bingen 1998; Karl 2002; Tefft 2004). Others, however, are of a quite different opinion. Docking (2005) argues that the SYCOV's leadership has been "embraced to death" by too much foreign funding, causing it to neglect its domestic base. "Well-intentioned international [NGOs] perverted the development of an organic cotton farmers' movement" (ibid., 198) and turned it into a tame and coopted bureaucracy.

Parallel to the restructuring of irrigation management, the cotton sub-sector has been reformed as well. In 2001, following a "farmers' boycott and slash of cotton production in 2000–2001" (Bingen, Serrano, and Howard 2003), a new law on cooperatives was promulgated to encourage and facilitate the development of cooperative business activities (Akeratane 2005). In 2003 the government presented a plan for the liberalization of cotton trade. The parastatal CMDT (the Malian Company for Textile Development), while maintaining its monopoly on cotton trade (Tefft 2004), was to withdraw from extension work and input supply and transport activities, which were to be privatized. The new policy also aimed to "create cotton producer associations which are united by a common productive interest and are more focussed groups than village associations based on neighbourhood and affinity" (Zoundi 2004, 5).

Since cotton is grown in the more accessible, high-potential southern part of the country, and because cotton farmers represent the most prosperous households in Mali (Tefft 2004), the policy reversal may well succeed. However, the cotton-producers' union has apparently been weakened (Docking 2005), and producer groups will need time to accommodate to the new situation. At present, they "require financial and management training" (Akeratane 2005, 2). A precondition for establishing effective, private-sector agricultural support services is the existence of sufficiently organized smallholders, whose associations are able to express demand adequately and handle a contracting mechanism (Zoundi 2004). This seems not yet to be the case. "The cotton sub-sector restructuring process in Mali is being held just at a time when cotton producer organisations that are supposed to be participating in the process do not exist" (ibid., 6).

Ghana

The history of cooperatives in Ghana mirrors the common experience in sub-Saharan Africa of far-reaching government interference (Oppong-Manu 2004). Various governments have used cooperatives to pursue their own agendas through "restrictive laws and government interventions that have stifled their efforts since colonial rule" (Taylor 2003, 1). In Ghana, as in many other African countries, this has led to a cooperative crisis where the state-controlled system faces a "gradual replacement of official commerce by parallel marketing and a retreat by farmers into subsistence production" (Khor 2006, 10, 2). Hence, prior to reforms "the majority of farmers had long since abandoned the government-run cooperatives in Ghana" (2006, 2). Of the ten thousand cooperatives that were registered in 1991, half of which were in the agricultural sector, "only 10% of cooperatives of all the sectors put together and 4% of agricultural cooperatives were active" (Le Coq 2003, 12).

In recent years Ghanaian cooperatives have been (partially) liberalized. Most parastatals were dismantled in the 1980s (Hitimana 2004), and since 1997 cooperatives enjoy the freedom of association and of non-association, that is, local cooperative societies can be freely formed and are no longer required to belong to a district, regional, or national association (ICCSL n.d.). A new law on cooperatives was enacted in 2004. Taylor commenting on the draft law, found that it was "marginally better than the [previous] law" and that many problems remain, "especially in the area of too much government control" (2003, 3). In 2004, there were more than twenty-two hundred registered cooperative societies in Ghana, half of which were in agriculture (Oppong-Manu 2004). Most primary societies are small (ICCSL n.d.) and are hampered, among other things, by lack of financial resources, as is the Ghana Cooperative College, which is "extremely lacking in resources" (Dunn 2004, 1) and has difficulties in meeting its education and training needs (Oppong-Manu 2004).

Moreover, although the government of Ghana officially supports the formation of groups, associations, and cooperatives, "the procedures for establishing a legal entity—e.g. a cooperative . . . —are complicated, time consuming, cumbersome, and often require legal assistance and/or going to Accra" (ICCSL n.d.).[1] An Apex organization, the Ghana Cooperative Council, representing eleven national cooperative organizations, has been established as the umbrella organization for all cooperatives in Ghana. However, since it "receives almost all of its funding from the Government," its independence is undermined (Oppong-Manu 2004, 3). The government's financial contribution may not be so great, however, since the Ghana Cooperative Council's activities have been on the low side for a number of years (Gabby Mills, personal communication). These findings confirm Bingen's conclusion that "there does not appear to be a clear-cut government commitment in Ghana to promote cooperatives, producer organizations or . . . NGOs in supporting farmer-based programs" (2003, 17).

This indifference on the part of the central government, in combination with the inactivity of the Ghana Cooperative Council within the new, somewhat liberalized environment, permitted the establishment of a parallel Apex organization, the Apex Farmers' Organization of Ghana (APFOG), which was established in 2003. According to Biney, the reason for building an alternative structure was that, after the change of government in 2000, there was a strongly felt need to form an independent and representative farmers' organization (2004, 1). The then-existing farmers' organizations, which had been on speaking terms with the previous government, were suddenly no longer involved in decision-making. Since this had been the case also in earlier changes of government, "it was found necessary to create an a-political independent apex organization" (ibid., 2). In 2004, "with the main aim of lobbying and advocating for favourable agricultural policies," APFOG represented about thirty organizations primarily engaged in "agriculture, livestock, forestry, fisheries and agro-processing" (ibid., 1). At the time of writing APFOG, represents some eighty thousand farmers in thirty-eight farmer-based associations, most of which operate at local or regional level. Its most important objective is to establish a platform for farmers' associations to advance the interests of farmers (Gabby Mills, personal communication).

Apart from this split into parallel structures, in recent years associational development in Ghana has seen also another bifurcation, which will be illustrated below by evolutions in the cotton and cocoa sectors, respectively.

Cotton Groups

As part of the SAPs, the cotton sub-sector, which previously had been controlled by the parastatal Ghana Cotton Development Board, was gradually privatized and opened up to limited competition in the 1980s. The Ghana Cotton Development Board was transformed into the Ghana Cotton Company in 1985. At present, there are twelve cotton-marketing companies in the country (Khor 2006). These companies—of which the Ghana Cotton Company is the largest, with 60 percent of total national output (GIPC 2006)—provide inputs on credit and buy cotton from growers at the end of the season (New Agriculturist 2004; Sikpa 2005).

This is primarily done by way of out-grower schemes in which farmers are encouraged to form a society with an elected chairman and a secretary in each connected village. "These leaders not only act as spokesmen in dealing with [the company], but also exert group pressure on the members to ensure compliance

with the rules and objectives [as laid down by the company]"
(Sikpa 2005, 2). The logic behind the group-based approach appears not to be a question of empowerment or of strengthening
organizational skills among the farmers. On the contrary, the
group approach aims primarily to "cut down on operational costs
to the company" (ibid.), especially since it is not communities
that are affiliated but "reliable and trustworthy farmers" (ibid.,
4). This usually means larger and wealthier farmers.[2] An indication that this is the case also in Ghana's cotton out-grower
schemes is that the Ghana Cotton Company, while concentrat-
ing on commercial relations with producers, has no connection
with national research centers and only provides one extension
worker for every ten thousand farmers (Hitimana 2004). Circumstances like these have led various authors to conclude that,
in Ghana, decentralization "does not motivate more local 'self-
help'" (Lentz 2006, 901), that "producer organizations are still
rare" (Spore 2005, 1), or that those that exist are "not strong"
(World Bank 2006a). Lyon (2003), however, found that incentives—and, hence, groups—are stronger in well-connected regions
and weaker in remoter areas.

Kuapa Kokoo

Whereas Ghana's cotton-growing regions are mainly in the poorer
and remote inland areas, cocoa production primarily takes place
in the wealthier and more accessible south (World Bank 2006a).
Ghanaian farmers engaged in cocoa production and their organizations—notably Kuapa Kokoo—have attracted widespread attention in recent years. When, in 1992, the government
announced liberalization of the cocoa market, this liberalization
was only partial. Internal cocoa trade was privatized, but the
Cocoa Board was not dismantled. It lost its monopoly, but it still
has the largest share of the domestic market (Khor 2006).
Whereas internal cocoa trade was liberalized, the government
retained its monopoly on external trade. Worried about the consequences of the reform, "a number of leading farmers, including a visionary farmer representative on the Ghana Cocoa Board,
. . . came to realize that they had the opportunity to organize,
as farmers, to take on the internal marketing function . . . while
the [state-owned] Cocoa Marketing Company . . . would continue
to be the single exporter" (Tiffen et al. 2004, 14).[3]

Founded in 1993 as a cocoa producers' cooperative with members in twenty-two villages (Tiffen et al. 2004), Kuapa Kokoo has experienced extraordinary growth in a rather short time. In 2006 it involved more than forty thousand farmers in over one thousand villages.[4] Also, having begun as a producers' cooperative that sold its cocoa to the Cocoa Board (Divine n.d.), the organization's activities have since expanded to encompass a farmers' union (buys cocoa from member farmers); a trading arm (for cocoa exports); a credit union (provides credit and banking services); and a farmers' trust (provides funding for community projects) (New Agriculturist 2004). Kuapa Kokoo is also a major shareholder in the UK-based Day Chocolate Company (Oxfam 2006).

This remarkable development could not have been accomplished without strong and effective links to external supporters. When the cooperative was launched, "there were considerable obstacles to overcome to comply and obtain a licence to trade," and, initially, lacking both capital and credibility, the "farmers attempting to start a new, collectively organized company had been effectively thwarted in their efforts" (Tiffen et al. 2004, 14, 15). The founding chairman then linked up with two foreign NGOs, SNV in the Netherlands and Twin Trading in the UK. With financial backing in the form of a loan from the latter, Kuapa Kokoo was established in 1993. Operating at a loss during the first years, in 1995 it began to make profit. In 1998 (with the aid of Christian Aid and Comic Relief) Kuapa Kokoo joined with UK Fair Traders, Twin Trading, and the Body Shop and decided not only to market cocoa but also to produce its own chocolate for the Western market, and the Day Chocolate Company was established (Oxfam 2006). Initially, Kuapa Kokoo owned 33 percent of the company, but in 2006 Body Shop International donated its share to the cooperative, which now owns 47 percent of Day Chocolate Company (Rättvisemärkt 2006).[5]

Apart from dealing with cocoa and chocolate, Kuapa Kokoo has invested in a wide range of projects to improve the livelihoods of individuals and communities. For example, "100 000 people, both members and non-members, have received free medical attention under [its] healthcare programme" (Tiffen et al. 2004, 31). Other projects involve village infrastructure and social services, hand-dug wells, nurseries and school projects (ibid.). Having faced initial bureaucratic obstacles but turned a difficult start into a success story, the Kuapa Kokoo cooperative has attracted not only foreigners' attention:

> Each year officials from the government and the Cocoa Marketing Board have attended the annual general meeting of Kuapa Kokoo to pay their respects, explain and answer for government policies and offer congratulations. Kuapa Kokoo has the best overall credit track record to date of all new buying companies. (Tiffen et al. 2004, 21)

After implementation of SAP, cooperatives in Ghana have developed in different directions. Some are still hampered by bureaucratic obstacles and governments' control attempts, while others have carved out a much wider room for maneuvering. Many are still small and financially as well as managerially weak and/or dominated by company-controlled out-grower arrangements. At least one—Kuapa Kokoo—has achieved in a rather short time remarkable and multifaceted accomplishments in a number of fields.[6] This has attracted wide attention from abroad, which appears to overshadow the otherwise precarious situation facing the majority of associations in the country. It is noteworthy, on the one hand, that Kuapa Kokoo was established by a group of leading and well-connected farmers who were able to mobilize external support aimed at empowerment. In contrast, cotton producers' societies, which also have experienced external support, cannot claim to have been empowered through the current arrangements. They rather appear to be disempowered. On the other hand, it is also worth observing the geographical aspect of these differences. Farmers' associations have been much more successful in high-potential (cocoa) areas than in poorer and more remote (cotton) areas with less infrastructure and less developed markets.

Burkina Faso

Peasant associations, rural cooperatives and grassroots' movements in Burkina Faso have attracted a great deal of attention during recent decades, and the country has often been seen as a forerunner in development from below. It is thus commonly held that local organizations in Burkina Faso are numerous, progressive, and truly representative of the rural population. As this section shows, the picture is a bit more nuanced.

Rural cooperatives in Burkina Faso date back to colonial times when they were established from above in order to meet French interests. After independence an unsuccessful attempt was made to promote development through regional development organizations and a decentralized system of village groups. Since many of these groups were dormant or had been closed down, a new effort was made in the 1970s. This new system of informal groups engaged in a wide range of communal activities (such as boring wells, constructing roads and maternity homes, and marketing farmers' products). These small and informal groups were deemed to represent "the most dynamic aspect of the cooperative movement" in the country (COPAC 1981, 17).

Actually, as shown below, since the 1970s there has been a veritable explosion of farmers' groups and unions in the country. Also, Burkina Faso "is likely the West African country with the greatest presence of external partners working with village organizations" (Bernard, de Janvry, and Sadoulet 2005, 23n14). Nevertheless (or precisely therefore), establishing a Department of Rural Institutions inside the Ministry of Rural Development in 1979 and drafting a new law on cooperatives were interpreted as a determination by central authority to bring cooperative development under its direct control (COPAC 1981).

In 1998, however, the government adopted a new national policy to promote cooperatives. This time the aim was to extend the freedom of association and to transfer tasks that had previously been provided by public-sector companies to "producer organizations and other partners [such as NGOs]" (SWAC 2005, 80). For example, this allowed in 2000 (in response to the formation of a sesame exporters' cartel) the establishment of SOFROFA (Society for the Promotion of Agricultural Networks), a government-supported cooperative (Oudet 2002). However, it has also been noted "despite a few success stories in the area of access to innovation, it was generally felt that most producers' organizations did not have the capacities needed to provide better agricultural support and consultation services" (ibid., 81). With these highly diverging interpretations of the status and capacities of farmers' groups, it is necessary to look more closely into what has actually been going on. In order to assess the qualities and potential of Burkinabé rural associations, distinctions will be made between cotton farmers and other peasants, as well as between the grassroots level and the union level.

Cotton Farmers' Associations

Cotton, which is primarily grown in the southern and southwestern parts of the country, is the mainstay of Burkina's economy, and the government has a strong interest in controlling this sector. Burkina gains more than 50 percent of its foreign exchange earnings from cotton, which is marketed by a parastatal, SOFITEX (World Bank 2006a). Inside the country cotton production is divided into three zones, each controlled by a separate cotton company. These companies control all steps of the harvest and extend credits for the purchase of inputs. Although cotton growing is comparatively lucrative for peasants, it appears to be a very exploitative system, and farmers, despite being organized, have very little influence.

> Interest rates are roughly on par with loan sharks, and credit allows companies to dictate rules surrounding harvest: the company chooses who grows cotton. SOFITEX . . . will only do business with cotton farmers' associations, called Groupement de Producteurs de Coton (GPC). Each association must contain at least 15 growers with at least two years cotton experience, and members must harvest at least 40 tons of cotton, requiring about 40 hectares. (Liebhardt 2005, 2)

This confirms the common experience that out-grower schemes tend to be governed by top-down management on a take it or leave it basis with little room for empowerment. Apart from having little influence and being the victims of "questionable accounting practices," cotton growers are also being exploited since they are "forced to pay 20 percent above market value for fertilizer and insecticide" (Liebhardt 2005, 3, 4). If their organizations had more members, they might be able to negotiate better terms of trade. However, there is a built-in mechanism that mitigates growth. There is no coordination among groups. "Each of the farmers' associations (GPC) negotiates its own credit arrangement, which forces newer, less experienced groups to pay higher interest rates, often between 10 and 20 percent" (ibid.).

The Naam Movement

Outside the cotton districts a quite different type of farmers' association, which has been widely recognized as composed of genuine grassroots' organizations, has evolved. The Naam movement, which was rather famous in the 1970s and 1980s, is the most widely known of them but there are several movements active in the country. Triggered by the big drought in 1973, but actually "inspired by a method created in 1967 by rural leaders of the Yatenga in the north of the country" (Ouedraogo 1989, 2), the Naam movement and the Six S, a support organization, were formed in 1976 by a former extensionist and teacher, Bernard Ouedraogo, and a French development worker, Bernard Lecomte. Six S (Se Servir de la Saison Sèche en Savane et au Sahel—Using the dry season in the Savanna and the Sahel) was based on the idea of using the dry season (which could last up to nine months), when peasants have no job, to promote village development. "Due to the drought, the dry season, traditionally the period for numerous social activities—festivals, funerals, marriages—became a dead season" (Lecomte and Krishna 1997, 80). Initially, this often meant to work together in order to cope with the immediate difficult situation by way of installing soil and water conservation measures that would improve agricultural production during the coming wet season. Later, it was extended into a wide spectrum of village projects (Uemura n.d.).

For practical reasons, Six S was financed as "an international association under Swiss law, but with Sahelian peasants and cadres as a majority of its administrators" (Lecomte and Krishna 1997, 81). It is a federation of peasant organizations like (and including) Naam from nine countries in the region (IISD n.d.b).[7] It provides support for self-help efforts and village groups in West Africa. It does not, however, assist in the formation of groups but "cooperates with ones that exist or spring up in villages, based on traditional patterns of local cooperation" (Lecomte and Krishna 1997, 75). Its mission is to "remove three obstacles to peasant mobilization: lack of technical know-how, lack of 'negotiators' to dialogue with government and aid agencies, and lack of funds to implement small projects" (IISD n.d.b).

The Naam movement "bases its approach on the wisdom and tradition of *Kombi-Naam,* an ancient association in which all members are truly equal" (IISD n.d.a, 1). The Naam group, thus, is "a traditional village body composed of young people . . . [with] highly developed cooperative characteristics" (IISD n.d.b, 1). Uemura points out that the Kombi-Naam aimed at "both developing moral qualities such as solidarity, cooperation, friendship and loyalty in the young, and at the same time accomplishing socially useful tasks for the village" (Uemura n.d., 1). Actually, the Kombi-Naam groups appear to have been common village age-group institutions. Traditionally, "young people were ordered to carry out construction work and harvesting and to organize festivals. . . . [Kombi-Naam] provided a sort of practical schooling in the working of society ... [but] they never got involved in improvement of the village" (Toborn 1992, 23).

In contrast, the modern Naam groups involve all people in the village and aim at "accomplishing economic, social and cultural changes without rejecting African values" (Toborn 1992). Their starting point is a "respect for traditional peasant knowledge and technical expertise" (Shaw 1990). In Burkina Faso many peasant organizations "have come to occupy an important political space at the local level" (Hårsmar 2004b, 3). At the national level, however, Naam received no direct government support (Toborn 1992). Actually, establishing the Naam movement was not easy. It met "the usual problems of initial official opposition" (IISD n.d.b) and "there were many attempts to bring it down" (Uemura n.d., 2). Although Naam is nonpolitical, "in 1975 . . . any organization that showed signs of autonomy or threatened to form a peasant movement was unacceptable to government" (Lecomte and Krishna 1997, 81). Emphasizing practical issues such as communal water and soil management (for example, stone bunds and plant pits, local innovations, and mutual learning,[8] the Naam has, however, managed to thread carefully and avoided catching the (then) "evil eye" of the state.

The movement grew rapidly. Established in 1976, by 1978 there were reportedly over twenty-five hundred groups in Burkina Faso's Yatenda area, with over 160,000 members (IISD n.d.b, 1). By 1988, Six S comprised approximately 3,560 village groups in seventy-five zones, spread over four countries: Burkina Faso, Senegal, Mali, and Mauretania (Uemura n.d.). Four years later, in Burkina Faso alone there were "more than 4,000 associations with no less than fifty persons in each association" (Toburn 1992, 23). Since then, the rate of growth has slowed, but in 2003 there were reportedly about 4,700 Naam groups in Burkina Faso alone, the majority in the northern part of the central plateau (Schweigmann 2003).

Their accomplishments are frequently reported as highly impressive.

> Naam groups have built wells and dams, set up vegetable gardens, planted a village woodlot, established village shops and mills. They also promote savings for village development. . . . They have a village health agent, pharmacopoelas, and a cereal bank. . . . The Naam movement has altered gender and inter- and intra-generational relationships. (Uemura n.d., 3)

To these accomplishments can be added roads and schools (Lecomte and Krishna 1997), as well as reforestation, animal breeding, handicraft, libraries, theaters and football, and various measures to prevent overgrazing, such as keeping sheep in stables and prohibiting goats (Toburn 1992).

All this could not have been accomplished with recourse only to local ingenuity. Through the Six S, the Naam movement has had access to external funding. However, and in contrast to many other projects, this money has been made available through a flexible funding system, which means that funds are made available to self-help groups without advance knowledge of the projects for which the funds will be used (Uemura n.d.). Moreover, the Naam movement rejected "desicionmaking at the level of a single village because it tends to be the center of parochialism and egoism. Six S chose to work at the level of thirty or so villages, with 15—20,000 inhabitants spread out over distances that could be covered on foot in one day" (Lecomte and Krishna 1997, 82).

These traits, however, are not enough to explain the movement's success. Every Naam investment "should have two children—a 'son' and a 'daughter.' The surplus of a Naam production is invested in two ways. One of them [the son] is used for maintenance or a new investment in the village. . . . The other part, [the daughter], is saved to be used for investment in another village" (Toborn 1992, 24). Thus, by working at the grassroots level and honoring traditional rules about sharing and reciprocity, the movement has been able to introduce novelties and, to some extent, change the economic and institutional landscape in which it operates. For example, "Naam's emphasis on 'participative learning' rather than a transfer of technology [is said to have] had an impact on the government's policies in Burkina Faso" (Schweigmann 2003, 16). Despite all this, the developmental and empowering impact of Naam appears to be less than commonly assumed. While Naam built much of its initial strength on its ability to root innovative projects in indigenous institutions, "the customs upon which the organization built its strategies of change also included strong hierarchical components. So when the strongman decided to move and do other things, the major part of the movement fell down" (Hårsmar 2004a, 232; also see below).

Other Burkinabé Associations

Whereas Naam is the most well known of the Burkinabé peasants' associations, quite a number of other associations and federations have sprung up as well (see, for example, Bingen 2003). Essama thus highlights a recent World Bank supported project to disseminate the use of *zaï* (planting pit) technology in Burkina. *Zaï*, she says, is "one of the most appreciated techniques by farmers in northern Burkina Faso" (2005).[9] In order to accomplish this goal, the World Bank supports the AVAPAS (Association pour la Vulgarisation et l'Appui aux Producteurs Agroécologistes au Sahel—The Association for the Popularisation of and Support to Agroecologists in the Sahel), which is active in three provinces in central Burkina Faso. Another such organization is the Association des Groupements de Zaï pour le Développement du Sahel (Association of *Zaï* Groups for Development of the Sahel), which was formed in the Yatenga region of the central plateau in the early 1980s (Ouedraogo and Sawadogo 2005) and whose objective is to spread the use of an improved version of the *zaï*. However, it has also been stated that the association was established "primarily in order to mobilize external financial or material support for spreading the . . . technology." In this objective, and in contrast to AVAPAS, it has been only "modestly successful" (ibid., 2). It is revealing that these two *zaï* associations are presented as innovative and different despite the fact that the Naam movement has long been "particularly active in soil and water management projects, like . . . the *zaï*" (Schweigmann 2003, 16). In part, this reflects the evolution of a lucrative market for organizations looking for external funding.[10]

In Burkina, as elsewhere, the large influx of financial support to associations has led the number of organizations, federations, and unions to mushroom; it has also increased patron-client organizations, tightly controlled by their leaders but with little influence for or benefits accruing to the grassroots (Hårsmar 2004b). In these cases, it is nevertheless a sign that social structures are undergoing change. In the cases referred to by Hårsmar (ibid.), it was not the question of traditional leaders using their positions to prevent change and preserve their own privileged positions. To the contrary, recent developments have allowed for a new kind of social mobility to emerge. Charismatic persons with good external connections but outside the traditional power structures, by way of establishing externally supported local "associations," have managed to reinforce their social standing in the local community. The local "participation" (which is necessary to obtain foreign funding) "was assured through a combination of material compensations, cooptations and social pressure" (2004b, 10). The "participating" peasants, however, were hardly aware that they belonged to an organization; they thought that whatever benefits accrued to them were due to the leader's personal benevolence (ibid.).

The reputation that the Naam movement has gained appears to overshadow the above-mentioned quite different situation for those peasants engaged in cotton farming in the southern parts of the country and/or paternalistic tendencies in some other organizations. However, not even the Naam movement has been able to withstand too much external attention. As pointed out by Schweigmann, it "runs the risk of becoming the victim of its own success. It is significant that internet searches on the Naam movement result in references to success stories only. The organization runs the risk to develop into a bastion, organized in a top-down manner" (2003, 18). Uemura found several remaining problems in the Naam: increasing delays in loan reimbursements, lack of training, heavy dependence on a few key persons, and women being under-represented in governing roles. Tasgian suspects that Naam might have lost its innovative character, since "everyone is doing the same kind of project" (for example, growing onions or potatoes, making jam or cheese). But, because marketing is neglected and rural demand for such products is limited, groups/projects do not last very long (Astrig Tasgian, personal communication).

One of the founders of Six S appears to be worried. Success, he says,

> has sown some seeds of failure. An excess of enthusiasm fuelled by donors practically lining up to provide funding has stretched the organization out too fast. Many new groups have not taken the time they need to organize themselves and generate the collective self-discipline expected from them. Increasingly, groups have enlisted with an eye on the funding alone, which has reintroduced the element of dependency that Six S has been trying to avoid. (Lecomte and Krishna 1997, 77)

In literature, farmers' associations in general and the Naam movement in particular are often depicted as the guardians of "African values" such as community, openness, friendliness, and solidarity. A 2001 World Bank report (quoted in Schweigmann 2003, 18) forces us to reevaluate this reputation:

> There was also a notable absence of collaboration among the local organizations in Yatenga, even within the same village. For example, there was no coordination between Groupements Villageois and Groupement Naam even though both groups were undertaking similar projects in the village, usually with external state or NGO partners. At the same time, each of the groups tended to be exclusive in their membership patterns. In fact, researchers noted several village groups creating more than one organization with the same people to solve the same problem. This was explained as necessary because "each outside partner wanted their own groupement."[11]

Senegal

Like Burkina Faso, Senegal is frequently considered a showcase of political development and a veritable NGO paradise. Reflecting such superlatives, McKeon finds that

> with 35 years of civic freedoms to its credit, and 25 of experimenting with decentralization, [it is the home of] an autonomous farmers' movement boasting over two decades of history. Both the level of engagement between rural peoples' organizations and official institutions and the degree of self-awareness with which it is being charted are more pronounced than in many other African countries. (1999, 333)

The road leading to such a prominent position has, however, not been straight.

As in many other West African countries, cooperative structures in Senegal were an invention from above. "The agricultural cooperative decree of 1959 was a vision of a prosperous mechanized agriculture. . . . Eight hundred cooperatives—which the farmers were totally unprepared to manage—[were] established with the flourish of a pen." Following a common pattern, the cooperatives were officially managed by government appointees but were "largely controlled by local elites affiliated with the ruling party" (McKeon, Watts, and Wolford 2004, 10).

Following a common pattern, but also aggravated by the Sahel drought, by the early 1970s the system was in crisis. Among other things this led to the formation of the first autonomous peasants' associations alongside the state-promoted cooperatives (McKeon 1999; McKeon, Watts, and Wolford 2004).[12] A practice of exchanges and visits among many of these local associations led to federations at the district and the regional levels and, in 1976, to the formation of a federation of Senegalese NGOs at national level, FONGS (Féderation des ONGs Sénégalaises). The name was imposed by the government because "any reference to farmers would have risked encroaching on the primacy of the official cooperative union" (McKeon 1999, 336). Its legal status was obtained in 1978.

"By 1990, FONGS had expanded to include 24 regionally-based associations throughout the country totalling 2031 village groups" (RDFS 2003, 1). Originally, FONGS's objectives were to reinforce solidarity among peasants' associations and to serve as a link between them and the outside world (McKeon, Watts, and Wolford 2004), and the federal process developed without reflection on public national policies (Destrait 2003). For practically a decade, FONGS limited itself to operating training and exchange programs for its members (McKeon, Watts, and Wolford 2004). However, with the implementation of SAP, its objectives were broadened, and FONGS began to seek a voice for small farmers in the negotiations under way (RDFS 2003). In 1983 the government signed an adjustment credit with the IMF and the new agricultural policy (NPA) of 1984 obliged the state to withdraw from all "productive" functions in agriculture (Luzzati 2002; McKeon, Watts, and Wolford 2004). In the same year a new law was inaugurated in order to reform the state-run cooperatives (Luzzati 2002). Peasants and their associations, alongside the private sector, were to take over those functions that were abandoned by the retreating state.

The number of groups and associations expanded. Liberalization of the economy "fostered rapid private-sector growth both upstream and downstream of agricultural production with new entrepreneurs forming cooperative groups." Moreover, "farmer organizations have been able to re-organize themselves to meet the challenges of the market, whereas earlier they had been mainly concerned with seeking the advantages [e.g. tax exemption] that stemmed from running an association" (Bélières et al. 2002, 12, 15).

At the same time

> northern NGOs were pressing FONGS to operate as an inter-mediary structure, processing the thousands of individual microprojects that were landing on donors' desks. The result was a period of rapid growth as FONGS took on a series of functions for which it was not necessarily prepared and which escaped the control of its member associations. A crisis of confidence broke out in 1989. It led FONGS to engage in a self-evaluation, which paid off in a strengthened and refocused organization. (McKeon, Watts, and Wolford 2004, 13)

As a consequence, FONGS introduced "a reflection on the involvement of farmers' organizations in the definition and implementation of agricultural and rural development policies"

(Destrait 2003, 2). In other words, it became more outward oriented and began to engage in politics.

The government, however, was not willing to let it take part in the ASAP discussions "on the grounds that it was not the only national federation representing rural people" (McKeon, Watts, and Wolford 2004, 13). FONGS, for its part, realized that in order to have a say, it needed to develop its own understanding of the crisis in agriculture and make alternative proposals (ibid.). It then turned to the FAO and requested that it extend to FONGS the same technical assistance that it normally reserved for member states. The FAO agreed and "helped FONGS to translate the language of SAP into terms comprehensible to farmers, and to carry out a reflection on peasant reactions on the NPA" (ibid.). The outcome of this process was presented at a national forum—What future for Senegal's farmers?—in 1991, a forum at which, for the first time, a peasant movement brought together representatives of peasants, government services, and donors to a public debate. FONGS severely critiqued both the Senegalese agricultural policies and the SAP. Its membership, however, "did not oppose the state retrenchment that accompanied SAP. But it claimed the right to participate in the redefinition of policies and programmes, and the support it needed to take on new functions" (ibid.).

This all led, after weeks of intense negotiations between the FONGS and leaders of the different associations, to the establishment, in March 1993, of a national platform, the CNCR (National Council for Rural Dialogue and Cooperation). In 1994 the CNCR launched its platform with a "Letter on Agricultural Development Policy" urging the government to adopt a policy favoring family farming. The ministry of agriculture, however, "expressed reluctance to accept any of the CNCR proposed policy measures, and a subsequent four month CNCR boycott of the [SAP] negotiations (a boycott supported by the World Bank negotiators) was resolved only after the President agreed to negotiate directly with a CNCR delegation" (Bingen 2004, 11). Since then, periodic meetings with the government have been institutionalized, and the CNCR has become the "undisputed spokesperson for Senegal's rural population in national, regional and international negotiations" (RDFS 2003, 2). For example, "the State-established cooperatives . . . have been left essentially to their own devises, bereft of government support" (McKeon 1999, 344).[13] Because of these developments, while the CNCR has prioritized policy negotiation, the FONGS has come to focus more on concrete support to village associations and farm families (RDFS 2003). The CNCR's achievements are commonly depicted as formidable:

> In the 10 years following its establishment, the CNCR accumulated a remarkable list of accomplishments. It bound a disparate series of rural federations into a national platform. It overcame a century of oblivion and won recognition for peasant farmers by the government and development partners, and a place at the negotiating table. It used this position to achieve a real impact on policies and programmes affecting rural development. In a political context marked by the rule of a single party, it . . . demonstrated that its role is an institutional one, not dependent on party relations. It spearheaded the construction of a regional peasant movement and made its presence felt in key global forums. . . . it is an extremely impressive record and probably unique in sub-Saharan Africa. (McKeon, Watts, and Wolford 2004, 8)

The CNCR derives its position from a number of sources. It has benefited from "a flexible and intelligent form of [foreign] programme support" (McKeon 1999, 347). It has emphasized its role as a professional as opposed to a political organization (RDFS 2003). It has successfully avoided antagonizing a suspicious state (McKeon, Watts, and Wolford 2004). And it has cooperated with local governments (ibid.). While constantly forwarding the interests of small producers and the logic of family farms, its role has been a mediator rather than a challenger (Destrait 2003). With this role, its "strategic choice was to join forces with the National Union of Agricultural Cooperatives and the other farmers' structures originally established on State initiative, in order to create a single, authoritative interlocutor" (McKeon 1999, 339).

Regional Cooperation

Successful regional cooperation among West Africa's farmers' associations is another issue that has attracted much attention and that often is presented as another proof that West African rural associations lead the developing world in the right direction. The CNCR in Senegal, apart from its accomplishments at the national level, in no small degree derives its reputation from its supra-national engagement. As mentioned in the quotation above, the CNCR has spearheaded the construction of a regional, (West African) peasant movement, notably ROPPA (West African Network of Peasants' and Producers' Organisations). There are several such networks in West Africa (see, for example, Bingen 2003), but ROPPA is the most important. Not only was the CNCR active in its creation, but "Senegal is the country where the participation of farmers' organizations [in ROPPA] is most advanced" (Ndiogou Fall, interview in RDFS 2003, 3).

ROPPA, bringing together farmers' associations in ten West African countries,[14] was formally established in July 2000 and is headquartered in Ouagadougou, Burkina Faso. It parallels a wider process of regional integration among states, symbolized by the launching of the Economic and Monetary Union of West Africa in 1994. Membership in the ROPPA network is "reserved for a single platform per country, which is expected to group all of the existing national federations" (McKeon, Watts, and Wolford 2004, 18). Each national forum elects seven representatives to ROPPA's General Assembly, which elects an executive committee with twelve members, at least two of whom must be women (Destrait 2003). According to Destrait, the objectives of ROPPA are to

- Promote and defend the values of smallholder agriculture based on family farms;
- Encourage and supervise farmers' and producers' organizations in each country to enhance their participation and involvement in policy formulation;
- Promote solidarity among West African farmers' and producers' associations;
- Ensure representation and defend the interests of members in national, sub-regional, and international levels.

"ROPPA seeks to create a policy voice for West African smallholders in discussions to standardize the Common Exterior Tariff, OHADA and judicial systems, and the preparation of a sub-regional Agricultural Policy" (Bingen 2003, 6). ROPPA has thus forcefully denunciated "the unequal competition to which

African agriculture is subjected by the exporters of industrialized countries, which benefit from subsidies denied to African farmers." ROPPA is also "seeking to ensure that small producers' interests are reflected in the agricultural component of the New Economic Partnership for African Development (NEPAD) and the trade agreement [with] the European Union" (McKeon, Watts, and Wolford 2004, 19).

In this pursuit ROPPA is "insisting on the term 'family-based farming systems' . . . little used in Africa in the past. It signifies support for a certain agricultural model to counter the danger of integration and concentration associated with liberalisation" (Bélières et al. 2002, 4). Actually, many have been tempted to see this as a sign that West African "rural producers' organizations are at the forefront against globalization" (McKeon, Watts, and Wolford 2004, iv).[15]

This is all very impressive. However, the above-sketched development did not occur without tradeoffs, and there are fractures in the constructs. These are of various kinds, partly economical, but in large degree they have to do with representation and accountability. Concerning the CNCR, ROPPA's "mother," McKeon found that the organization was "understaffed and underequipped [and] . . . overwhelmed with dossiers that need to be analysed and followed" (1999, 345). As the organization grows and communication becomes more intense, this situation is likely to be exacerbated. Another aspect is that—although the World Bank considers the CNCR to be "truly representative" of the majority of Senegalese producers (Bosc et al. 2002, 35)—"questions can be raised about the representative nature of the CNCR. Who or what groups does it really speak for?" (Bingen 2004, 23). It has been pointed out that the "relationship between the social base and the formal base is far from neat." Some of CNCR's member federations suffer from "anomalies in leadership" and "very few of [them] can claim documented, dues-paying membership and regular means of communication with members" (McKeon, Watts, and Wolford 2004, 20). Actually, "it is widely recognized that individuals at the local level are unaware of either what the CNCR does, or what positions it represents in their name" (Bingen 2004, 24). Nevertheless, McKeon et al. conclude, "The CNCR has, by all accounts, acted in the interests of peasant farmers even though it has not systematically consulted nor explicitly received its mandate from them" (2004, 20). These weak chains of accountability and representativity may turn out to be the organizations' Achilles' heel, both internally and in its external relations.

ROPPA appears to be in a similar situation as the CNCR, although the above-mentioned constraints are magnified because of more difficult communication at the supra-national level. "ROPPA is considered to be a network, but its pyramidal organisational model is more similar to a confederation of organisations" (Destrait 2003, 5). Difficulties with communication together with long chains of representation and gaps in the institutional set up within and between countries lead to high consultation costs, but "ROPPA cannot wait for all farmers to be informed" (ibid.) or give it a go-ahead when that would be needed, for example, in negotiations with external parties. A related problem is that ROPPA relies heavily on technical and financial external support. Hence, its capacity to strengthen national platforms and influence policy "derives in no small way from the broader international backstopping through . . . Europe based networks" (Bingen 2003, 19).

It may be convenient—that is, practical—for donors to have one party to deal with instead of many, but how much self-reliance does this actually provide? Although often treated as the voice of the West African farmers, ROPPA at present cannot claim to be the spokesperson for all farmers in West Africa. With priority given to promotion and defense of smallholder agriculture based on family farms—and their organizations—this objective "specifically and deliberately sets ROPPA apart from efforts to promote commodity-based groups and networks, especially for cotton" (Bingen 2003, 6). Paradoxically, whereas Western supporters often believe that ROPPA is a means to stifle globalization, commodity-based organizations are exactly the ones that have been able to challenge Western interests (see Chapter 6 herein).

Summing Up

West Africa's experience with organizations is diverse and sometimes contradictory. The fate of formerly state-managed rural cooperatives is a case in point. While previously often neglected by governments and abandoned by peasants, contemporary policies toward cooperatives point in different directions. Officially liberalized, their (potential) activities are often stifled by bureau-cratic obstacles and, as in Ghana and Nigeria, by continued at-tempts at control by the national government. The devolution of authority—and, hence economic responsibility—from state to farmers' groups and cooperatives in large-scale irrigation schemes appears sometimes to have been implemented for obscure rea-sons (such as transfer of costs) not necessarily aimed at devel-opment or enhanced efficiency. In any case, they have been too hastily implemented (in no small degree due to donor pressures), and "ownership" was transferred before the organizations sup-posed to take over existed or, if they did, had acquired the capac-ity to do so. Apparently, in these cases the cards have been stacked against success. In some cases, an exploitative parastatal system for strategic crops, such as cotton, has been replaced by an equally exploitative system of "group-based" outgrower-schemes, which, moreover, does not encourage empowerment, demand-drivenness or local ownership of organizations.

It can, of course, be argued that this doesn't matter very much since the farmers affected are a small minority. But the sky is clouded by conclusions that recent reforms have not led to an upsurge in self-help projects or group initiatives. Instead, a ten-dency for smallholders to retreat into parochial and clientelist security systems or to link up with NGOs has been observed. Foreign NGOs are happy to step in, and several countries in West Africa have been designated as NGO paradises. But NGOs tend to compete rather than cooperate, and they often undermine genuine self-help efforts at the grassroots level. Hence, a com-mon notion is that local organizations are weak in West Africa. However, they seem to be more successful in high potential and/or well-connected regions.

At the same time, West Africa has seen the birth of some ex-ceptional endeavors at domestic organization building, notably the Naam movement in Burkina Faso, Kuapa Kakoo in Ghana, the FONGS and the CNCR in Senegal, and ROPPA on the supra-national level. Their accomplishments are impressive indeed. Nevertheless, questions have also been raised about their sustainability (Naam), and their accountability and repre-sentativity (CNCR, ROPPA), indicating that the full story has not yet been told. Chapter 6 aims to take us one step further in that direction.

Six

Interpreting the West African Experience

> Institutions . . . determine the possibilities that
> exist in a society. Organizations are established
> to make use of these possibilities.
> —Douglas North, 1990

This chapter summarizes the West African experience with organizations for development. It seeks to answer the question: Is the West African experience in any significant way different from that in other parts of sub-Saharan Africa? Many writers contend that it is. If that turns out to be the case, it also seeks to assess whether West African NGOs are a role model for others to follow. Or could there perhaps be other factors involved, affecting both organizations and their environment in a way that is conducive to development? We begin by taking a closer look at the success stories that have given the region its reputation.

Success Stories

West Africa is frequently depicted as a veritable NGO paradise with a multitude of strong, effective, and representative farmers' associations fulfilling a wide range of functions at both the grassroots and higher levels in society. It is true that West African farmers' associations have, in some cases, made remarkable achievements. The Naam movement in Burkina Faso and the Kuapa Kokoo in Ghana are two cases in point. They appear to be practically oriented, the former primarily toward soil and water management and community projects, and the latter toward the market, albeit (at a later stage) including also important community objectives. On a different level the FONGS and the CNCR in Senegal, and the ROPPA on a supra-national level have been successful in influencing policy and forwarding the values and perspectives of the small family farms, which constitute the backbone of the West African economies. Beside these, it is also pointed out that, especially in cotton-growing areas, strong producers' organizations have evolved (Hussein 2004).

This, however, doesn't exhaust the list of success stories. In March 2005 a panel of WTO trade judges ruled (in response to a petition filed by Brazil) that US subsidies to American cotton farmers is a violation of international trade rules. Brazil's complaints were the culmination of a "long path to victory [that] began with cotton producers' associations across West Africa" (Smith and Rice 2004, 1). In 2003 these associations, with several West African governments in the lead, had brought the case to the WTO at the Cancun meeting but failed to get the backing of the rich countries. The case was then successfully carried by Brazil but "it started with West African producers" (ibid., 2; see also Heinisch 2006).

This, no doubt, has added to the reputation of cotton-growers' associations as being strong. However, as the previous chapters have shown, not all cotton-growers' associations are strong. Due to the economic importance of cotton in West Africa, many governments still retain monopolies on cotton trade and cotton-growers' groups tend to be disempowered and exploited through out-grower schemes (Burkina Faso, Ghana, Mali). Others are dominated by local elites, and although effective in many ways, they may not really reflect the interests of the majority of smallholder peasants. Nevertheless, success stories are repeatedly being told and, indeed, there are some remarkable experiences of associational undertakings in West Africa. How can this be explained?

Why the Successes?

One factor for success is that West African farmers' associations—and foreign NGOs coming to their assistance—have a longer history than those in ESA. The Sahel drought in the 1970s (and another one in the 1980s) forced many farmers to try to find new solutions to prevailing adversities. Among the measures taken were experiments with new forms of organization. A possible consequence could be that, with this longer organizational history—and, hence, a longer learning period—many initial missteps have now been overcome, resulting in higher efficiency today. A contributing factor may also have been that SAP came later to West Africa than to other parts of Africa. Therefore, during the most critical learning period, the institutional landscape in West Africa was calmer and when the SAP-induced disruption of markets, support systems, and so on eventually set in, many of the new organizations had already developed routines and found their modus operandi.

While these may have been contributing factors, they are not likely to be the major reasons for the apparently successful associational performance in West Africa. More important seems to be that most associations have chosen a non-confrontational approach. West African governments have not always been as benign as the contemporary conventional wisdom suggests. "In several countries there is more freedom of expression and organization, even if this is still sometimes only window dressing" (de Honoré 2004, 55). Suspicion, indifference, and even hostility toward independent organizations can still be found in some governments, and despite some liberalization, the playing field is not all that level. This is particularly clear in relation to formal cooperatives, where some governments have found it difficult to relinquish control.

While a number of federations have ventured into advocacy and policy dialogue, they have, in most cases, avoided taking on the role of watchdogs to monitor and criticize governments. In Benin, "the majority of NGOs do not have political agendas" (Bierschenk, Brüntrup-Seidemann, and Hoffmann 1999, 429). In Ghana, Mali, and Burkina Faso the approach of associations and federations has often been non-confrontational (Alebikiya 2004; R. J. Bingen 1998; Lecomte and Krishna 1997; Roche 1991). In Senegal, federations such as the FONGS and the CNCR have consciously chosen to emphasize "development rather than politics" (McKeon 1999). This, typically, concerns their relations with national governments.

At the grassroots level the situation is blurred and authority in flux. Unclear institutional setups and an ambiguous mixture of arrangements have allowed not only traditional and formal sources of authority to coexist; in some cases farmers' organizations have actually assumed authority that one normally would expect to find with other actors. However, it would be premature to believe that, at this level, local organizations would be able to assume an outspoken role as watchdogs. In most cases it is not possible to establish organizations that have a confrontational character without the consent of local elites.

In contrast, when it comes to external relations, the approach has often been deliberately political. The above-mentioned success in bringing US cotton subsidies to the WTO is a case in point. Farmers' associations and federations in Ghana have repeatedly criticized the World Bank for trying to sell out domestic resources to foreign corporations (Amenga-Etego 2004), and/or have denounced the unfair trade policies imposed by the WTO (Kareweh 2004). "Instead of blaming policy makers, [their task is] rather [to] engage them in sensitisation processes" (ibid., 53). In Senegal the president of the FONGS stresses that "international institutions should not take the responsibility away from governments" (RDFS 2003, 1). Also, in Senegal, "the CNCR . . . has made it clear that it considers the state its primary partner and has consistently defended the sovereignty of the state as national policy maker" (McKeon, Watts, and Wolford 2004, 48). And at the supranational level ROPPA has attacked "the unequal competition to which African agriculture is subjected by the exports of industrialized countries, which benefit from subsidies denied to African farmers" (ibid., 19).

This, obviously, has given West African farmers' associations and producers' organizations wider room to maneuver on the national scene and given *some* organizations bigger clout in national policy negotiations. As mentioned above, most governments in West Africa are weak, lack financial and managerial resources, and control only part of their national territories. It would be easy for organizations of various kinds to try to use this power vacuum to confront governments and/or to bypass them in internal struggles for power and/or independence. This has also often happened at local level. But on the national level many West African associations and federations have adopted approaches that strengthen the states. In so doing, they have no doubt significantly contributed to the creation of an enabling environment. The strong emphasis in many associations on family farms and smallholder peasant values apparently contributes to this. Such expressions are simultaneously overtly populist and sufficiently vague to be non-confrontational. Moreover, peasant values are commonly associated with solidarity, community, and shared destiny. Such slogans fit perfectly with the as-yet-unaccomplished project of nation building that, on a higher level, remains the governments' task. This, no doubt, has been a successful approach—for some.

Possible Success Stories

Still, with de Janvry and Sadoulet (2002) we must ask: "Why, with so many success-stories told and with such a rich institutional landscape," is there so little material wealth in West Africa? In both Burkina Faso and Senegal—the most frequently mentioned successes—the incidence of rural poverty remains among the highest in the world. Have all these organizations (NGOs, FOs, POs, CBOs) been without impact? A part of the answer, de Janvry and Sadoulet suggest, is that "the thickness of the institutional landscape is endogenous to poverty," that is, "many organizations have been introduced in response to [external] interventions . . . aimed at combating poverty" (ibid., 8). This, however, is far from the whole story. It is correct that poverty has led to a large inflow of donors and foreign NGOs that have created local associations and/or assisted in their creation. However, not all groups and local organizations have resulted from foreigners' interventions.[1] The Naam movement began largely as an indigenous project and, in Senegal, an independent rural association of local organizations was established in 1963 (Luzzati 2002).

Everything is not a success—not even those associations or movements that we have become accustomed to regard as successes. The CNCR in Senegal and the regional association ROPPA—frequently referred to as the successful guardians of peasant values and the small family farms—have problems with representativity and accountability.[2] Luzzati (2003) argues that the organizations that were the founders of the CNCR are all in crisis, that some exist only on paper, that others have not held any annual meetings for years, and so on. He further proposes

that it is unlikely that the CNCR and ROPPA will be able to up-
hold this role as protector of the small farmers because rural
stratification is already under way, and it is becoming increasingly difficult for the small producers to have a voice in these
organizations.

The Naam movement in Burkina Faso is frequently referred
to as a West African success story. Nevertheless, Bernard, de
Janvry, and Sadoulet, in a study of village associations in the
Mossi region—the homeland of the Naam movement—found that
their contribution to village-level poverty reduction appears to
be limited. This, they say, "is evident in Burkina Faso, where
92% of the rural households have access to at least one village-
level organization, 57% are actual members of such VOs, but
only 32% have received monetary benefits from one organization and, when they do, those benefits are usually quite limited"
(2005, 2).

In many cases members of government, army and administration set up their own NGOs, and the new associations may
not be as independent as it sometimes seems. The dependence
on foreign NGOs tends to be very high among local organizations, and there are often reasons to wonder whose agenda they
aim to fulfill. It is not at all uncommon that their sensitivity—
and that of the supporting INGOs—to local needs and priorities
is weak, and that they often tend to impose their own timetables
and their own ideas of what should be done and how. There may
be reason to ask: What is a success? A case from the Sahel is
illustrative.

Birchall (2003, 57–60) reports about a program run by an international agency for more than twenty years (1978–2000) in
six countries in the Sahel region. Initiated after the big drought
in the 1970s, it is presented as a success story that benefited
more than eighty-five thousand people, who are members of over
two thousand grassroots organizations. The program aimed to
strengthen the capacity of local communities to manage natural
resources, secure increased access to basic services, and improve
storage and marketing of food products. The guiding principle was
to act in partnership with local people, to make joint diagnoses, to
plan and evaluate in a participatory way, and to plan for withdrawal once the rural population was able to take full control.

Reportedly, self-managed cotton markets now sell 80 percent of Sahelian cotton output; more than three hundred village grain banks have been created; as have savings and credit schemes, village irrigation schemes, and village resource-management committees. More than half a million trees have been planted, and more than fifty thousand self-employment opportunities have been created. Projects have also extended upward from these core activities into new regional and national-level representative bodies. The aim of reducing poverty has been achieved, the standard of living has improved, agricultural output has increased, food security has been enhanced, and natural resources are better managed. The program ended in 2000, and new, locally owned NGOs have been set up. They have the skills needed in training and cooperative organization and have begun to contract directly with aid agencies (Birchall 2003).

With Birchall, it would be easy to conclude that this is, indeed, a success story. However, as the last sentence reveals, the local organizations involved are far from self-reliant and capable of standing alone when the supporting agency leaves—after twenty-two years! As he also points out, it is questionable whether "the indigenous networks and NGOs that have replaced [its foreign supporter] will preserve and consolidate the gains made" (2003, 59). Among other things, the people and organizations involved suffer from "social disputes [and] ethnic conflicts," and "there are problems concerning the local communities, of conservatism and aversion to change." The gains made "are certainly quite fragile" (ibid., 59–60).

But we should not prematurely blame this on mediocre foreign assistance. Actually, this example illustrates several things. First, there might be too many success stories being told. Often the supporting agencies are the ones reporting about programs and achievements, and, hence, there is reason to be skeptical about what they tell us. Others may have a vested interest in showing that "peasants can" or that "groups function"—and therefore they should be supported. But, as Lyon points out, the assumption that group support is the superior way to bring aid or development assistance (which are not always the same thing) is "based on the impact of certain flagship, highly publicized, inspiring cases of 'best practice' community development that are reported uncritically, with details given of the multiple benefits, and a lack of attention paid to [failures and mistakes or to] the processes by which the cooperation took place" (Lyon 2003, 324). Second, there are indeed communities and groups that may have a strong aversion to change, especially when "development" is to be initiated or supported from outside (see below). Third, the flooding of rural West Africa with NGOs and NGO-channelled development aid, may well have contributed to undermining indigenous initiatives and, hence, delayed development. We have already seen that donors and NGOs compete for clients and opportunities to spend development money, and often create parallel groups and committees for the same purposes in the same villages. In various ways they, intentionally or not, tend to take the initiative away from their "beneficiaries." Spontaneously established local organizations may be slower to evolve but, generally, they are more sustainable (Astrig Tasgian, personal communication).

It has been stated that "most West African NGOs . . . are driven by donor agendas. NGOs rely on the resources given to them, but are often disconnected from the communities and local economies in which they are working" (Bertone 2000, 2). To the extent that it is true that self-help is only taken as a last resort, this may be extremely counterproductive. Many NGOs and externally supported associations are driven by the logic of rent seeking rather than of development. NGOs need to spend money (on groups) in order to get the much-sought-for project support from donors. On the one hand, readily available development aid, thus distributed, "may well result in the emergence of new forms of [dependence and] informal local despotism, however, rather impotent as regards . . . mobilizing capacities" (Bierschenk and de Sardan 2003, 147). On the other hand, "the Third World poor are sophisticated consumers of development projects [and very skilful in] . . . playing NGOs against each other to see which one would give them the highest cash incentive" (Michener 1998, 2113). With so many willing spenders around, it may seem more worthwhile to wait for the next spender to arrive than to take the initiative. There are signs that, at least in some locations in West Africa, attitudes reminiscent of Melanesian cargo cults have evolved.[3] J. Bingen reports:

Over the last 10 years there has been a veritable explosion of largely NGO-supported farmer and village groups throughout [West Africa]. Depending on the concentration of NGOs in a region, it is common to find farmers who 'belong' to four, five or six associations. In fact in some areas, so many little projects have come and gone for so long that farmers joke about just waiting for the next project or group to join. (2003, 11)

Also, de Janvry and Sadoulet found that household members typically belong to a constellation of associations. Hence, they propose that "participating to organizations . . . can be a significant requirement in time allocation that competes with direct productive activities" (2004, 3). Bierschenk, Brüntrup-Seidemann, and Hoffmann, reporting from Benin, found that "most NGOs are not created in order to solve any specific problem, except for the problem of finding employment for their 'owners'" (1999, 422). And, at the grassroots level the "cargo culture" flourishes. As one villager explained, Yes, they had created groups, but "the group lies fallow until an outsider comes to cultivate it" (1999, 428).

This tendency is strengthened when INGOs and NGOs with foreign economic backing pay people to attend meetings and provide generous per diems to workshop participants. This is motivated by the need to reach the poor. The poor struggle to make a meager living and are usually unable to take time to participate in meetings. The idea is that they can be empowered if they are compensated for income foregone during meetings. The ambition is admirable, but this strategy tends to backfire. When INGOs and supported NGOs compete for clients, this diverts the target groups' attention from development and entices them to join the highest bidder irrespective of the appropriateness of projects. Moreover, since not everyone is invited to workshops, it becomes increasingly important to "own" a CBO—that is, to be the chairman[4]—no matter how miniscule or inactive that CBO is. For the fortunate few, "this is often more profitable than the tedious struggle for development" (Astrig Tasgian, personal communication). Since payment is instant while the benefits of development are distant and insecure, the effect is often a lopsided agenda.

Such anti-development attitudes are, thus, often the result of NGO activity—not the circumstance that brought them there. However, they are not likely to reflect group or community approaches everywhere. To the extent that people want to preserve their lifestyles, this desire is likely to be stronger where these lifestyles, institutions, and safety nets are still intact. In other areas grassroots are likely to prioritize real development projects. However, NGO competition remains a problem. In order to be able to explain the different outcomes of support to associational development, we need to look more closely at where these differences occur. According to our hypothesis, geography matters.

Geography and Associations

J. Bingen distinguishes among three types of producers' organizations present in West Africa: (1) largely commercial groups, (2) mixed farming groups, and (3) subsistence-oriented groups. The commercial groups, he says, are export-oriented farms, usually run by civil servants and often with retirement money that enables them to be well capitalized. Membership in their associations is generally contractual. The mixed farming groups are composed of members that operate small-scale and diversified-production enterprises with less capital available. While producing their own food, they depend heavily on marketing of a single cash crop. It is convenient for them to engage in joint marketing of this product and, perhaps, arrange joint purchases of inputs. The subsistence-oriented groups are made up of a wide variety of self-help or mutual labor associations, usually village or community-based and oriented toward individual and collective well-being. There is no or little marketing, and labor may be the primary and often only asset. NGOs tend to be involved in establishing these kinds of groups (Bingen 2003).

De Janvry and Sadoulet have tried to distinguish different kinds of groups and associations in "West Africa's rich organizational landscape." They identified a mixture of state-organized peasant cooperatives, NGO-driven organizations, traditional community organizations, and professional producers' organizations. "Household members typically belong to a constellation of these institutions to satisfy their needs and maximize actual or potential opportunities" (2002, 3). That, however, is likely to be an exaggeration. At least the poor would have little benefit from professional organizations, and they often tend to be excluded from or at least to be marginalized in other types of associations (see, for example, Botchway 2001; Luzzati 2003; Lyon 2003; Wennink, Nederlof, and Heemskerk 2007).

Moreover, according to our assumptions, these different types of associations are likely to evolve (or at least to be more common) in different environments. For example, the Naam movement in Burkina Faso would be largely representative of Bingen's third category (or community organization in de Janvry and Sadoulet's language) and it originally evolved largely in the poorer and more peripheral parts of Burkina Faso. In contrast, the Kuapa Kokoo in Ghana (a market-oriented organization in the vocabulary of de Janvry and Sadoulet) is a kind of organization that resembles Bingen's category two (mixed farming groups), and it evolved in the more well-connected, commercialized, and high-potential areas of the country. It appears that strong organizations tend to be (modern) producers' organizations, whereas weak organizations (from a development perspective) are community oriented.

Bernard, de Janvry, and Sadoulet have highlighted the importance of the institutional environment for organizational success. Their study was carried out in 281 villages in Burkina Faso in 2002–3, which were the home of 647 village organizations, 327 of which were community oriented,[5] and 320 market oriented. The difficulty these village organizations have in delivering the expected economic benefits to their members, they explain, is a consequence of "community conservatism" together with a "generally low level of financial resources available" and "the lack of complementary public goods and institutions" (2005, 2). The latter two factors suggest that these are peripheral areas. Indeed, there was a strong resistance to commercialization and, particularly, against privatization. They further found that "COs are more evenly distributed across villages" than market-oriented organizations and that "a large village has 40% greater probability of having an MO than a small village [and] a village with high social homogeneity has 20% less chance of having one" (ibid., 7, 2). Since large villages are likely to be better connected to roads, markets, public institutions, and so on, this also indicates that the spatial variable is a strong determinant for which type of organization we are likely to find where. Even if there were many market-oriented organizations, they faced strong barriers of social resistance. In order to overcome these obstacles, most market-oriented organizations found it necessary also to pursue some community-oriented activities, which no doubt rendered members' personal enrichment more acceptable to fellow villagers but also limited their economic efficiency.

Of further interest—and to the disappointment of many—is the observation that "the impact of an external partner on the way decisions are effectively taken in the organization is limited" (Bernard, de Janvry, and Sadoulet 2005, 24). But this was not because the villagers were tradition minded per se or unwilling to play by new and different rules. To the contrary, with a common tendency to idealize "community" and a preference for participatory democracy, which permeates many INGOs, "external partners appear to be more effective in influencing the performance of COs through participatory rules of governance than in influencing that of MOs which requires more leadership in the decision-making process" (ibid.). From a development perspective, this may be just as well. "Even though external partners press for more participatory forms of governance, the most efficient cooperatives are those with strong leadership" (ibid.).

However, it seems as if Bernard, de Janvry, and Sadoulet to some extent misinterpret their findings. Community-oriented associations have bonding purposes and typically deal with issues of a more general concern, that is, projects and undertakings that have a public-good character. Here, influence has traditionally built upon consensus arrangements involving (more or less effectively) a wide range of stakeholders. Hence, it is no surprise that community organizations find it easier to accommodate NGOs coming to teach them "participation." They practice that already.[6] The market-oriented organizations, on the other hand, are of a bridging nature and are established in order to link up and/or compete with entities of which their members normally have little knowledge and with which they have no affinitive ties. Such arrangements often demand quick decisions (also in the home countries of foreign NGOs) and give less room for participation. On many occasions it would be tremendously impractical to let all the stakeholders be involved. But this is not to say that community organizations are less effective than market-oriented organizations. The two types of organizations have different purposes and their effectiveness ought to be measured with different instruments. The geographical implications of this—which type of organization are we likely to find where?—should, however, not be overlooked.

What's So Fascinating about Community?

Market encroachment and external penetration are often seen as some of the currently most severe threats to West African agriculture and lifestyles. Many associations try energetically to preserve family farms and peasant values, thereby being "at the forefront of mobilization against globalization" (McKeon, Watts, and Wolford 2004, iv). At the same time they are believed to "shift the balance of power in favour of poor rural people" (Bigg and Satterthwaite 2005, 144). However, many of the organizations that lead this struggle are professionalized economic actors, only loosely anchored to their smallholder base (Luzzati and Altare 2006), and community cooperatives are underrepresented. This is seen as problematic because community cooperatives are believed to be the type of association that is the most compatible with the "African mentality" (Luzzati 2003). Actually, it is maintained, "traditional communities . . . offer the breeding ground for the successful operations of new communitarian enterprises" (Luzzati 1999, 139). Hence, it is concluded, rather than the market-oriented organizations, it is the community-oriented associations that should be strengthened and promoted (Luzzati 2002).

Whether communitarian enterprises really offer breeding grounds can be questioned. Two examples of collective undertakings in social environments where bonding traits are strong are presented below. Hårsmar provides an example from Burkina Faso.

Although located on the densely populated Mossi plateau, this is a peripheral region. Poverty is more prevalent than in other areas, and the government has no effective jurisdiction over land distribution. Sharing practices, gift giving, and so forth play a prominent role in the local economy. A large dam has been built, which makes cultivation of vegetables possible throughout the entire dry season. Those with rights to the land very seldom grow vegetables on more than a fraction of the land they control. They do, however, retain their land for the cultivation of cereals in the rainy season. Vegetables are primarily grown by seasonal migrants, who move into the area for that specific purpose. Many of them stay only during the dry season. There is no land market, only the practice of lending land. No fees are involved, but some kind of gift is expected after the cultivating season.

The most common way to access land is by creating peasant organizations, which negotiate with the original inhabitants for the right to use a piece of land close to the dam. No lasting arrangements exist. The groups are usually formed after an official call at the local market at the end of the rainy season. Whoever has the ability to work one or more vegetable plots, and has the means to pay the fee for the motor pump, may join the group. When the group has been formed, decisions are made on the number of members that will be allowed, the fees that will be charged, and the vegetables to be grown. Apart from that, no coordination is undertaken in the buying of farm inputs, cultivation, or marketing of produce. Every member works on an individual basis except for the irrigation system.

While this system gives a certain social security and provides more people with access to land, it tends to discourage soil management and productivity-enhancing investments. The land under negotiation is usually not the best, and the conditions for the use of this land are not very stable. On the one hand, this constrains those borrowing the land. If they manage to increase its fertility and get good harvests, they run the risk of losing access because those with the original rights to the land may very well reclaim it.

On the other hand, it also constrains those lending the land. Given the strong social pressures against personal enrichment and the fact that the profitability of agricultural investments is often quite low, it may be a more profitable "investment" to give gifts to relatives, friends or even strangers. The returns on these 'investments' may be substantially higher than returns from agricultural markets. Lending land has the same function. This is not to say that no changes take place. There are tendencies for a more market-oriented approach to vegetable gardening. However, they are clearly marginal (Hårsmar 2006).

Dennis Galvan has studied the life cycle of a local peasant association (APT) in Tukar, Senegal. He provides excellent insights into the workings of the "economy of affection" or, more precisely, of how the new merges with—or allows itself to be absorbed by—the already existing. A short résumé follows.

The association was founded in 1986 in Tukar, a large village of three thousand inhabitants, by a group of young men and women in their late twenties and thirties. They had tried their luck in Dakar or other urban centers for some part of the previous years. Frustrated by lack of achievement, but also by a desire to avoid marrying someone from another ethnic group in urban Senegal, they returned to their home village. Some of them were also motivated by a feeling that they wanted to "make something happen" that would enable them to stay in the village.

The immediate catalyst for forming the APT came from an outbreak of cholera in the spring of 1986. Although none of the eventual founders of the APT had specialized training in public-health matters, they understood the link between the disease and contaminated water. They organized public-health-awareness campaigns, orchestrated hand-washing campaigns, and convinced people in the community to use a few drops of chlorine bleach to purify drinking water.

Encouraged by this experience, the core group of seven, young men who belonged to the village elite, started to discuss possibilities in Tukar. They enrolled another dozen or so people of about their age in the community, making sure to include women and at least a few members from the low-status occupational castes. They then prepared a document outlining the goals of a proposed peasant association, which was officially registered. An older brother of the secretary general had a university classmate who worked for a Franco-Senegalese NGO in Dakar. The APT was just the sort of local, grassroots organization this NGO liked to support. Eventually, it helped the APT formalize its top priority plan (a basin for storing rainwater to be used for an irrigated vegetable garden in the dry season). The proposal was funded by an international NGO in 1990, and an enormous basin was dug. The project, however, suffered from poor soil analysis, and the basin never held water for more than a month or two. The APT moved on to other activities. It received grants to establish a revolving credit fund to help community members buy, raise, and sell cattle. This project continued for a number of years.

In the mid 1990s most of these resources were reinvested in buying and running a local "boutique," or general-goods store. The APT took on this task, for which it was not particularly well suited, in response to a community crisis: ethnic unrest on the Senegal-Mauretania border had resulted in the forced expulsion of most Mauretanians in 1989. With them gone, there were no shopkeepers. In spite of considerable debate and dissent within the organization ("Serer people don't run shops!"), the APT shifted most of its resources into reopening and running one of these shops. It was a constant headache keeping the store stocked, finding APT members to staff it at all times, and perhaps more critically, managing the free flow of credit to customers. The shop was forced to shut down on a number of occasions because, having given most of its inventory away to relatives and friends on credit, the shelves were bare and there was no reserve left to stock. In the years since the shopkeeping experiment, the APT has tried to return to its cattle-raising revolving credit scheme, but it has lacked the capital needed. By 2005 the organization had become moribund save for a malaria-prophylaxis purchasing arrangement, run on a shoestring by some APT women.

Galvan, however, stresses that community-based organizations as effective as the APT in its heyday are rather unusual. This, he says, is because it was not revolutionary. Rather, a key ingredient of leadership success in this case was neo-traditionalism; it combined institutional elements of more than one sociocultural origin. This peasant organization, in one guise egalitarian, was also in fact a remobilized circumcision age cohort. These young men were already linked in a durable, local, historically embedded and meaningful set of institutional practices. Along the same lines, it was no accident that APT's leadership group gave pride of place to a member of the lineage of the village founder/resource manager, as well as the son of the highest-ranking local political official. The APT gained access to the plot of land used for the irrigated farming experiment thanks to a donation from the head of the founder's lineage.

By the late 1990s the APT began to fragment, losing both its leadership position in community-development efforts and its ability to mobilize various sectors of Tukar society. Galvan, however, is reluctant to view this as a failure. Instead, he stresses, it had a different primary function and its syncretic quality—a redeployed age cohort engaged in development—may have doomed it to irrelevance when it became less a tool to secure status and resources for an upcoming generation and more an "economy of affection" network of social support among an already established local elite (Galvan 2007).

Local organizations often fill other social functions and are sometimes established for purposes quite different than their external promoters take for granted. Galvan underlines that this case study does not, at the end of the day, give us reason summarily to dismiss local empowerment and community organizations. Rather, it reminds us that outsiders might have exaggerated expectations and that it may be a mistake to focus too much on the institutionalization of particular community organizations. He goes on to say that the demise of an organization like the APT, rather than being a sign of the ephemeral nature of the experiment, may be a natural, expected, and even useful part of the overall dynamic of community-based development. "Generational change and life cycle dynamics might make the rise and fall of any given CBO over a period of years not an indicator of dysfunctionality, but the norm" (Galvan 2007, 80–81).

So much for community-based development. As has been the case with so many other externally initiated experiments with community organizations, the APT did not have a lasting developmental impact on the village. If associations are the key to development—a widely held belief these days—it may be more effective to shift focus from the organizations themselves to the environment in which they perform. Organizations act and react according to possibilities and obstacles that they confront, not because they are exposed to some kind of allegedly superior rationality or because they are empowered to do things differently by some external supporter. As argued above, the environment—in terms of social norms, infrastructure, access to information, markets, and new opportunities, but also exposure to new challenges and competition—does matter. Therefore, manipulating the environment will, most likely, yield more than efforts to manipulate organizations. I will return to this issue in the concluding chapter.

Summing Up

The organizational landscape in West Africa is extremely diverse, and it is thus not a straightforward task to sum up the status of peasant associations and related organizations in the region. As this chapter has shown, there is an abundance of associations in the region, but it is very hard to generalize about them. In litera-ture West African countries have variously been labeled "NGO paradises," "showcases in democracy"; the region's associations are said to be "leading the Third World"; and an abundance of "success stories" are presented, although mostly reporting about the same associations.[7] Indeed, some associations have made remarkable achievements (for example, Naam, Kuapa Kokoo, CNCR, ROPPA, and the joint victory of cotton producers' organi-zations at the WTO). This, however, does not imply that all asso-ciations are strong. Actually, there are just as many reports about weak and dependent organizations in the region as there are success stories. For some reason they have gone largely unno-ticed in mainstream literature on West African associations. It is important that both sides of the coin are accounted for so that the development potential of associations can be properly assessed.

Two circumstances in particular have spurred associational development in the region: the Sahel droughts and SAP. The former led to the spontaneous setting up of a great number of associations to cope with food crises and environmental stress. Mostly these were of a bonding type aiming to solve practical, immediate problems but with little ambition to foster socioeco-nomic change. At the same time support NGOs, domestic as well as foreign, flooded the region, initially with an outspoken relief orientation and less of a change orientation. SAP, to the contrary, has had a somewhat different impact. State involve-ment in productive sectors has been reduced (although it is still maintained for strategic crops), formal cooperatives are in cri-sis, and with varying degrees of success they are being replaced by private-sector producers' organizations. In several cases such reorganizations appear to have been pushed too rapidly (due to donor pressures), before there had been established farmer-owned associations capable to take over. In other cases local organization-like creations for cotton growers are subject to remote control by out-grower schemes.

There is an abundance of NGOs operating in West Africa, and although some of them have been found to be very effective, many have a very limited geographical outreach and most of them appear to be heavily dependent on outside funding and remote agenda setting. There appears to be a marked difference in successfulness between Francophone and Anglophone West Africa as well as between more progressive and market-oriented associations in easily accessible areas, on the one hand, and more community-oriented ones in remote and poorer areas, on the other. The great majority—and in some countries perhaps the *only* type of organizations—are of the bonding variety. For various reasons many foreign NGOs appear to have a naive perception of community and therefore prefer to support these less progressive associations. Hence, they tend to contribute less to development than could be expected. At the grassroots level community-oriented, "bonding" organizations dominate, whereas the more progressive, "bridging" organizations (those that strive to take on a role as change agents) remain a minority.[8] "Briefcase NGOs" and small rural committees waiting to be cultivated by a donor illustrate a growing problem and a new variant of the dependence syndrome. Not even the Naam movement has been spared this reorientation.

At the same time as there is a strong—and perhaps growing—donor dependence among both domestic NGOs and local organizations, this literature review also revealed an outspoken emphasis on macro-level federations, unions, and platforms at both national and supra-national levels. These high-level associations have commonly been seen as proof that West African farmers' movements are strong, influential, and representative. This appears to be an exaggeration. To a not insignificant degree West African farmers' federations gain their "strength" from not seriously challenging governments and their links to the grassroots—and, hence, their representativity—are weak.

Thus, the organizational landscape of West Africa is extremely heterogeneous and difficult to generalize about. Notwithstanding the above-mentioned shortcomings, the frequently reported success stories are part of reality too. In many ways they indicate that important steps toward development are being taken. *Shortcomings* is not the proper word, however. It refers to expectations, and expectations seem often to have been too high. Development is a slow process, especially when expected to come about from below with the help of the grassroots and their own organizations. The various kinds of successes so frequently reported about might give the impression that shortcuts can and have been taken. However, if the overall socioeconomic environment in which organizations are created remains largely unchanged (governments only control part of their territories; markets do not reach remote areas; due to an absence of alternative social security systems there are strong obstacles to altered social relations; and so on), local associations will be less progressive than many external supporters hoped for. But this is not to say that conservative and bonding organizations are failures; rather, it illustrates that organizations cannot be seen in isolation from the environment in which they are operating. Does this environment differ significantly from that (those) in ESA?

Are West African Associations Leading the Way?

Indigenous organizations in West Africa are often regarded as stronger, more progressive, and generally more successful than organizations elsewhere in sub-Saharan Africa. However, within West Africa, organizations in former French colonies are sometimes said to perform better than their counterparts in Anglophone West Africa. Apart from the previously presented proposals that this is so, Develtere and Fonteneau (2001) found a much higher prevalence of member-based health-insurance associations in West Africa than in other parts of sub-Saharan Africa. They further noted that, except for Ghana, all success stories were in Francophone West Africa, and that their numbers were increasing. Thus, there seems to be good reasons to believe that indigenous organizations in (Francophone) West

Africa do indeed perform better than organizations in other parts of Africa. If that is so, how can it be explained?

As suggested above, one factor could be that NGOs (of all kinds, not only intermediaries) have a longer history in West Africa and therefore are likely to have gained more experience than organizations elsewhere in sub-Saharan Africa. NGOs in East Africa, for example, are mostly of a more recent date, and many still are experiencing "growing pains." But it is not only a matter of experience. The circumstances surrounding the "birth" of NGOs in different parts of Africa differ greatly and are likely to have had a strong impact on their performance. In West Africa, farmers' associations and NGOs were to a large extent formed to cope with the disastrous effects of the Sahel droughts in the 1970s. Even though governments were initially suspicious and reluctant to tolerate independent organizations, the situation was too severe and too complicated for governments to deal with alone. They therefore had to allow room to organizations outside their control.

On a few occasions external supporting organizations—donors and INGOs—also have made unusual concessions and allowed more room for maneuvering for some West African peasant organizations. Both the Naam in Burkina Faso and the CNCR in Senegal have enjoyed flexible external funding, which has allowed for local ownership and demand-led projects. Financial contributions without strings attached are extremely unusual and in ESA appear to be conspicuous only by their absence. Even though rare also in West Africa, they are shared characteristics among (most?) success stories.

At the same time, rural organizations such as the Naam appear to have been (in the early days) preoccupied with solving practical problems in rural areas and were less inclined to blame governments for difficulties encountered. Drought was perceived as a natural phenomenon rather than a social construct. This appears to have given many West African farmers' associations an advantage over organizations in ESA, which were new and inexperienced when SAP was introduced in the 1980s.[9] To a large degree NGOs in ESA have a rather different origin. They did not spring up spontaneously in response to locally perceived needs. On the contrary, the NGO boom in ESA came with externally imposed structural adjustment measures. To use an expression from Hettne, many of these associations were formed during a period of intense "government bashing" (1992). Moreover, whereas in West Africa an early emphasis was on rural, local organizations, in ESA much more attention was given from the start to the urban and intermediary (NGO) level.

Therefore, NGOs and farmers' associations in ESA have often had a more confrontational attitude toward governments than have their counterparts in Western Africa. Moreover, in ESA, NGOs were to a much larger extent promoted by external forces, and expectations that newly formed, independent organizations should assume the role of watchdogs and keep a critical eye on governments were often pronounced. Hence, in ESA, governments have been more suspicious of independent organizations and control attempts have been—and remain—more common. In West Africa, to the contrary, NGOs have in many cases been supportive of governments and directed their critique more against outside agents such as the World Bank and donors. This has given (some of) them greater visibility, and many commentators see this as a sign of their stronger positions in society.

There are several circumstances that could support and explain such claims—but only if it can be shown that West African rural organizations indeed are stronger than their counterparts elsewhere on the continent. Whereas it would be premature to state that West African organizations are role models for the subcontinent, it is sometimes maintained that associations in Francophone West Africa perform better than do their counterparts in Anglophone (West) Africa. It is typically only former French colonies that are labeled NGO paradises, and virtually all success stories about farmers' associations in West Africa emanate from Francophone countries (with Kuapa Kokoo being the outstanding exception).

Fulginiti, Perrin, and Yu (2004) are apt to explain such differences by reference to countries' different colonial heritages. They found, for example, that agricultural productivity in sub-Saharan Africa varied greatly between former French and British colonies. At first sight it appears as if Anglophone sub-Saharan Africa performs better, but if Nigeria and the Republic of South Africa are excluded,[10] the former French colonies performed best with a higher average productivity gain per year. One must,

however, be careful with using colonial heritage as an explana-
tory factor, at least if it is interpreted as a direct cultural influence. Other factors, although linked to earlier colonial affiliations,
seem to be more important. Although it occurred relatively recently, quite a few authors point at the importance of the de-
valuation of the CFA franc in 1994 as a major stimulus for
agricultural growth and for the formation of producers' organizations in Francophone West Africa (Ruijs 2002; Couture, Lavigne
Delville, and Spinat 2002; Toulmin and Guèye 2003; Tefft 2004).

On top of this, there seems to be a potentially important difference in the nature of external agricultural trade patterns in
Francophone and Anglophone Africa respectively. Zoundi et al.
found that "producer organizations in Francophone countries
tend to be more strongly involved in the service offer than in
Anglophone countries. In the latter, agribusiness is more developed" (SWAC 2005, 47). This, while mirroring historical patterns
of dominance, apparently has more to do with contemporary
external relations than with cultural influence. "French importers of green beans to this day prefer to source crops from smallholder farmers in Burkina Faso, while British importers endorse
bean production within large-scale, often white-owned farms in
Zambia" (Scott 2006, 650). Hence, for those involved, incentives
to form modern and bridging producers' organizations at the base
level appear to be stronger in Francophone sub-Saharan Africa.
On the other hand, the proportion of peasants involved in this
kind of trade is not overwhelmingly great.

Nevertheless, one circumstance that could explain the suggested superiority of West African associations is greater market
access in West Africa and therefore a larger share of bridging,
commercialized and progressive organizations there. It is noteworthy that Ruijs (2002) found that in Burkina Faso the transport costs for cereals only amount to between 5 and 20 percent
of the consumer price. In contrast, in Tanzania transport costs
for maize are as high as 50 percent or more of the retail price in
Dar es Salaam (Isinika, Ashimogo, and Mlangwa 2005). Here it
definitely looks as if West Africa has a strong advantage. It is also
worth observing that in relation to total land area, West Africa
has higher road density (six-tenths of a mile of road per 38.6
square miles) than does Eastern Africa (UN 2004; World Bank
2006a). On the one hand, this is likely to have contributed to the

fact that West Africa on average scores better than other parts of Africa in the Global Hunger Index (Wiesmann 2006). On the other hand, it is an indication that accessible areas occupy a larger proportion of total land in West Africa and that peripheries are proportionally larger in ESA. As suggested above, this is likely to have a strong impact upon what kind of organizations one will find.

Seemingly contradicting such claims is a World Bank report that found significant differences between West Africa and the rest of Africa in the "ease of doing business," where conditions in West Africa were deemed worse than elsewhere on the continent (World Bank 2006b).[11] This also seems to be reflected in Transparency International's 2005 Corruption Perceptions Index, where East Africa scored better than West Africa. Measured this way, it appears that West Africa is more corrupt and a worse place to do business than is the rest of sub-Saharan Africa. It could be objected that, since this kind of index is based on comments from a large number of businessmen and others (foreigners) who deal with these countries, such valuations are irrelevant for the present purpose. There are good grounds to say that urban and international businessmen and the rural grassroots live in worlds apart. Then, however, the impression that West Africa is a better place to do business would be strengthened. On the other hand, since many NGOs are urban based and display weak contacts with grassroots, it is probably fair to see them as part of the more corrupt, urban business climate.

Admittedly, these considerations are somewhat speculative, and it would be premature to interpret this as proof that West Africa presents a more unfavorable environment for organizations. These indexes are crude measures and, moreover, they are of alien origin; what counts as corruption from an outside viewpoint might not be so from within. In the right environment corruption may even present a strong incentive for small economic actors to join forces and together overcome irregularities and eventually to establish order. Since political power and decision making tend to follow both formal and informal channels, and informal influence normally is preserved for powerful economic actors, smallholders make better use of official channels (Toulmin and Guèye 2003), preferably by getting organized. Thereby they are likely also to strengthen the formal system and contribute to its enhanced reliability and inclusiveness. This process may take time, however.

Moreover, as pointed out by Teorell and Hadenius (2006), the democracy-corruption relationship is not linear but J-shaped; that is, corruption is lower in strongly authoritarian states than in states that are partially democratized (and lower again when democracy is "fully" realized). Hence, a high level of corruption may indicate a generally more tolerant and, therefore, enabling environment, which is beneficial also for organizations. If, furthermore, indigenous NGOs and farmers' associations have been less politicized and less confrontational, as indeed they have been in West Africa, this seems to confirm the proposal that West African associations are leading the way. Less corruption and more attempts by governments to control organizations in ESA indicate more autocratic regimes there and a less enabling environment for associations. However, this does not permit the conclusion that the apparently more enabling environment in (Francophone) West Africa is the result of NGO activity. It is rather the other way around. Moreover, there are great differences among West African organizations' ambitions and abilities. As the previous chapters have shown, there is an abundance of weak farmers' associations also in (Francophone) West Africa.

Even if there are differences in associational performance between eastern and western sub-Saharan Africa, these differences might not be as great as is sometimes suggested. Moreover, it seems these differences are becoming less pronounced over time. Whereas West Africa in general and Francophone West Africa in particular may have had an early advantage, the difference seems to be diminishing. It is possible that this reflects contradictory trends in East and West Africa, respectively. In ESA we have seen tendencies toward enhanced professionalism and self-reliance among (some) rural associations. Here, different authors point at the contemporary emergence of a "new breed of organizations"—more dynamic and confident and apparently with a more outspoken development orientation. Chapter 3 presented a number of cases where newly formed or reformed East African rural associations have proved to be both independent and innovative.

In West Africa, to the contrary, what has generally been interpreted as a strong start of indigenous associations in the 1970s appears to have been weakened and corrupted as time has passed. Guèye found that "participatory development in Francophone Africa is beset by a number of problems . . . [and] its impact . . . has been disappointing" (1999, 10). Once self-reliant organizations are increasingly trying to attract external financing, are losing initiative, and are becoming dependent on artificial life- lines, enthusiastically provided by donors and foreign NGOs. This not only reduces their independence, but it tends to pervert ambitions at both the grassroots and intermediary levels, and the development potential of indigenous organizations is lost or at least reduced.

This is not to say, however, that West African associations are weaker than associations elsewhere in Africa. Instead, it seems as though differences are becoming reduced and that a conver- gence is under way—at least in the sense that whereas West Af- rican local organizations are becoming more directly dependent on foreign support and domestic NGOs increasingly assume the role as dependent intermediaries in a delivery chain, (some) East African associations appear to be becoming less so. The general picture is in any case one of generally weak indigenous associations. Success stories, although frequently reported, ap- pear to be exceptions rather than the rule.

Part IV

ANOTHER WORLD
IS POSSIBLE

In the Introduction to this book, it was emphasized that more is believed than known about NGOs and their role in development. At this point it can be concluded that, more often than not, NGOs are not what they are believed to be. And civil society organizations might not be as civilized as has often been assumed. Organizations, moreover, are not stable and unchanging entities. To the contrary, they are dynamic and sometimes develop in strange and unforeseen ways. While this to some extent serves to explain the many misconceptions encountered, it also means that the final story has not yet been told.

Expectations about development from below and about what NGOs (of all kinds) are and can do have been far-reaching and often misinformed or unrealistic. As this book has shown, their record leaves a lot to be desired. Some of the reasons for this are to be found within the organizations themselves. Others are of a structural nature and belong to the contexts—both local environments and the international political economy—within which organizations find a niche to occupy. But it is not only NGOs and INGOs that have questionable records; donors and the Northern governments behind them are an obscure bunch and behind all the bold declarations of solidarity and support, one often wonders whether development is what they really strive for.

The stated objective of virtually all those involved in the "NGO approach" is development—a concept that has many meanings. Despite this practical inconvenience, it is now time to assess if, how, and to what extent the NGO approach has contributed to development in Africa. This concluding section summarizes the findings, puts observations in context, and draws—as far as this is possible—conclusions of a more general validity about what organizations can do in and for Africa. It highlights the global environment and the role of donors and Northern and international organizations for African development and points at some conditions that need to be fulfilled for African organizations to be able to realize their potentials as development vehicles. Finally, suggestions are made about what donors and INGOs can and/or should do and what they should refrain from doing insofar as they still believe that organizations are essential for development.

Seven

Another World Is Possible

> The greater the challenges facing FOs, the greater
> the need for external support, but the greater the
> likelihood of it subverting and undermining long
> term FO development.
>
> —Chirwa et al., 2005

Development Trends and Potentials among African Rural Organizations

Sub-Saharan Africa's experience with organizations is rich and varied. So are the potentials of indigenous, rural organizations to be part of—let alone initiate—development. This study has confirmed the existence of a wide range of CSOs and associations on the subcontinent. It has also shown that these exist at various levels of society and in different environments, and that they tend to differ widely in terms of objectives, resources, and ways of doing things. Some are spontaneous creations. Others are the result of external assistance—or interference. Hence, it is not a straightforward task to generalize about their roles, accomplishments, or potentials. But generalize we must.

There is no doubt that sub-Saharan Africa is in dire need of development—half the subcontinent's population ekes out a living below the poverty line. There is also no doubt that rural organizations have important roles to fill in the development of sub-Saharan Africa. In terms of settlement, livelihood, and so forth the subcontinent remains predominantly rural. That is also why development has to start in rural areas. Moreover, it would be difficult to speak of development if a majority of people were not included. Organization means some kind of collective undertaking, and organizations have a potential not only to speed up development, but also, and foremost, to bring it closer to the people—at least if organizations are created from below.

The number of rural associations in Africa has grown at an extraordinary pace during the last decade or two. Not only have numbers grown, but it has also been declared that "farmers' organizations . . . now increasingly voice the needs of their members in various fora on policy-making and orienting service provision" (Wennink and Heemskerk 2006, 5). Also, it is claimed that "in many SSA countries, national agricultural innovation programmes are moving into a new phase through empowered farmer organization at all levels based on the mobilization of social capital at village level into 'Farmers Fora'" (Heemskerk and Wennink 2004, 13–14). This could easily be seen as proof that sub-Saharan Africa is currently in the midst of a process of intensive development. It also could be and has been interpreted as proof that (1) African development is finally an indigenous process, and (2) farmers' associations, cooperatives, and other grassroots organizations have taken the lead in development. As the preceding chapters have shown, this is far from the truth. There are cases such as Heemskerk and Wennink write about, but so far they are exceptions. One reason is that the rapid growth in numbers of associations reflects excessive external penetration and forced birth of organizations more than signifying a truly indigenous response among grassroots to changing circumstances. Hence, we should not take the purpose of organization for granted.

Indigenous organizations have shown quite diverging ambitions, strengths, and weaknesses as tools for development. In fact, not all associations are aiming at development. Some are more oriented toward preserving relations and lifestyles than with finding new ways to deal with the world. The World Bank's assertion that there are rural producers' organizations presently active in 65 percent of villages in Senegal and in 91 percent of villages in Burkina Faso (2007) should be taken with a grain of salt. This is likely a misconception, since many are community-oriented organizations rather than market-oriented organizations or real producers' organizations. It gives an inflated picture that serves to give the impression that the NGO approach to development is more successful than it really is.

Among donors, INGOs, development researchers, and all kinds of Northern NGO supporters there is a widespread belief that it is a straightforward task for organizations to change the environment in which they operate. This is also one of the major reasons why "organization" has been assigned such prominence in contemporary development theory. However, this seems largely to be a misunderstanding and reflects wishful thinking rather than sound analysis. Instead, the surrounding environment exerts a stronger influence on organizations than vice versa. One doesn't need to invoke determinism to admit that the room for innovation tends to be much narrower than has often been expected, and that in large parts of sub-Saharan Africa the environment in which associations are being formed is not as enabling as frequently assumed. This can be so for different reasons, for example, strength of social institutions, neocolonial economic structures, relations to governments, and nearness or remoteness. Primarily, it has to do with the presence or absence of incentives.

Nearness and Remoteness

A common shortcoming in studies and reports about African organizations is that they generally do not distinguish among the types of environment in which farmers' associations operate; that is, much that has been written about African rural associations pays too scant attention to the often considerable differences in options and constraints present in remote and accessible regions. Webster, for example, in a far too generalizing manner, claims that in recent decades far-reaching changes in collective action have occurred:

> Rural social movements whose objectives were previously concerned with the defence of a way of life, of a type of production, of a community from the intrusions and demands of a state have been replaced with social movements that cut across spatial boundaries and delineate new political and cultural spaces. . . . [Nowadays] the objectives of social movements are to change policies, their implementation and their outcomes, rather than to demand the

retreat of state and government from "their" locality. (2004, 2)

Hence, it is suggested that where not so long ago a largely uncaptured peasantry was keen to preserve its independence, "the politics and practices of the rural poor today is to engage with the state" (Webster 2004, 4). In the same vein, many supporters of NGOs and peasants' associations in sub-Saharan Africa believe that these are at the forefront in the struggle against globalization (see, for example, Luzzati 1999; McKeon, Watts, and Wolford 2004).

This is wishful thinking at best. A more accurate statement would be that NGOs—and INGOs in particular—are part of globalization. Not only have they "become a transnational community itself" (Mitlin, Hickey, and Bebbington 2007, 1703), but "in some significant ways [access to global resources and influence in global forums], NGOs have benefited from the process of globalisation" (Tandon 2001, 55; see also Holmén and Jirström 2009). Nevertheless, the idea that NGOs fight globalization is widespread.

Such statements perfectly illustrate the self-image and ambitions cultivated among Northern "radicals" and within many Northern and international NGOs. With the collapse of the Soviet union many Marxist scholars turned post-modernist and began clouding their analyses in an obscure language. Many post-Soviet NGO-supporting political academics in the North began either idealizing "community" or using (imagined) "social movements" as a substitute for class.[1] Class, as we have seen, has little practical relevance in the daily workings in rural Africa. Hence, from this perspective, "social movements" do not mirror the African associational reality. Moreover, whereas in other parts of the developing world it may be relevant to talk about rural social movements, it appears to be less so in sub-Saharan Africa. There are numerous reports suggesting that smallholder peasants in sub-Saharan Africa rather than engaging with the state—or, for that matter, with the formal economy—take the exit option and "seek their survival in the informal sector" (Leysens 2006, 33; see also Hydén 1995). The dominance in large parts of rural Africa of bonding community organizations over bridging market organizations points in the same direction. Moreover, when

African smallholders do engage with the wider society, the concern of their associations is not focused on fighting globalization. As the examples of Kuapa Kokoo, CNCR, ROPPA, and the Maasai movement have shown, the aim is to become part of it, albeit on better terms.[2]

According to Leysens, "The majority of . . . Africa's inhabitants are economically marginalized." He further stresses that "the political protest potential of the marginalized is lower than that of the economically integrated, they are more tolerant of authoritarian political [regimes], and . . . inclined to accord somewhat more legitimacy to the state than are the integrated" (2006, 31). With limited presence of central governments in large parts of rural areas, it is likely that in Africa south of the Sahara, social movements are primarily urban phenomena. To the extent that they also have a rural base, this is in those limited areas with good accessibility, that are already integrated with a larger polity and economy. Many rural organizations are both limited in size and have a strong ethnic profile. Such less integrated associations in more remote areas are also more likely to be content with preserving lifestyles and independence and less likely to form social movements.

In any case, it is not helpful to equate local organizations or community groups with social movements. The minimum requirement for the existence of a social *movement* is some kind of shared belief and an outreach that goes beyond the locality. A social movement, by definition, is broad based both ethnically and geographically. The question of size is important, and most rural groupings in sub-Saharan Africa—also the NGOs—have a very limited spatial coverage and do not constitute movements. Local and/or community associations are usually too isolated to do so, and networking is undeveloped. And the NGOs, while generally in agreement that they—as a category—should have a greater say in national (and even international) policy formulation, often pursue conflicting agendas and compete for funds, clients, and market shares. Hence, the notion of movement seems ill founded.

And why—now that the state, after structural adjustment, has been rolled back and bereft of its former resources—should the "politics of the rural poor" be to engage with the state? This doesn't make sense—neither to me nor, it seems, to most rural Africans.[3]

Rather than engaging with the state, rural Africans in some cases (some regions) have become more self-reliant, take their own initiatives, and embark upon a rather autonomous process of development from below. In other cases (regions), people/groups withdraw or sit back and wait for NGOs, backed by foreign funding, to come and engage with them. They even joke about how much more profitable this is than alternative options (such as engaging with the state). Moreover, in large parts of rural Africa, the state is hardly there to engage with.

The mixed and often unsatisfactory experiences with NGO activities and externally supported village development projects have many causes. One that should not be overlooked is that many NGO programs "focus on strengthening agricultural systems in marginal farming areas" (Practical Action 2005, 24). Marginal farming areas often mean remote areas. Many INGOs and donors have, in their efforts to reach those most in need, ventured to support—or introduce—organizations in remote areas. The outcomes of such efforts have generally been meager, and they often turned out to be charity work rather than development.

INGOs and NGOs have sometimes been (temporarily) effective in introducing agricultural technologies that increase peasants' production and productivity. However, since transport infrastructure and markets often are poorly developed, peasants find it difficult to dispose of the surplus and thus risk economic losses despite improvements. The surplus produced is wasted when crops are left to rot in the fields because there is no market where they could be disposed of. This discourages further investments and productivity enhancements as well as innovative organization building. In such situations there is likely more to gain from investing in physical infrastructure (roads, bridges, warehouses) so that transport and transaction costs will be reduced and private traders and/or collective marketing associations will have a better chance at survival than in directly tampering with local organizations in order to render them more "effective."

The peripheries in sub-Saharan Africa are much larger than most writers about the virtues of organization would have us believe. Africa is a huge continent. The Sahara desert is about as large as the US mainland, whereas Sudan and Congo each almost equals Western Europe in size. Not only is it huge, large parts of sub-Saharan Africa have low population densities where the majority of the population is engaged in low-productivity agriculture mainly for subsistence purposes. Hence, the costs of investing in transport and communication infrastructure are high.[4] In the early 1990s the density of sub-Saharan Africa's road network was only one-sixth of what India's had been in the 1950s, prior to its green revolution (Hazell and Fan 2002). In terms of road and railroad density and quality, sub-Saharan Africa still lags behind all other major regions of the world (Goldstein and Kauffmann 2006). Consequently, information is slow and hard to obtain, transport and transaction costs are high, and, in large parts of the subcontinent, markets are rudimentarily developed. In such environments there are few incentives to adopt market-oriented rationality.

With the help of external supporters, many rural associations have been formed in remote areas where contacts with the outside world are irregular and unreliable. In such areas the pressure to alter the ways things are done and/or to challenge established institutions and power structures have been comparatively weak. Even though some organizations—for example, the Naam movement—have been (almost) spontaneously formed, they seem to have been predominantly occupied with preserving and reproducing rather than altering known ways of life. As was suggested in the introductory chapter, associations with a higher developmental potential are likely to be found in more well-connected and commercialized regions. The preceding chapters have also shown that this is indeed often the case.

In more remote areas there appears to be little scope for establishing bridging organizations as long as the links with the wider society are weak and occasional. It needs to be underlined that discussion of high-potential, well-connected areas versus peripheries is done for reasons of simplicity. It is important to realize that this should not be regarded as an absolute dichotomy. In reality, different regions are more or less central and more or less peripheral, and these criteria may change over time. It is thus more a question of degrees of centrality or remoteness than of either/or. Hence, any type of environment is likely to be the home of different types of organizations, albeit with a predominance of one type or another.

It is therefore no surprise that, for example, Bernard, de Janvry, and Sadoulet (2005), in their study of rural organizations in Burkina Faso, found a coexistence of both community-oriented and market-oriented village organizations, although they didn't exactly step on each other's toes. However, since they also found a strong resistance toward undertakings that could lead to socioeconomic differentiation, they found more community-oriented organizations than market-oriented organizations. The relevant observation is that the predominance of one type of organization did not preclude the existence of the other type. Noteworthy is, however, that, in this rather peripheral area, market-oriented organizations were not only fewer, but many had to include some sharing elements or public good in their activities to be socially acceptable. Interesting also is that supporting NGOs, although they tried, found it very difficult to influence the way decisions were taken in the two types of organizations (in community-oriented organizations there was no need to teach villagers participatory methods since that was already practiced; in market-oriented organizations villagers understood that a much quicker and more flexible type of decision making was needed).

Development from below can take many forms and directions. It can be based on some kind of social movement, or it can be effectuated through groups or individual entrepreneurs. Whatever the case, it is likely to be slow rather than abrupt. Similarly, the difference between an enabling and a constraining environment is not only a matter of degree. It is also a matter of process. From a capitalistic perspective, a suboptimal and only partially market-oriented community cooperative (Luzzati 1999; Chapter 1 herein)—which suffers economic disadvantages but enjoys a higher degree of social respectability—appears to be an ideal albeit temporary solution in more or less peripheral areas. It is, however—in contrast to what many communitarians hope—less likely to represent a serious challenge or a sustainable alternative to "modern" enterprise. Rather, it represents an intermediary form of association, which, while less likely to be competitive in the long run, has every potential to make the transition to a different system smoother and therefore more acceptable to the grassroots. Hence, not all peripheries are hopeless cases.

Neither are all potentially favorable regions the fertile seed-beds for progressive grassroots' organizations that might have been expected. Larsson, for example, reporting from Mount Meru, "one of the most favourable areas for agriculture in Tanzania," as well as one of the "richest," found an outspoken "unwillingness by farmers to organise along cooperative lines" (2001, 453, 21, 213). Part of the explanation might be the discouraging earlier experiences of state-led "cooperation"; partly it may be the undeveloped markets and the comparatively high costs of transportation in rural Tanzania (Isinika, Ashimogo, and Mlangwa 2005) and, indeed, in ESA generally. Rural SSA remains predominantly peripheral.

INGOs, NGOs, and Development

As long as development aid has been a project, one major concern has been that technology transfer is a highly problematic matter. As far as organization goes, this seems to be even more the case. Pre-SAP promoters of cooperatives in developing countries learned the hard lesson that undifferentiated transfers of institutions and organizations are no less problematic than transfers of production techniques (Kötter 1984). This lesson now seems largely to have been forgotten. Despite good intentions, success with externally organized organization building in Africa has usually been far below expectations. Korten (1980) stressed flexibility and opined that there is not one model to follow, not one set of key factors to explain success. Success, he emphasized, instead depends on "organizational fit," that is, on how well an organization fits in the context or environment where it operates. To a large degree externally initiated—or transferred—organizations appear to be misfits in sub-Saharan Africa.

Prominence by Default

It is perhaps symptomatic of the aid industry that the prominence given to NGOs as forerunners in development was not based on their good record as development instruments. When, in the 1980s, NGOs were given this privileged role, there was simply too little experience of NGOs as development agents to do so. This experiment then, when it was launched, can therefore best be characterized as a strategy by default. Disappointment with conventional development aid, which typically had been channeled to and through the state in receiving countries, mounted high in the 1980s. In particular, the receiving governments were blamed for lack of development. Not only were they criticized for being ineffective, but they were increasingly depicted as crooks and kleptocrats and as obstacles to progress. Anything that could be labeled *non*governmental was by definition good.

Sanyal (1994) has pointed out that this critique of the African state was flawed. Not because African governments do not deserve critique, but because the critique was often misdirected and/or ideologically motivated. Western politicians, donors, and scientists needed a scapegoat. Sanyal suggested that critics were angry when their fine theories about development (and especially about the nature, options, and prerogatives of the state) turned out to be worthless. Theories about the state in developing countries are often detached from the environments where these states operate, instead constituting textbook idealizations with little real world relevance.[5] Conveniently forgetting that development aid has seldom been given without strings attached and that, during the Cold War, aid had been used as a tool in superpower competition, these Northern scholars, politicians, and so on needed someone to blame for lack of development, and the state looked like a suitable culprit—if governments do not behave as predicted, blame the governments.

Based on very different ideologies and theoretical foundations, this critique came from many directions. Mackintosh (1992) noted the existence of an unholy alliance, made up of both leftists and neo-liberals. The neo-liberals, ideologically biased against any state, wanted an enhanced role for NGOs because they would reduce the role of the state and draw on charitable funds and unpaid work to reduce costs and the call on taxation. The leftists, concerned instead with class and power, found the state only to be serving the powerful and saw NGOs (sometimes mistaken for social movements) as a countervailing force. NGOs, supposedly exercising political leverage on behalf of the poor and the powerless, could transfer power and resources into the hands of the needy. Or so it was hoped.

Ill-founded Optimism

Hence, while not agreeing on much else, a consensus emerged that it would be better to bypass the state. This was not confined to aid-receiving countries. Donor countries also have had their fair share of structural adjustment. At the time critique was also aired against ineffective aid, and the public in many donor countries was showing signs of aid fatigue—not so much of aid per se as of conventional, bilateral aid (Earthscan 1995). Little was known then about NGOs. This opened up a new possibility for the aid industry to remain in business (Schmale 1993). If aid could be given to—or channeled through—NGOs, it could appear as less questionable and jobs would be secured. Since NGOs were unknown, nobody had anything bad to say about them (Riddell, Bebbington, and Peck 1995). NGOs thus became the new "justifiers of aid" (Snrech 2001, 50) and provided a much sought for "humanitarian gesture" (UNCTAD 2006) to Northern governments. The number of Northern NGOs grew quickly. Donors not only became more appreciative of (Northern) NGOs, some were even established on their direct initiative (Riddell, Bebbington, and Peck 1995). One reason, given by the Swedish Minister of Aid at the time, was that "since aid had been so heavily criticized, more voices were needed to defend it on the home front" (quoted in Sandberg 1992, 8).

Despite the fact that little was known about NGOs, there were many who were quick to wave the NGO banner as the perfect solution to most if not all problems of underdevelopment. NGOs (usually no distinctions were made about the great diversity among them) were lifted to the foreground as some kind of silver bullet, being both the means and the end at the same time. Without being able to base judgments on experience, NGOs, so we were assured, were more flexible, more close to the grassroots, more participatory, more responsive, and more democratic, and hence more effective than conventional aid providers (for a review of arguments, see Holmén and Jirström 1996). In short they were seen, not least by themselves, to represent an (even *the*) alternative paradigm.

This, however, is largely self-deceptive. On the one hand, already in the 1990s mainstream and alternative paradigms in development theory tended to converge and, hence, there was

hardly an alternative to represent (Pieterse 1998). Shepherd further noted: "One would expect NGOs to be working in the new
paradigm. Some no doubt are, or are trying to; but at least in the
north NGOs have generally gone for growth themselves. . . . NGOs
are increasingly not looking as though they are the major vehicle for the new paradigm" (1998, 265). Recent studies comparing NGO aid and bilateral donor aid have found that "the allocation
of self-financed NGO aid reveals striking similarities to the allocation of official . . . development aid" (Nunnenkamp, Weingarth,
and Weisser 2008, 2). Similarly, Koch et al. observed that NGOs
"tend to replicate the location choices of official 'backdonors'"
and to "keep a low profile rather than distinguishing themselves
from other donors" (2008, i). Nevertheless, many people were
eager to believe that NGOs in some important sense are different. Even if such claims and expectations have often turned out
to be ill-founded, this image is still promoted today—not least by
INGOs and Northern NGOs themselves. And apparently the pro-
paganda works; hardly any official document or aid agreement
can today be presented without acknowledging the importance
of including NGOs/CBOs.

A more skeptical attitude now seems to be spreading. In the
early twenty-first century the awareness is slowly growing that
much more is assumed about NGOs than is actually known about
them and that their reputation has been based to a large degree
on what people want to believe. The 1980s, however, were permeated by optimism. At the same time as bilateral aid declined,
increasingly large funds were channeled to and through NGOs,
and their numbers mushroomed in both receiving and donating
countries. That the number of NGOs grew in Africa as a result of
changed financial flows is not surprising. After all, that was the
intention. The effects, however, have often been other than those
intended.

The record of NGOs as development initiators in sub-Saharan
Africa is mixed. Partly, this is because there are so many types
of NGOs and not all are development oriented. Many are engaged in relief and charitable work (and often do a good job in
this capacity) and, therefore, should not be criticized for not contributing to development. But also among those NGOs that have
a more outspoken ambition to "do development" there is certainly less to brag about than often has been assumed. Many

NGOs, both domestic and foreign, while purporting to do development, are actually operating as relief organizations. A large part of their work is done in peripheral areas and, while offering some temporary relief to poor people, they do not change their overall situation. At both the grassroots and intermediary levels it is also frequently noted that organizations lack resources, skills, and knowledge, and that intermediaries often have no close contact with grassroots. Far too often NGOs, supposedly assisting local groups, are understaffed and lack both vision and innovative capacity. Hence, their development impact is often negligible—or even negative. Many are fakes created with the sole purpose of tapping into the new and externally provided financial flows.

Opportunism and Development

Opportunism seems to characterize much contemporary NGO activities in sub-Saharan Africa. Apparently, it is common at both intermediary and grassroots levels. This need not be bad in itself. After all, development is about seizing opportunities, and that is often a question of being creative. The problem is rather a perceived lack of opportunities. This influences behavior and the meaning of organization in various ways. Sometimes it leads to passivity and to the emergence of a "cargo cult" where NGOs are turned into substitutes for development. On other occasions it fosters a desire to escape. In December 2006 a documentary on Swedish TV showed how mothers in Senegal and Mauretania were quite innovative in their use of local organizations. They formed small cooperatives (Tontin) in order to finance and organize the shipping of illegal emigrants (boat refugees), usually their own sons or relatives, to Europe because of a perceived lack of opportunities in the countries where they live (SRTV 2006). Whereas such organizations do not contribute to Africa's development, they may well represent the most realistic assessments of options available to their members.

For lack of alternative options to earn a living, the best solution may well be to start an NGO. Actually, it has been suggested that "the major reason for starting an NGO is to provide jobs for graduates" (John Kadzandira, personal communication). Not infrequently, INGOs and the NGOs they support also offer better payment than alternatives would do. Some NGOs (externally funded) are only there to provide their owners a salary. Even though that does not necessarily preclude them doing a good job, many NGOs have been established too hastily by well-intentioned enthusiasts with too little experience and too few skills and resources to do their job efficiently. Quite a few have also been registered by fortune hunters with no serious intentions to facilitate development. Such experiences lead to calls for precaution among donors financing NGOs and NGO-administered projects, and foster a tendency toward control and upward accountability. Thus, an approach that was (and still often is) believed to be bottom up runs the risk of being turned into its opposite.

At the same time, there are more encouraging examples of how organizations have been created for more forward-looking and developmental purposes. Even if success stories are few so far, they *are* there, and they need to be told. Recently formed producers' organizations, reformed cooperatives, member-operated commodity exchanges, and independent farmers' platforms are all proof of growing capability and self-reliance. Similarly, the common transfer of extension provision from governments to NGOs has often been criticized for being an abandonment of smallholders. But it has at least had the effect that extension now must be effective. Previously, extension agents had secure employment but reports abound about negligent and lethargic service providers. Now, because NGOs hire extension agents on short contracts (two or three years), they must show results or they will not be reemployed. Hence, despite many shortcomings, it is often correct, as others also have concluded, that NGOs often accomplish and leave behind more useful things in villages than governments have done. But then again, the record of governmental service provision was hardly impressive. It is, however, just as common that groups and accomplishments do not survive the project period and vanish when NGOs move on.

If the experience so far of this NGO experiment leaves a lot to be desired, one should be careful not to denounce it altogether as a failure. On one level the problem is not the African organizations. It is rather the often premature and exaggerated expectations placed upon them. "External partners often seem to expect from [Southern organizations] an unrealistic degree of perfection"

(Snrech 2001, 49). When performance does not match expectations, the external partners either "dictate the agendas of southern NGOs" (Bertone 2000, 1) or they "set up their own organizations which are easier to mould to their outlook, rather than try to work with existing local institutions" (Guèye 1999, 10; see also Mercoiret et al. 2001). Particularly constraining has been external supporters' impatience in combination with the common lack of infrastructure and undeveloped markets in areas where many local organizations operate. There are many examples where African NGOs have been effective in raising the productivity of smallholder peasants, but with unreliable markets the latter have not been able to dispose of their surplus. More would have been accomplished by improving the overall environment in which local organizations operate and thus creating opportunities, rather than by tampering directly with smallholder organizations.

Help to Self-help?

Paradoxically, the most severe problem accompanying this "participatory" attempt to realize development from below is an apparently widespread lack of trust among supporters. Africa has never owned its development policies. Outsiders, both official donors and NGOs, have used Africa as a full-scale laboratory, "a place where they can experiment with their political philosophies and ideas of new international, social and economic systems" (Borgin and Corbett 1982, 28). Before the NGO boom hit Africa, it was not uncommon that African governments had as many development policies as there were donors in the country (Simon and Radoki 1990). This still seems to be the case but now on a much grander scale. Today, "the state is placed on the same level as other so-called stakeholders, including NGOs" (Shivji 2006, 10). With hundreds of foreign NGOs invading Africa to "do development," African ownership of the development process appears to have diminished even further.

Not only are there many foreign NGOs in sub-Saharan Africa, but they often have very different ideas about why they are there and try to realize quite different objectives. Some try to link African peasants to markets; others decry development strategies that favor a market economy; some are "modernizers"; and others tend to preserve pre-modern structures and idealize community. Some try to introduce industrial/scientific inputs in agriculture, whereas others demand that peasants only use organic methods before they can be assisted. With the state rolled back and such diverging aspirations among those willing to help Africa, the policy situation is chaotic. One measure to mitigate this is the recent establishment of joint-donor platforms, where donors agree among themselves on shared priorities. Another is that, since NGOs depend on donors for large parts of their finances, there are some possibilities to steer NGO activities in the desired direction. Whether this will bring the development process closer to the Africans is a different matter altogether.

The sudden growth in the number of development organizations in sub-Saharan Africa could be a good sign, a promise that the subcontinent is now recovering from years of stagnation and dependencies. However, to a large extent this mushrooming of organizations is the result of external penetration. Redirection of aid flows has fed this growth, leading to the creation of some genuine African development organizations, but also contributing to the flocking of opportunists, crooks, and swindlers around the newly provided pork barrels. That some African governments have begun monitoring NGOs and threaten to de-register those that are found to be exploitative or cannot convincingly report development activities is sometimes decried as undue attempts at control. However, it is equally likely to be a sign of good governance.[6]

Whereas some INGOs have budgets in parity with donors, African NGOs operate on a much more modest level. For many, the situation is precarious. They "are operating hand to mouth at a subsistence level, making them highly risk averse" (James et al. 2005, 4). Not only does this often limit their area of operation in strict geographical terms, but it also sometimes limits their presence in time. On the one hand, the death rate among African NGOs is high; on the other, some NGOs engage in more projects and village activities than they are able to carry through. This leads to haphazard performance and interruption of activities. They may start up in a grand style when solvent, only to find that six months later they are out of money and their activities have to lie dormant until a new financial injection has been secured—often from a different INGO (African NGO worker, personal communication). This goes a long way to explain (1) their often limited impact, and (2) why the grassroots sometimes have a quite relaxed attitude to NGO activities, allow them "do their thing" while they are present in the village, and then wait to see what the next NGO might have to offer.

Haphazard performance should not be blamed entirely on the NGOs. Many are financed by donors in faraway countries but even if aid agencies try to work with long time perspectives and sometimes have a good understanding of the countries they are engaged in, aid priorities are often decided above their heads (for example, switching aid from Africa to former Soviet states, or from governments to NGOs and now, perhaps, back to the states again). Often such reorientations have little to do with on-the-ground realities. More often, they appear to reflect changes in Northern governments and/or a new fad in the donor community. This often puts NGOs in a precarious position. They "may be effective in facilitating group formation but . . . often do not provide for sustainability. Most NGO initiatives disappear as soon as the external supporting agency decides to withdraw support" (Heemskerk and Wennink 2004, 89).

Whatever Happened to Empowerment?

Empowerment and capacity building are high on virtually every NGO's and INGO's agenda. Going through literature on NGOs and development, one frequently encounters the implicit assumption, and sometimes bold declarations, that *"by their very nature,* NGOs are participatory, action-oriented—democratic—groups" (Africare 2005, 1, emphasis added). As a general statement, this is simply not true. Even if there are exceptions, NGOs frequently, perhaps even mostly, are neither as democratic nor as participatory or empowering as has commonly been suggested. This is so for a number of reasons.

Empowerment means local ownership and implies that the rural grassroots should identify needs and ways to solve them. This they can do by different means, for example, by establishing their own local organizations in order to initiate projects to deal with practical issues and/or to enhance the capacity to deal with external entities such as traders, public authorities, and INGOs. NGOs are supposed to assist with all this. This also implies that NGO services should be demand driven. In theory this is a beautiful approach. In practice it is often merely an illusion. The limited size and capacities of many NGOs lead to a situation where the grassroots and CBOs have to—and soon learn to—confine their demands to the limited range of services that "their" NGO is able to offer. Hence, in practice it is often the NGO (or the donor that finances the NGO) that is the ultimate decision maker.

That development should be participatory and demand driven is accepted by virtually all donors and INGOs today. It is widely propagated, and one easily gets the impression that it is widely practiced. That appears, however, not to be the case. Pantanali, commenting upon one major external organization's approach, found that "projects especially designed on a demand-driven basis have actually been in operation for only three or four years" (2004, 3). And this was mostly on an experimental basis; not all of this agency's projects were demand driven. Despite limited experiences of demand-driven development (DDD) and despite the fact that "not enough is still known about the . . . target communities, and about the best way to help them" (ibid.), attempts are now made to "spread, scale up and mainstream participation" (Pimbert 2004. 2).[7] With this rush among INGOs and donors to speed up the demand-driven process—a formidable paradox in itself—there is a great risk that a good idea will—again—be turned into "a low-overhead model of service delivery" (Perrett 2004, 6). Rather than community-based and demand-driven development, it often results in "supply-driven demand-driven" development (Mansuri and Rao 2004). Implementation "is increasingly pulled toward focussing on achievement of short-term . . . targets. Except in a few notable cases, longer term capacity building goals tend to be under-addressed" (Perrett 2004, v; see also Ebrahim 2003). While in practice DDD is often a chimera, tales of DDD are primarily for home consumption; that is, they serve to mask Northern dominance and to create an illusion of effectiveness in the North that pays for it (see Dichter 2003 for similar conclusions about microfinance).

A contributing reason for maintaining external control over local activities is fear of elite capture of local organizations and projects. And indeed, elite capture is frequently being reported. One should be careful, though, when blaming local elites for being overly selfish and lacking solidarity. At least in part the problem lies elsewhere. On the one hand, sub-Saharan Africa's rural areas have been flooded with myriad external or externally supported NGOs wishing to create local organizations and start projects, but often with "little or no experience in participatory development [and a] pressing need for quick and visible results" (Platteau and Gaspart 2003a, 1). On the other hand, the availability of rural people with the necessary skills to run projects, write proposals, head committees, and negotiate with donors and NGOs is often limited. Hence, the same people tend to turn up again and again as chairmen, secretaries, and treasurers in externally supported committees and organizations. Thus, the scale of outside intervention in itself leads, more or less automatically, if not to "capture" then at least to elite domination.

Besides this, Platteau and Gaspart claim that many local leaders have not only a "proclivity to view aid agencies as purveyors of money" (2003a, 5)—which, in fact, they often are—but they also find that local elites have a tendency to enrich themselves at the expense of their fellow villagers. Therefore, they say, external agents should discipline local leaders (ibid.; Platteau and Gaspart 2003b). They admit that this could be interpreted as "neo-colonialist pressure" (2003b, 1690) but apparently see no alternative. In their view the problem lies with the Africans, not with the external agents or this approach of intervention. This, actually, boils down to "blame the victim." Instead, the external agents should ask not only how far they are prepared to intervene, but also what right they have to intervene.

Calderisi's assertion that "the root of corruption is Africa's strong family ties" (2006, 86) completely misses the point. In large parts of rural Africa people have to make a living in risky and volatile environments. For their social security they depend on traditional social institutions such as kin, chief, and patronage, even if these are not as egalitarian as communalists sometimes want to believe. As long as these are the only structures available to provide social security, it would be asking too much to insist that local elites (or the grassroots for that matter) should disregard them and start distributing wealth along new and alien principles. In the case referred to by Platteau and Gaspart, a local chief had disproportionately distributed the gains from an NGO-led project in the village, allocating a lot for himself but only small amounts to the rest of the project participants. There was a trial, but the chief escaped punishment and was even re-elected as project leader. Platteau and Gaspart comment:

> Here is a clear illustration of the support that poor people are inclined to give to an elite member on the ground that they have benefited from his leadership efforts. That he apportioned to himself a disproportionate share of the benefits of the aid program is considered legitimate by most of them. They indeed think that without his efforts their own situation would not have improved at all. In particular, he created the village association which had to be formed in order to be eligible for external assistance. (2003a, 6)

If this is acceptable behavior in the affected communities, why denounce it? Could it be aid delivery that is the problem, not the recipient?

The position of domestic NGO leaders is often delicate. Since the NGO boom in Africa is a rather recent phenomenon, many NGO leaders are young and inexperienced. Commonly under-staffed and operating on a strained budget, they are caught among conflicting demands from clients, donors, and kin. Donors want to influence—or even decide about—projects. Clients and other planned beneficiaries may or may not act as true and active participants in groups and committees. And "a leader is expected to provide for extended family and kin through patronage and other forms of largesse. . . . Leaders are often directly obligated to a sizeable number of dependants on an ongoing basis, an inevitable situation in the context of mass poverty" (James et al. 2005, 15). Apart from perhaps confusing the NGO's budget with private budgets and creating jobs and sinecures for kin, it is not uncommon for NGO leaders to be "expected to extend the use of office facilities to their spouses and family members. Use of an office vehicle to take children to school, do weekend shopping or go to the rural areas to attend funerals and other functions is the expected norm" (ibid.). It is too easy for Western critics to denounce this as corruption and to call for disciplinary measures. The fact is that if NGO leaders did not live up to such expectations, on many occasions they—and the NGOs—would lose credibility and be unable to accomplish anything.

External supporters sometimes see this as proof that the grassroots do not understand their own good and therefore need "conscientization" before they can be entrusted to manage local organizations. This is as far away from DDD as one can come. Actually, what outsiders do when they urge rural inhabitants to behave according to an alien logic, is to demand that they should behave as if they lived in a society where they do not. Otherwise expressed, many well-meaning outsiders are actually trying to impose the norms and values of an educated, well-fed, and often spoiled urban middle class in a post-industrial welfare state to inhabitants in a poor, rural, semi-literate, and pre-modern peasant society. That this would work is hardly a realistic assumption. Why the rush to discipline? [8]

Institutions aren't so easily changed. Viewed from below, the local chief in the above-mentioned case did nothing wrong. Moreover, he and his fellow villagers were there first, and a little politeness wouldn't be out of place. The NGO arrived there of its own initiative. Local people should be allowed to be the masters in their own house while the guest abides by the local norms for conduct. If the guest doesn't like them, it is free to go elsewhere. Isn't that what "development from below" is all about—even if it turns out to be both slower and less smooth than assumed and even if it takes off in an unforeseen direction? Empowerment is indeed difficult, especially when initiated from outside.

NGOs, both domestic and international, usually depend heavily on donor funding. This has been found to undermine development from below. It is well known that he who pays the piper also calls the tune. Financial dependencies tend to make NGOs accountable upward rather than downward (to their clients). "Flexible funding" such as the Naam and the CNCR have enjoyed (allowing them to use funds at their own discretion) is an exception and far from the rule. Instead, there are signs that ownership of projects, and indeed of the entire development process, are even further removed from the grassroots, which, on the rhetorical level, are said to be its centerpiece. This is not because donors are inherently dictatorial. They have their own auditors watching over their shoulder to make sure that time schedules are kept and that taxpayers' money is not just given away but used according to plan. This is particularly problematic since "participation" loses its meaning when applied to time-bound and result-oriented development projects (Chhotray 2004).

Also, in order to stay afloat, poor African NGOs must be very sensitive to—and often develop great skills in observing—even small shifts in donor fads and jargon (African NGO staff, personal communication). Consciously or not, instead of making their own priorities and presenting their own projects, African NGOs and local groups tend to align their project proposals with donors' preferences. With pent-up competition among domestic NGOs, those organizations that gain support have structural or strategic advantages over other NGOs (Clifford 2001). However, it also leads African organizations to "spend considerable time chasing money that is not very useful to them" (Mitlin, Hickey, and Bebbington 2007, 1710). The implications for the indigenization of development are severe.

It is also not uncommon that NGOs and INGOs assist their client CBOs and committees with writing project proposals (see, for example, de Sardan 2005; also Astrig Tasgian, personal communication). This further strengthens the tendency to streamline local "initiatives" with external preferences. In terms of power, the relationships between indigenous organizations and external supporters are highly unequal and "partnerships between development agencies and indigenous [organizations] are often fragile, and tend to dissolve when they fail to meet the preconceptions of the developers" (Watson 2003, 287). As Shivji points out, "a substantial number of NGOs are set up to respond to what is perceived to be in vogue among the donor-community at any particular time. Donor driven NGOs . . . are perhaps the most dominant" (2006, 13).

Group formation is often a precondition for funding. This has led to "jump starting" NGOs and to forced birth of many local groups, CBOs, and village committees, which, however, remain totally dependent on continued external support.[9] This is a problem not only at the local level. It is well known that "outside pressures to form nationwide producer organizations tend to delay the already slow process of PO strengthening" (Pesche 2001, 37). Despite this, many donors, INGOs, and NGOs want local groups and CBOs to scale up their activities and address not only practical issues at the local level but also engage in lobbying and policy analysis. Advocacy has become "standard practice for development NGOs" (Edwards 2005, 3). There are many reasons why lobbying and advocacy have become so prominent on NGOs' agendas, not all of them leading to grassroots empowerment. Edwards suggests that it is because it is the "least costly form of scaling-up" (ibid.) Not only is it cheaper than running projects in villages, it also demands fewer skills. Many NGOs are urban based and have no close contacts with the rural grassroots. On many occasions they also do not know enough about farming, which is the main occupation of their rural clients. Hence, they lack the capacity to "do development" in rural areas. In any case, lobbying and advocacy are preferably done in urban settings—especially since donors "are not funding the popular sectors of society, but are strengthening a new African elite committed to the promotion of a limited form of *procedural* democracy" (Hearn 1999, 4, emphasis added).

Much NGO literature has emphasized the importance of empowering the grassroots to demand services from government. Considering that, simultaneously with the growth of NGOs, the state has been rolled back and has lost much of its former capacity to provide services, this seems to be largely deceptive.[10] But advocacy can be the beginning of a political career for urbanites as it gives NGO leaders a possibility to speak on behalf of the (rural) grassroots—although often without close contacts or a mandate to do so (Holmén and Jirström 2009). This is not to deny that INGOs and NGOs are often driven by a humanitarian zeal and that their staff is devoted to the mission. However, ideology is a strong driving force in many intermediaries, especially in INGOs. Empowerment, therefore, often means only that the grassroots should learn to see things the outsider's way.

Ideology, while often being a strong motivating force for those working in "alternative" organizations, can thus be a hindrance as well as an asset. The general idea is that "organizations promoted from the outside, with an 'instrumental' approach, gradually acquire knowledge, know-how and tools encouraging their independence from their guardians" (Mercoiret et al. 2001, 22). Kilby (2006) stresses that NGOs and INGOs are not one of a kind, and that the degree to which they actually empower their clients to become independent depends on the broad values—the *Weltanschauung*—guiding their activities. These values are not stable but "can be eroded over time as an organization grows, staff change, or donor preferences change" (ibid., 959). It is easier to maintain the value base in small organizations where people know each other well. But then again small organizations have a limited impact and many want to grow. By now, NGOs—and particularly INGOs—have become "a major growth industry" (Edwards 2005, 8). This has had an apparently far-reaching effect on their performance. "There is no doubt that many of today's INGOs are motivated by normative agendas. Insecurity and competition, however, often pushes them to behave in . . . rent-seeking ways" (Cooley and Ron 2002, 36).

Whereas it is often the case that donors and INGOs—despite their good intentions—find it difficult to accept local societies and indigenous institutions as they are, and worry about elite capture and the grassroots' improper prioritizations, it is revealing to try and see things from the other perspective. Harrison assumes the role as interpreter:

> Southern NGOs feel themselves to be the subjects of changing and imposed agendas. In addition, accountability is seen as a one-way street; southern NGOs spend inordinate amounts of time trying to meet the accountability requirements of diverse donors. There are suspicions that donor-supported projects are job creation schemes for [Northern] experts and volunteers when there are equally qualified southerners available. Lastly, the major concerns raised by southern NGOs are not demands for increased funding, but for increased transparency and respect. (2002, 591)

Whether domestic or foreign, NGOs want to remain in business. They compete for clients, market share, donor funds, and sometimes for political influence. They are thus keen to preserve what they "have," and this has sometimes been an obstacle to real empowerment as well. Primarily, it has limited networking and mutual learning among local groups and organizations that are linked to different NGOs. In many ways, therefore, NGOs in Africa have not made the great contributions to emancipation or empowerment of the poor that they were expected to do. Instead, they have often created new forms of dependency. In many cases it is relevant to talk about international patron-client structures in the NGO world (Holmén and Jirström 2009).

It is illustrative that, for all the lip service paid to the need to strengthen African organizations, many Northern NGOs "are opposed to aid being channelled directly to southern NGOs" (Manji 2000, 75).

In light of this, one should perhaps be less concerned with the shortcomings of African NGOs and farmers' associations and instead be impressed by what they have actually managed to accomplish. African NGOs, both intermediaries and local associations, are caught in a rather precarious situation. Most NGOs are "operating hand to mouth at a subsistence level, making them highly risk averse" (James et al. 2005, 4). In general, most African organizations are also of recent origin, and their staff and leaders tend to be relatively inexperienced. For most of them it is becoming increasingly difficult to compete with INGOs and donor-supported NGOs, and African development is rapidly becoming a matter of remote control. In addition, African local and popular organizations suffer from a severe brain drain. Not only are they often captured or crowded out by donors and INGOs, but they are also the victims of "high turnover of senior staff recruited by international NGOs and donors" (ibid.).

Donor requirements generally impose heavy costs on African NGOs, and only a small number of indigenous organizations can match external demands. Donors prefer to work with counterparts that "speak the same language," that is, with NGOs that "fit their criteria and understand their reference points and ideas, especially with regards to financial matters" (Chowdhury, Finlay-Notman, and Hovland 2006, 26). Grants and contracts go to the already well connected. Moreover, because donors and INGOs (1) are reluctant to pay "core funding" to the organizations they collaborate with and (2) prefer to only spend "aid money" on projects, capacity building in African NGOs falters, resulting in "an observable differentiation within the . . . African NGO sector" (Bornstein 2003, 393), with smaller NGOs being gradually excluded from participation. Fafchamps and Owens (2006) call this a "crowding out" of domestic NGOs by donors and INGOs. Instead of empowerment, according to Secknelgin, we often get

a critical disempowerment process in relation to NGOs' links with people. By becoming actors for service delivery, NGOs locate themselves into a set of social relations that are institutionalised at the international level. NGOs are exposed to "capacity building" exercises by donors who try to ensure that [the] "right" management tools are put in place to help achieve international policy targets. These tools help form NGOs and their functions in ways that international actors can recognise and access, but such a process paradoxically frustrates the ability of NGOs to respond to the needs of local people expressed within local institutional processes and relations. (Seckinelgin 2006, 724)

These new chains of dependency extend all the way from governments, aid agencies, and INGOs in the global North through NGOs to CBOs and grassroots committees in African villages. Within this chain of dependencies, Hearn (2007) does not hesitate to say that African NGOs fulfill the role of *compradors*—a new (dependent) bourgeoisie. Surely, there are such tendencies but it is likely an exaggeration to ascribe this function to all African NGOs.

For different reasons—some practical some egoistical—many of those involved in supporting local development find it difficult to relinquish control. African organizations, especially those at the local level that everyone supports in theory, have not earned much faith as vehicles for development. Their main function so far has been to offer an excuse for others to pursue *their* objectives and expand *their* businesses. A multitude of African as well as Western and INGO staff have found employment and career opportunities for themselves. Some have even found their way to a seat at the policy-negotiating tables. However, since it is a widespread experience that NGO projects often do not survive the disappearance of the supporting agency, they so far have contributed little to development. The irony of the matter is that whereas cooperatives and similar associations "traditionally" have often been created in order to avoid exploitation by middle men, this "NGO scramble for Africa" amounts to nothing less than the heyday of the middlemen. Opinions vary, however, as to how serious this is. Batterbury contends:

We cannot afford to dismiss externally funded development projects as irrelevant or wholly destructive to local interests . . . but neither can we say that the encounter between the occupants of Toyota Landcruisers and local people has been unproblematic, or free of the clientelism and self-interest that mars many efforts at rural development in Africa. (2005, 275)

Others are of a quite different opinion. Voices from the South are much more outspoken about the failure of the NGO approach to development (see, for example, Zaidi 1999; Aloo 2000; Amutabi 2006). One need not go as far as Shivji, who opines that the whole NGO circus represents a "reassertion of the imperial project" (2006, 16; see also Zeleza 2006; Nolutshungu 2008). It is enough to admit that expectations on NGOs have been naive and exaggerated and that there is no simple or "magic" solution to delayed development. In any case, it is not the question of one project being pursued, imperial or otherwise. There is certainly no conspiracy. There are simply too many helpers involved, all keen on grabbing a slice of the cake, all pulling in a different direction, and all eager to preserve their self-interests.

Implications for Donors

Which is the proper lesson to draw from this? That local organizations aren't the panacea to development after all and therefore should be abandoned? Is it time to make a new experiment? As this is being written, disappointment with local organizations and the allegedly community-based approach seems to be mounting (Blaikie 2006; Perrett 2004; Platteau 2004). Hence, there is a great risk that—again—the baby will be thrown out with the bathwater. Igoe and Kelsall point out that "in East Africa several bilateral and multilateral donors have quit NGO based aid, redirecting almost 100% of their budget to ministerial support" (2005, 2). Against the above-sketched background, this is hardly surprising. One nevertheless wonders: Is this because the African state has been found to differ significantly from what it was (described as) twenty years ago? Will such a turn-around bring development closer to the Africans? Or is it just a new effort to save the donors and the aid industry now that criticism of aid seems to be mounting again?

The sad thing about development aid is that it is almost never given without strings attached. Worse, the primary objective of aid is to serve the interests of the donor rather than those of the receiver. At the very least, it serves to enhance the goodwill of the donor. Aid is used as a means to enhance political influence and often also to create political allies or clients in the international patronage system. Apart from this egotistical political aspect, aid has lately become big business. This is not to deny that many individual employees in NGOs, INGOs, and governmental-aid agencies are altruistic and sometimes work for low salaries and/or contribute to groups and projects from their own pocket. But the organizations in which they work need foremost to remain in business, and apparently donors' and INGOs'/NGOs' most important mission is to boost their own reputation. I have long found it disgusting that, for example, the US government writes on every sack of maize and every can of cooking oil donated that this is "a gift from the American people." Traveling through Africa, it is equally disturbing to see road signs announcing that "this project is financed by the European Union." And now I find that some INGOs do the same. When visiting women's groups in Tanzania in 2007, they showed me equipment on which it was written in big letters: "DONATED BY [*NAME OF INGO*]."

During the Cold War the superpowers, in their competition for allies and vassals, by distributing "development aid" provided benign as well as dictatorial and clearly anti-developmental governments with artificial lifelines. This detached these governments from their constituencies and lessened the pressure on them to develop resources and human capital within the territories they were supposed to govern; that is to say, donors prolonged the life of neo-patrimonial regimes. With the end of the Cold War, the rationale for providing aid diminished, the big players lost interest in Africa, and it was suddenly "discovered" that African leaders were crooks who needed to be disciplined. Aid was reduced, conditionalized, and redirected (which gave myriad NGOs and INGOs unexpected prominence as subcontractors and watchdogs). Now this approach too is being questioned. The competition for vassals in Africa is reemerging.

Apparently—as was the case when the NGO-scramble for Africa set in some twenty years ago—this recent reorientation of aid away from NGOs and back to the state appears to occur for reasons that have nothing whatsoever to do with NGO/INGO performance. But it is likely to have far-reaching consequences for them. Two circumstances in particular serve to explain this apparent U-turn in Northern aid policies: China's ascendance as a major player in sub-Saharan Africa, and the terrorist attack on the World Trade Center in New York on September 11, 2001.

Asian Flu

China is suddenly presenting itself as a potential superpower and has shown strong ambitions to gain a foothold in Africa. It has become a new and perhaps unpredictable donor. By 2006, China had signed aid agreements with more than forty African states, and it "appears to be one of the most active countries . . . in Africa" (Mahmoud 2007, 2). China deals directly with African governments and it does not demand "good governance" from partners. This has influenced the behavior and policies of Western donors. The Paris Declaration on Aid Effectiveness was presented in 2005. It officially reinstates the state in the driver's seat, calls for harmonization of donors with recipients, and says that enhanced aid effectiveness is to be achieved through "increasing alignment of aid with partner countries' priorities" (2005, §3, ii). One is advised to be skeptical about such bold declarations. Aid is still a part of foreign policy, and foreign policy is there to safeguard the interests of the policymaker, that is, the donor. Remembering how donors have striven to coordinate NGOs and to align them with their own objectives, one would wisely expect joint donor platforms to become instruments for aligning recipient governments' policies with donors' priorities. It is in any case hard to believe that coordinated donors—in real life—would abstain from using this platform for such purposes. De Renzio's comment is revealing: "Donor pressure works best when the international community speaks with one voice and acts together, and the recipient government cannot easily resort to alternative funding sources" (2006, 2).

Apart from that, this reorientation has caused worries among INGOs for a number of reasons. On the one hand, smaller Northern NGOs have argued that this emphasis on effectiveness—the requirement for strong managing-for-development results—demands greater professionalism and "such an approach leads to increased 'bureaucratisation' simultaneously creating an access barrier for CSOs that lack capacity to fulfil the extensive MfDR requirements" (Wright-Revolledo 2007, 4).[11] Thus, there is a process of crowding out NGOs also in the global North (see also Holmén and Jirström 2009). INGOs are worried also because they envisage a reduced role in policy negotiations and because it gives less space for *Northern* values (Hauer 2006; emphasis added). This, however, is probably an unwarranted worry (see below).

The Paris Declaration can be seen primarily as a direct response to the Chinese presence in Africa. China emphasizes that its activities in Africa are based on the principles of *cooperation* and *mutual benefit*. It is no coincidence that China's manifestation of its intensified engagement with Africa, FOCAC (Forum on China-Africa Cooperation), launched in 2000, was followed in 2001 by the birth of the Western-supported NEPAD (New Economic Partnership for African Development). And it is no coincidence that the Paris Declaration followed soon after. Neither is it surprising that whereas FOCAC emphasizes cooperation, NEPAD emphasizes partnership. The difference between the two approaches, however, is that whereas Western donors still emphasize good governance (but are becoming more permissive), China promises to be hands off (it does not tell aid recipients how to run domestic affairs). And China certainly needs no watchdog NGOs to keep governments in line. Suddenly, NGOs are becoming a menace to Northern donors, but this appears to have more to do with China than with the NGOs.

"You are either with us or against us."

These infamous words by the former US President George W. Bush, uttered immediately after the terrorist attack on New York on September 11, 2001, perfectly illustrate another recent change in Northern aid policies. Not only did President Bush declare that in order to be eligible for American aid, governments in the global South must gather under the banner of American-led War on Terrorism, but Canada, Great Britain, and the European Union also have tied their development assistance to anti-terrorism considerations (McMahon 2007; Aning 2007).[12] This has several implications for NGOs. For example, according to the 2006/2007 INTRAC annual report, "in North America NGOs are on the defensive, under increased scrutiny and required to sign up to supposedly voluntary codes of conduct." In June 2003 President Bush "informed American NGO leaders that they were in fact 'an arm' of the US Government—and that they had an important job to promote US interests" (Igoe and Kelsall 2005, 5; see also Klein 2003). Donor capture of INGOs and NGOs is intensified, and it is becoming increasingly difficult for them to represent some kind of alternative development.

History repeats itself. There is a clear risk that the global powers will again be tolerant of repressive and anti-developmental regimes as long as they serve the interests of the donor. After all, development is not so high on the agenda. Under this scenario the recent policy shift is not so much a question of strengthening the African state as it is of aligning it with Western values and security considerations. INGOs will face some hard times, while not much support is likely to be given to African organizations at the grassroots. It thus seems as if the NGO struggle for Africa might have reached its peak. This, paradoxically, may be just as well.

The Bumpy Road to Success?

The problem, as argued here, is neither the African NGOs nor the African smallholders and their local organizations. Instead it is twofold: (1) expectations on NGOs/INGOs have been unrealistic and exaggerated, and (2) grassroots' organizations have seldom been given a real chance to be the owners of local development. In fact, they have often been embraced to death. Based on ideology and improper analysis, in the early 1980s the decision was made that only *non*governmental activities should be promoted. This, however, led much development aid astray. It diverted attention from important aspects of African development and failed to "recognise the limits of community-based approaches in the context of wider state-building objectives" (ID21 2006, 1). The widely advocated opinion that rural grassroots shall own the development process and formulate their own development agendas clashed with the need to "integrat[e] disparate autonomous communities into one central political unit" (Murunga 2000, 110). But this was only one of many mistakes.

What Africa needs is simultaneously to build state, markets, and indigenous organizations. These are projects that sometimes clash, but they need not be antagonistic. Poor peasants at the grassroots level hardly formulate their own development agendas—that is a much too complex and long-term project. They are fully occupied with finding solutions to more immediate problems. Hence, hundreds of helpers scrambled for Africa with the ambition to implement development agendas. This, however, diverted attention from the more important aspect of *self-help.* In this sense many NGO activities have actually become substitutes for development. Moreover, organization building was often done as a substitute for both state and market. This has been detrimental to African development, especially when donors and INGOs "have rather unrealistic expectations—about the pace of institutional innovation in the public sector, of private sector development, of management capacity to cope with innovation and complexity, and the speed of social change at the community level" (Perrett 2004, 8).

It is time to turn African development into an indigenous process—or, rather, into a multitude of parallel processes initiated and owned by Africans and their associations in many different localities simultaneously. Donors and concerned outsiders can— if they tread carefully—do a lot to facilitate such processes, but should *avoid getting directly involved in projects and local organizations.* There seems to be little need to teach Africans to help themselves. What they need is more opportunities to do so. It may be tempting to intervene in order to speed up processes or to see to it that the "proper" projects will be initiated and that the "proper" decisions will be made. Virtually all experience we have tells us that this is counterproductive. So, we now know, is throwing money at organizations. Unless done with extreme caution, external funding only attracts fortune hunters and leads to ill-prepared projects and unsustainable organizations.

Africa is not a hopeless case. It is not only critical researchers like myself and Northerners with many years of experience from within the INGO community (for example, Dichter 2003; Lockwood 2005) who are becoming increasingly skeptical about the NGO approach. A growing number of African intellectuals also are becoming increasingly weary with the present situation. And African organizations show signs that it is time to take the lead in development. A recently established Pan African Farmers Platform found that "Africa continues to be oriented more toward the outside than inwardly," but also concluded that "there are no alternatives to the mobilization of our own human resources and our own financial resources" (PAFP 2008, 2, 3). The road ahead might be both bumpy and winding, but this bodes well for the future.

A precondition is, of course, that Africa is allowed to become self-reliant. This study has highlighted the impact of environment on organizations, their orientations, limitations, and potentials. Some environments offer more incentives for innovative and progressive organization than do others. It has also shown that, in the right environment, African smallholders have the will and capacity to establish their own organizations for self-help purposes that make them part, and to some extent owners, of development. It therefore seems that, in order to spread development and reduce poverty in sub-Saharan Africa, much more could be gained by *creating incentives* for local action and organization rather than by spending time and energy on trying to make the grassroots form organizations where such incentives are largely absent. This study has given evidence confirming the suggestion that organizations are much more likely to mirror their environments than to reshape them. Hence, more will be gained by manipulating the environment than by manipulating organizations.

Manipulating environment may not sound particularly humanitarian. It certainly doesn't sound participatory. But it depends on how—and where—manipulation is done. Of course, it is no panacea either. But the issue has to do with who owns the initiative. A benevolently manipulated environment is likely to induce people to be innovative, to find solutions, and to form the kinds of organizations they have use for. But it will be *their* organizations, erected in order to fulfill *their* objectives. In that sense the outcome of development will not be predetermined. In order to render the environment more enabling, donors and INGOs would probably achieve more by pursuing an approach to development that is much more hands-off than hitherto. And donors, IFIs, and African governments could invest more in human capital and key public goods such as research and education, roads and communications infrastructure, and facilitate market development, thereby shrinking the periphery and rendering it easier for local organizations to bridge gaps and link remote communities to the world. "What is lacking in [sub-Saharan Africa] is not the potential for good ideas or the propensity to enterprise but the supporting environment, the climate that will activate latent entrepreneurs" (Baume 1996, 220).

Sub-Saharan Africa remains predominantly rural. Hence, African development must start in its rural areas. The subcontinent, although presently poor and undernourished, has a great but untapped potential to increase significantly its agricultural productivity (Holmén 2005; Larsson 2005). That this potential now, after structural adjustment, has not been made use of is due to both internal and external causes. Internally because of undeveloped transport infrastructure, missing or unreliable markets and a vast periphery; externally because the cards have long been stacked against African development. Creating markets is not confined to changes within Africa itself. Donors can help by establishing a creative environment also—and foremost—by keeping their own house in order.

Structural adjustment was imposed upon African governments due to their perceived bias against agriculture (Kreuger, Schif, and Valdes 1988). However, since then, the policies of donor governments have displayed an equally strong bias against African agriculture. Despite all declarations about a willingness to support poor people and nations, Northern aid flows for African agriculture fell by half between the late 1980s and the late 1990s (Haggblade 2005). Support to agriculture fell even more. Whereas the effectiveness of aid can be disputed, this shows that donors' commitment to agricultural development in sub-Saharan Africa has not been a high priority.

Apart from reducing aid to agriculture, rich countries subsidize their own farmers while denying poor countries the right to do the same. Rich countries also continue to dump their subsidized agricultural products in poor countries, thereby undermining the development of domestic markets. As if this weren't enough, trade barriers are maintained against would-be export products from African countries, thus preventing the evolution of export markets as well. The International Food Policy Research Institute predicts that "an end to rich-country support in agriculture would generate annual gains of US$40 billion for developing countries, with Sub-Saharan Africa, the world's poorest region, gaining US$3.3 billion" (IFPRI 2003, 5). With such export earnings forgone, it is no wonder that, in large parts of sub-Saharan Africa, preservationist community-oriented organizations remain more common than innovative, market-oriented producer organizations.

For decades, bilateral donors and the IFIs have advocated free trade and forced poor countries to do away with subsidies and protectionist trade policies. But donors seldom practice what they preach. Their stated belief in the virtues of the free market has not affected their own behavior. For Africa, the effect is devastating. "To protect its farmers, the European Union spends $350 billion a year, an amount equal to Africa's entire annual income and fourteen times the aid the continent receives" (Calderesi 2006, 15).

All in all, it has been estimated that "those policies by industrialized countries have displaced about US$40 billion in net agricultural exports per year from developing countries and reduced agricultural incomes in these countries by nearly US$30 billion" (IFPRI 2003, 25). A substantial part of this would have accrued to sub-Saharan Africa.

But it is not only a question of income forgone. African governments are also drained of resources in order to honor external debt-repayment obligations. Hence, their abilities to invest in development are reduced—sometimes severely so. Some small steps have been taken to reduce the debt burden; however, they are far from enough, and demands for debt repayment appear to be maintained primarily for political reasons. Repayment is not crucial for the survival of rich countries. Actually, "the international community could immediately write off debt without the complications and objections that have been raised. That would save Africa $10 billion annually in debt service payments over the next decade or so. Those savings would offset half of the aid that Africa now gets" (Mistry 2005, 675).

As long as this situation prevails, it seems rather meaningless to provide development aid—and it would be difficult indeed to maintain that aid aims at poor-country development. It is, rather, the case that aid is there to mask exploitative, neo-colonial relations. Africans and African organizations are probably wise regarding donors and INGOs as cargo deliverers. Some Northern NGOs and INGOs have criticized the above-outlined situation, but at the same time many appear to have found comfortable niches within the system. Normally they make pleas for more aid, not less. And this aid, of course, should be channeled through those making this plea. This is yet another reason to question whether INGOs really represent an alternative.

These policies and this situation need to be reversed. If Africa were offered fair trade and a fair chance to realize its potential, I am convinced development would no longer be a mirage but a reality.

The most effective way in which Northern governments and international institutions can help Africa is not to "do development" but to remove obstacles and then leave development to the Africans and their organizations. Likewise, on many occasions INGOs and Northern NGOs would help Africa more by pressing for policy changes in the global North (which some already do) than by interfering in Africa proper. African governments must be allowed to protect their emerging markets from overwhelming and often unfair competition, and donors should refrain from undermining market development in poor countries. Debt cancellation should become a reality, not an intention. It would also make sense for African governments to invest in infrastructure and human development, and to level the playing field for new organizations—CSOs as well as private-sector enterprises. Organizations can accomplish a lot, but they cannot carry the whole development process. If outsiders really were concerned about reducing poverty in sub-Saharan Africa, that would be a good place to start. With that done, Africans could safely be entrusted with the task of organizing for self-help.

Notes

1. The label NGOs, here, is not restricted to intermediary organizations but is meant to be taken literally, that is, *non*governmental, and to include large and small, formal and informal associations.

Part I
INTRODUCTION

One: Development and Peasants' Associations in Sub-Saharan Africa

1. It appears that many of those who advocate community-based development do so with the, often implicit, hope that Gemeinschaft-type social relations can be preserved or re-created on a grander scale as development proceeds. The question is whether this is a realistic assumption.

2. It is revealing that despite all the participatory rhetoric in contemporary aid and development prose, structural adjustment was never negotiated with but was imposed upon aid-receiving countries. African governments (as could be expected) were skeptical about SAP. But many African NGOs, which could expect to benefit from the reform, also "condemned the imposition of . . . SAPs as no less than a form of *re*colonization of the continent" (Hoogvelt 2002, 181).

3. In recent years this tendency to retreat and abandon forward-looking engagement may have been exacerbated by the prevailing AIDS pandemic. Reporting from Malawi, Bryceson and Fonseca found that "a sense of powerlessness concerning their vulnerability to HIV/AIDS leads to concentration on the more immediate concern of trying to ensure [the smallholders'] day-to-day staple food needs. Changing rural land and labor patterns are militating for more transaction-based rural livelihoods" (2006, 1565).

4. However, the same document also reveals that most of its funding activities have been directed to European NGOs that in some way support or cooperate with Southern NGOs and local organizations. Hence, it appears that the idea of the delivery chain has not disappeared

as quickly as language has changed. This may also reflect a tendency toward cultural imperialism. Not only are European NGOs preferred over African NGOs, but faith-based organizations are increasingly being recognized as important to development, donors' support has focused disproportionately on mainstream Christian organizations (Clarke 2006).

5. The early community development approach—intended to be based on locally perceived needs and on community participation—which was common among donors in the 1950s, was abandoned by the mid 1960s because communities were found to be less egalitarian than expected and this approach was found to strengthen the economic position of the elites and was unable to improve the situation of the poor (Holdcroft 1978). Despite this experience, the community approach is currently being revived, not least because many Northern NGOs and academics display a romantic view of primordial, "indigenous" and allegedly "communitarian" local societies.

6. This, however, is a misreading of Hydén, who explicitly states: "The economy of affection has nothing to do with fond emotions *per se*" (1983, 8). Being founded on a non-capitalist rationality, it denotes "a network of support, communications and interaction among structurally defined groups connected by blood, kin, community or other affinities, for example, religion" (ibid), relations that often are reciprocal but seldom egalitarian.

7. To illustrate this, I recall a conversation I once had with my Egyptian landlord about nepotism. I asked him about his opinion about former president Anwar Sadat's habit of directing generous public investments to his home village and of arranging sinecures in the administration for relatives—a behavior that in my country would have been denounced as misuse of office. Knowing that my landlord was no admirer of the former president, I expected the answer to be depreciative. To my surprise he instead burst out: "If President Sadat did not take care of his own family, how could he be the father of the country?!" Contrary to what (Western) advocates of "good governance" used to proclaim, this "adverse" behavior was a precondition for political legitimacy. From a non-Western perspective, it may even be labeled good governance.

Part II
THE EASTERN AND SOUTHERN AFRICAN EXPERIENCE

Two: The ESA Experience—Part I

1. *Introduction to Part II:* This is not entirely true. While it is correct that none of the household surveys conducted mentioned LOs or CBOs of any kind, in Malawi we did encounter one group of half a dozen smallholders who had made a joint purchase of a diesel pump for

irrigating their (adjoining) fields where they grew maize and vegetables. This was (so far) the only joint undertaking within this group, which moreover was too small and informal to be perceived as an organization by the villagers.

2. An exception to this rule is Zambia, which since 2002 uses cooperatives to distribute subsidized fertilizer.

3. ILO/ICA (2003) also emphasizes the need to establish or strengthen apex organizations. A possible, or at least contributing, explanation could be that both the ILO and the ICA are distant international organizations and in need of national representatives with whom to communicate.

4. The following summary is based on Flygare (2006).

5. Countries included in the report were Ethiopia, Kenya, Lesotho, Malawi, Swaziland, Tanzania, Uganda, and Zambia.

6. Previously, Kenyan cooperatives were commodity based (for example, coffee, milk, pyrethrum), and the notion of community based only indicates a break with that tradition. It should, however, not be confused with the previously made distinction between organizations oriented toward satisfying individual goals and community-based organizations. Members can now be drawn from the same village irrespective of the crop they grow or the service they want to utilize.

7. Seemingly echoing the strategies of the past, in 2002 the new government of Zambia introduced the Fertiliser Support Programme. Although the president of the Zambia Cooperative Federation warned against formation of cooperatives on political lines (*Times of Zambia* 2005), cooperatives again appear to be assigned noncommercial objectives. Under the program peasants receive a subsidy of 50 percent on seeds and fertilizer, provided that they are members of a farmer group or a cooperative, which they are free to initiate and form by themselves. So far, the program suffers from inadequate and untimely supply of inputs, poor marketing arrangements, and lack of reach to remote areas. Reportedly it has had very little impact on food security and poverty reduction (CSPR 2005).

8. Even if many smallholder peasants do sell small quantities of vegetables or maize at harvest time (to repay loans, for example), they need to buy maize at a later time when their own food supplies are exhausted. Such "distress sales" do not indicate that these smallholders are market oriented in their strategies.

9. Contract farming, presently highly favored among donors and IFIs, will not be dealt with here because it commonly has a "take it or leave it" character and therefore rarely contains an emancipatory component.

10. The long-term aim is that a focal area should be made up of about two thousand farmers. Only during the initial phase was the figure four hundred deemed sufficient (Cuellar et al. 2006).

Three: The ESA Experience—Part 2

1. I have not been able to acquire information about how James et al. distinguish a development NGO from other NGOs.

2. Whereas there may be good reasons to question Moi's reasons for questioning the mandate of NGOs to try and influence policy, he still may have a point.

3. Whereas many supportive INGOs put advocacy and lobbying high on their agendas (Holmén and Jirström 2009), it is more than likely that successful lobbying depends less on the message and more on contacts and access to patronage. This implies that only those already well connected can make use of this option, but at the same time it will likely preserve or strengthen neo-patrimonial structures rather than introducing something new.

4. In Uganda, a few years ago, I met with a group of women who were using microcredits for small businesses. They had all received individual loans from an NGO but were collectively responsible for repayments. The women were very happy about the arrangement because, as they told me, they were subsidized by 25 percent, that is, they were only required to repay 75 percent of the amount borrowed. However, the accountant of the NGO told me that the interest rate was in fact above 30 percent (varying somewhat depending on the length of the loan period). This means that the women would have to repay to the NGO almost twice the amount they expected. I cannot say whether this discrepancy was due to misunderstanding, lack of communication, or worse (patronage building and/or a trick to control local entrepreneurs). In whatever case, the women were in for a surprise, and the viability of the scheme must be cast in doubt.

5. In the above-mentioned KDDP program, support organizations stayed in the area for at least eight years.

6. It is not only NGOs that may stay only a short time in the villages where they run projects. So, sometimes, do their staff, and occasionally one gets the impression that development tourism is more attractive than development assistance for (some of) those who work for INGOs. In Malawi, I came across a group (actually two couples) of young, foreign NGO workers. The young men were working with pumps and wells while the young women were engaged with home economics. None had previous experience in developing countries or with this kind of work. They had recently completed their educations and had been in the country less than a year, but they were already planning to move to Madagascar and take up jobs for another NGO there, because they had "heard that it should be very nice there" (anonymous, personal communication).

7. It seems not only at the base level. According to Tripp (2001a), in Tanzania 80 percent of registered NGOs are women's organizations.

8. Igoe, based on Bayart, contends that extraversion is "symptomatic of a political system that is externally oriented as a result of long-standing dependency on external resources. African elites have long derived power and authority from their access to external institutional resources, which frequently means access to resources that can be used to build and maintain patronage structures" (Igoe 2006, 401). On the one hand, this perfectly illustrates the dilemma of aid. On the other hand, it is misleading to limit extraversion to governments. Extraversion—being a sign of dependency—represents a general tendency to expect solutions to come from outside, the Melanesian cargo cult being its most extreme expression. Other expressions are, for example, the tendency for many African scholars and politicians to blame everything that is problematic on colonialism and globalization, thus relieving them of responsibility and/or legitimizing inactivity. Moreover, as I see it, there is a very strong tendency toward extraversion among NGOs in contemporary Africa, as they strive for external recognition, funding, and contacts.

9. This comparison of versions is in no way intended to belittle the work of Ellis and Freeman. Most likely this alteration is due to some peer reviewer's comment. We are all faced with demands to follow such advice, even if it sometimes appear to imply a form of censorship.

10. One should be careful, though, not to depict public servants as invariably disinterested and lethargic or automatically to give governments all the blame for lack of progress. Snyder reports: "When I delved deeper into why [the] residents had voted these officials into office, when they had a reputation for not doing much work and spending all their time in the local beer halls, one man stated 'That is why we voted them into office. We don't want government officials bothering us with their development projects'" (2008, 296).

Part III
THE WEST AFRICAN EXPERIENCE

Four: Decentralization and Organizations in West Africa

1. Other sources give much higher figures for the number of participants in this event. Destrait, for example, claims that as many as fifty thousand people were mobilized in the protest (2003, 6).

2. The above paragraphs concern NGOs, to be distinguished from farmers' associations. The latter will be dealt with in Chapter 5.

3. In the first democratic election in 1991, Kérékou was defeated by his prime minister, Soglo. However, in 1996 Kérékou surprisingly returned to power after some opposition politicians crossed the floor in his favor. He was reelected president in 2001.

4. There may indeed be reasons to be skeptical about the seriousness of the Nigerian government's willingness to tolerate independent
organizations. Various attempts by the central government to deregister
trade unions and to limit the freedom of association have been repeatedly reported (IJCSL 2004; ICCSL 2006).

Five: Farmers' Assocations in West Africa

1. The ICCSL was founded in 2003 so, although the referred-to document is undated, the information provided is deemed valid for the
present situation.
2. Studies from elsewhere have found that over time small producers tend to be excluded from out-grower schemes, which gradually concentrate on the larger and most productive farmers (see, for example,
Pagaran [1994] on tomato out-grower schemes in the Philippines).
3. The government later introduced "partial liberalization of the export of cocoa, with effect from 2000/1" (Khor 2006, 8). This has, for
example, allowed Kuapa Kokoo to export about one thousand tons of
its yearly output to the European Fairtrade market (Divine n.d.).
4. Figures on membership are impressive but nevertheless inconsistent among sources. Whereas Jones (2005) mentions forty-five thousand members, Rättvisemärkt (2006) says forty-seven thousand cocoa
growers in twelve thousand villages are members of Kuapa Kokoo.
Oxfam (2006), on the other hand, gives a figure of forty thousand members in the same year.
5. While this is indeed a remarkable development, it should also be
noted that the Day Chocolate Company occupies (as yet) a miniscule
niche in the British chocolate market. Lockwood reports that in 2004
the market share of 'Divine' fairly traded chocolate was only just over
0.1 percent (2005).
6. Kuapa Kokoo seems to be the exception that confirms the rule.
In 2006 Kuapa Kokoo had some forty thousand (possibly as many as
forty-five thousand) members. The total number of cocoa growers in
Ghana has been estimated at about 800,000 (Toulmin and Guèye 2003,
42), which means that Kuapa Kokoo only represents about 5 percent of
the total number. The remaining 95 percent still need to establish their
own organizations. Perhaps Kuapa Kokoo can inspire them to do so.
7. Benin, Burkina Faso, the Gambia, Guinea Bissau, Mali, Mauretania,
Niger, Togo, and Senegal.
8. As explained by Bernard Ouedraogo (1989): "If I give you an egg
and you give me an egg, each of us has one egg. But if I give you an
idea and you give me an idea, each of us has two ideas."
9. Zaï is a relatively small planting pit, the dimensions of which vary
according to the type of soil. Pits are dug during the dry season, and

the number of pits per hectare varies from twelve thousand to twenty-five thousand. After the pits have been dug, organic matter is added at an average recommended rate of 0.6 kg/pit, and after the first rainfall, the matter is covered with a thin layer of soil and seeds placed in the middle of the pit. The *zaï* fulfills three functions: soil conservation, water conservation, and erosion control for encrusted soils. Being ideally suited for degraded land, the application of the technique can reportedly increase production by about 500 percent if properly executed (Essama 2005).

10. At the same time, a pertinent question is why the World Bank and other external supporters are so keen on financing new—single message—organizations when, for example, the Naam movement has promoted this technology successfully for decades. One cannot avoid the suspicion that this illustrates a tendency among external supporters to capture indigenous initiatives and subordinate them under a foreign agenda—or, at least, to take credit for what is already happening anyway. It is illustrative that Akande (2006) concluded that the World Bank has been successful in relocating the base for African rural development to outside the continent.

11. Accordingly, folk humor has given a new meaning to Six S: *Se Servir de Sous Suisse Sans Soucis* (how to spend Swiss funds without remorse).

12. Luzzati proposes that a parallel structure of peasant associations *(foyers)* was begun in the early 1960s. Local *foyers* gradually developed into an association (Asescaw) in 1976. According to Luzzati, this was the most important organization in rural Senegal until the late 1980s (2002).

13. In the process, they could also have been left without *any* organizational support. The then-prevailing strategy "was not universally accepted even among the leadership of FONGS, some of whom felt that the *Union des coopératives agricoles du Sénégal* (UNCAS) was unredeemable and that the platform would be better off without them. [However, UNCAS remained and] . . . tagged along . . . out of fear of isolation" (McKeon, Watts, and Wolford 2004, 15).

14. ROPPA's aim is to include other national farmers' and producers' platforms. At the time of writing, its members are made up of national executives of farmers' and agricultural producers' forums of Benin, Burkina Faso, Cote d'Ivoire, Guinea, Guinea-Bissau, Gambia, Mali, Niger, Senegal, and Togo. See the roppa-ao.org website.

15. It remains to be seen how effective ROPPA will be in bringing family farms to the forefront in the policy forums that matter. As reflected in the titles of many recent publications, there is, however, no doubt that the CNCR and the ROPPA have had a strong impact on recent literature concerning West African development (see, for example, Bélières et al. 2002; SWAC 2005; Toulmin and Guèye 2003; and Defoer 2006).

Six: Interpreting the West African Experience

1. According to Bernard, de Janvry, and Sadoulet (2005, 24n15), "More than 30% of the organizations in the surveyed areas [in Burkina Faso] were created at the impulse of the State, an NGO, or a bilateral donor." In other words, approximately two-thirds of these organizations were "spontaneously" established.

2. The same is reported, for example, about the umbrella organization CCOF (Co-ordination Framework for Rural Producer Organizations) in Burkina Faso, where "lack of funds limits the amount of grassroot consultations it can carry out" (Conway et al. 2003, 22).

3. See Igoe and Kelsall (2005) for a similar conclusion regarding NGO-activities in developing countries more generally.

4. Actually, chair*woman,* since many donors and INGOs find it important to reach women and to formulate special projects for empowerment(?) of women.

5. They classified a community-based organization as an organization that *never* had engaged in market-oriented activities, a rather severe delimitation.

6. This is not to deny that there often is a "democratic deficit" with local chiefs and male heads of family having disproportionately strong influence while the voice of women and/or the young weigh less.

7. Kuapa Kokoo cocoa growers cooperative is a frequently cited success story. Perhaps because it is exceptional, many have found it necessary to spread its gospel. On October 23, 2006, Google had more than thirty-five thousand hits on "Kuapa Kokoo." Similarly, the Naam movement has been written about extensively. Google had more than one hundred thousand hits on "Bernard Ouedraogo."

8. It is important not to confuse the different uses of the term *bridging* that appear in literature on organizations and development. Putnam's (1993) study of organizations in Italy used "bridging" to designate associations that bridged the gaps between families, clans, and so forth, and therefore contributed to enhanced trust and a growing social capital in northern Italy. In southern Italy, on the other hand, such bridging organizations were rare and both citizenship and social capital remained weak. Putnam thus used "bridging" in an "introvert" sense creating linkages between segments of a local society. Some would call this a bonding trait. The World Bank, for its part, uses "bridging" in an "extrovert" sense to emphasize the links between local communities and the outside world. Although one use does not necessarily exclude the other, the World Bank primarily focuses on bridging geographical distance, whereas Putnam focuses on bridging social distance.

9. This advantage was also enhanced because SAP came later to West Africa, a circumstance that further extended the pre-SAP learning period for rural organizations there.

10. Due to their sizes, they distort the general picture in Anglophone countries' favor. Nigeria and South Africa represent on average 17 percent and 13 percent of sub-Saharan Africa agricultural output respectively over the period 1960 to 1999 (Fulginiti, Perrin, and Yu 2004).

11. If Southern Africa is excluded, the difference between West and East Africa is significantly reduced; East Africa, however, still has a slightly better ranking.

Part IV
ANOTHER WORLD IS POSSIBLE

Seven: Another World Is Possible

1. There are differences though. Whereas Earle (2007) differentiates between NGOs and indigenous social movements, Onsander (2007, 12) uses the expression "popular movements/NGOs."

2. The success of West African cotton-growers' organizations when their complaints were raised at the WTO over unfair US trade policies was not because they opposed globalization. To the contrary, success was attained because they referred to the free-trade agenda and showed how the United States violated the rules it pushes hard to impose on others. Whether this was a real or merely a symbolic victory is debatable, however. WTO regulations are totally binding for signatories, and countries that are found to violate them must compensate the negatively affected country or be "punished" in the form of trade sanctions. "It is not, however, the organisation WTO who punishes anyone, it is the country which has won the dispute who is permitted to introduce trade barriers against the erring party. Consequently, if a small country wins a dispute against a larger one [e.g. Burkina Faso vs. the USA], in practice it has almost no chance of introducing trade sanctions by itself which are severe enough to affect the larger country" (de Vylder, Axelsson-Nycander, and Laanatza 2001, 80). As always, the WTO is there to protect the powerful.

3. Unless, as has happened in West Africa, they do so in order to *defend* the state against the imposition of hegemonic demands from donors and IFIs.

4. Here, I believe, is one of the few cases where donors could contribute to African development in a meaningful way. African governments cannot yet raise the necessary financial resources for maintaining a sufficiently dense road network, let alone extend it.

5. Booth proposes that the situation might have improved since the heyday of government bashing, at least to some extent. "Some donor agencies have become more interested than they were in understanding domestic politics and the political economy of state formation in

the countries where they work." But he also points out, "It remains still to be seen how far even the more politically informed agencies will allow the conclusions of this type of analysis to drive what they do" (2005, 2).

6. In order to be registered as an NGO—and enjoy tax-exemption status—an organization normally must be nonprofit. If it cannot show that it is, it will lose this privileged registration.

7. Also in relation to participation, it has been noted that these approaches often become an instrument for contextless social engineering. They "have largely been driven with a focus on refining participatory methods and left out the role of attitudes and community—and of institutional cultures as constraints or opportunities for [development]" (Friis-Hansen and Boesen 2001, 11).

8. There is nothing wrong per se with values such as human rights, (gender) equality, democracy, transparency, or good governance. They are all worthy of striving for. But they are time- and space-specific social constructions. Maslow's "hierarchy of needs" tells us that basic needs (for example, food, shelter, and health) are fundamental and that, in poor societies, issues like democracy, participation, transparency, equality, and stakeholder involvement are of secondary importance as long as secure access to basic requirements is not guaranteed. In this sense many NGO and donor priorities are Northern and urban priorities. Moreover, their satisfaction is likely to be the *result* of development rather than its "trigger." In this sense the common demands for transparency, participation, and gender mainstreaming as a precondition for development (aid) put the cart before the horse. But, again, this is for home consumption and serves to legitimate aid and INGO activities in their home countries. The problem, thus, is not the "faulty prioritization" of rural Africans but rather the strength of Northern middle-class missionary zeal and its unquestioning conviction that its values and priorities (whether religious or secular, colonialist or emancipatory) always have universal applicability and therefore can be easily transferred to other cultures and societies. Why this is so is, perhaps, a theme worthy of further investigation.

9. This is not the only way that forced birth of local organizations takes place. As shown above, too hastily implemented decentralization of public irrigation schemes in Mali, Niger, and Malawi, and devolution of responsibilities to local producers' organizations before such organizations had been established were results of pressures from the IFIs to speed up decentralization.

10. Moreover, it is likely to divert effort from more effective avenues. Bayat, for example, found that, in the Middle East, CSOs have been much more effective in changing the course of events through direct action, "the quiet encroachment of the ordinary," rather than by resorting to demand-making movements. Whereas demand-led social

movements have been permeated by hierarchy and clientelism, direct action has created "realities on the ground that the authorities sooner or later have to come to terms with" (Bayat 2000 iv, v). There is no reason to believe that the Middle East is unique in this respect.

11. Indirectly, this is an admittance that many NGOs and INGOs are not as professional as they and their supporters would want us to believe.

12. Actually, President Bush was *not* waging a war on terrorism. His government was merely fighting some acts of terrorism and some terrorists while endorsing others. When it suits its interests, the US government has so far encouraged terrorism or at least turned a blind eye—and it has sometimes actively engaged in terrorism itself (for example, kidnapping and torturing of Swedish citizens by the CIA; freezing suspects' bank accounts without telling them why; years-long detention of "suspects" without telling the prisoners what they are accused of; secret trials and nondisclosure of "evidence"; indiscriminate acceptance of "collateral damage," and so on). In May 2008, President Bush found that torture—an act of terror—is perfectly acceptable when practiced by US armed forces.

Reference List

Abdillahi, M. S. 1998. The emergence of local NGOs in the recovery and development process of Somaliland (northwest Somalia). *Voices from Africa* 8 (December). Available at the un-ngls.org website.

Abernethy, C. L., H. Sally, K. Lonsway, and C. Maman. 2000. *Farmer-based financing of operations in the Niger Valley irrigation schemes.* Research Report no. 37. Colombo, Sri Lanka: International Water Management Institute (IWMI).

Adeyemo, R., and A. S. Bamire. 2005. Savings and investment patterns of cooperative farmers in Southwestern Nigeria. *Journal of Social Sciences* 11, no. 3: 183–92.

Adeyeye, V. A. 2001. *Micro-credit sourced through cooperatives and rural poverty: Evidence from Family Economic Advancement Programme in Osun State, Nigeria.* Niser Monograph Series no. 7. Ibadan: Nigerian Institute of Social and Economic Research (NISER).

ADF (African Development Foundation). 2005. *Connecting rural coffee farmers to the American market.* African Development Foundation.

African Development Fund. 2005. *Federal Republic of Nigeria: Agriculture and rural institutions support project.* Appraisal Report. Agriculture and Rural Development Department. Central and West Region. OCAR. April.

African Union. 2005. *Status of food security and prospects for agricultural development in Africa.* Addis Ababa: African Union.

Africare. 2005. *Democratic ideals from the grassroots up.* Available at the africare.org website.

Agrisystems. 2003. *Study of focal area development committees (FADCs) and common interest groups (CIGs) within NALEP.* Nairobi, Kenya: Ministry of Agriculture and Livestock Development.

Aipira, C., A. Feyissa, A. Kawash, and D. O'Malley. 2008. Cooperative sustainability: The cases of Malawi's NASFAM and Ethiopia's Oromia. Seminar paper. LUMID. Lund, Sweden: Lund University. Mimeo.

Akande, T. 2005. The Role of the state in the Nigerian Green Revolution. In Djurfeldt et al. 2005, 161–79.

———. 2006. *Food policy in Nigeria: An analytical chronicle.* Ibadan: The New World Press.

Akeratane, M. A. 2005. Cooperatives, development and decentralization in Mali. *SDdimensions* (February). Available at the fao.org website.

Akindele, S. T., O. R. Olaopa, and A. S. Obiyan. 2002. Fiscal federalism and local government finance in Nigeria: An examination of revenue rights and fiscal jurisdiction. *International Review of Administrative Sciences* 68: 557–77.

Alebikiya, M. 2004. Changing approaches to agriculture in Ghana: The experience of ACDEP. In Diakonia, 63–66.

Aloo, F. 2000. The NGO movement in Africa. *The ACP-EU Courier*, no. 181 (June-July): 58ff.

Amenga-Etego, R. 2004. Grassroots sensitisation and civic education: The experience of ISODEC Ghana with the 'water for all' campaign. In Diakonia 2004, 28–30.

Amha, W., T. Abebe, and M. Demeke. 2008a. Afrint II: Macro study. *Agrarian structure and commercialization in Ethiopia.* Draft.

———. 2008b. Afrint II: Macro study. *Agricultural intensification in Ethiopia.* Draft.

Amutabi, M. 2006. *The NGO factor in Africa: The case of arrested development in Kenya.* New York: Routledge.

ANC. 2002. Evaluating the WCAR NGO forum (and preparing for the WSSD). Available at the anc.org.za website.

Andrae, G. 2004. Decentralisation by default: 'Localisation' of supplies and re-traditionalisation of regulation in the wake of privatisation of water provisioning in Kano, Nigeria. Paper presented at the workshop entitled Decentralisation in Practice: Power, Livelihoods, and Cultural Meaning in West Africa. Uppsala. May 4–6. Department of Cultural Anthropology and Ethnology. Uppsala: Uppsala University/IIED.

Aning, K. 2007. *Security, the War on Terror, and Official Development Assistance.* Accra, Ghana: Kofi Annan International Peacekeeping Training Centre.

Arn, A-L. 1988. *The making of institutions and leaders at rice root level: Inside the Rural Works Programme in southern Bangladesh.* CDR Project Paper 88:3. Copenhagen: Center for Development Research.

Arnesen, O., V. Kapelrud, and R. Øygard. 2002. *Support for organising producers in Southern and Eastern Africa: Status and possibilities for Norwegian assistance.* Final draft. NORAD.

Asiimwe, D., and B. M. Nakanyike, eds. 2007. *Decentralisation and transformation of governance in Uganda.* Kampala: Fountain Publ.

Aspelin, G. 1977a. *Tankens vägar: en översikt av filosofiens utveckling.* Vol. 1. Lund: Doxa.

———. 1977b. *Tankens vägar: en översikt av filosofiens utveckling.* Vol. 2. Lund: Doxa.

Assefa, T. 2005. Revitalizing market-oriented agricultural cooperatives in Ethiopia. A case study conducted in cooperation with USAID's Cooperative Development Program. ACDI/VOCA.

Atampugre, N. 1997. Aid, NGOs, and grassroots development: Northern Burkina Faso. *Review of African Political Economy* 24, no. 71: 57–73.

Atieno R. 2006. The limits of policy success: The case of the dairy sector in Kenya. Paper presented at the Future Agricultures Consortium Workshop on Politics and Policy Processes for the 2008 World Development Report on Agriculture. January 22–23. Institute of Development Studies, UK *The limits of success: The case of the dairy sector in Kenya.* Future Agricultures Briefing. Available (as The limits of success) at the future-agricultures.org website.

Bagré, A. S., H. Bary, A. Ouattara, M. Ouédraogo, and D. Thiéba. 2004. *Challenges for a viable decentralisation process in rural Burkina Faso.* KIT Development Policy and Practice Bulletin 356. Amsterdam: Royal Tropical Institute (KIT).

Barr, A., and M. Fafchamps. 2005. *A client-community assessment of the NGO sector in Uganda.* Working Paper. Oxford, UK: Global Poverty Research Group, Department of Economics, Oxford University.

Barr, A., M. Fafchamps, and T. Owens. 2005. The governance of non-governmental organizations in Uganda. *World Development* 33, no. 4: 657–79.

Barrow, O., and M. Jennings, eds. 2001. *The charitable impulse: NGOs and development in East and North-East Africa.* Oxford: James Curry; Bloomfield, CT: Kumarian Press.

Barya, J. J. 2000. *The state of civil society in Uganda: An analysis of the legal and politico-economic aspects.* Working Paper no. 58. Kampala, Uganda: Centre for Basic Research.

Bates, R. H. 1981. *Markets and states in tropical Africa: The political basis of agricultural policies.* Berkeley and Los Angeles: University of California Press.

Batterbury, S. P. J. 2005. Development, planning, and agricultural knowledge on the Central Plateau of Burkina Faso. In Cline-Cole and Robson 2005, 259–79.

Baume, S. K. 1996. *Entrepreneurship: A contextual perspective: Discources and praxis of entrepreneurial activities within the institutional context of Ghana.* Lund Studies in Economics and Management 28. Lund, Sweden: Lund University Press.

Bayart, J-F., S. Ellis, and B. Hibou. 1999. *The criminalization of the state in Africa.* The International African Institute/James Currey/Indiana University Press. London: Villiers Publ.

Bayat, A. 2000. *Social movements, activism and social development in the Middle East.* Civil Society and Social Movements Programme Paper no. 3, November. Geneva: UNRISD.

Beckman, B. 1988. The post-colonial state: Crisis and reconstruction. *IDS-Bulletin* 19, no. 4 (October): 26–34.

Bélières, J-F., P-M. Bosc, G. Faure, S. Fournier, and B. Losch. 2002. *What future for West Africa's family farms in a world market economy?* Issue Paper no. 113. October. London: IIED.

Bello, A. 2007. Agricultural sector reforms in Nigeria: Challenges, prospects and the way forward. In *Consolidating and sustaining the gains of reforms in Nigeria: Proceedings of a workshop,* ed. S. O. Akande and A. S. Olomola, 43–57. Ibadan: NISER.

Bernard, T., A. de Janvry, and E. Sadoulet. 2005. *Do community sharing norms constrain the emergence, configuration and activities of market-oriented organizations? A study for Burkina Faso.* Mimeo.

Bernstein, H., and P. Woodhouse. 2001. Telling environmental change like it is? Reflections on a study in sub-Saharan Africa. *Journal of Agrarian Change* 1, no. 2 (April): 283–324.

Bertone, A. 2000. *The case for empowering Southern NGOs: Interview with Ann Huddock.* Global Policy Forum. Available at the globalpolicy.org website.

Bierschenk, T., and J-P. O. de Sardan. 2003. Powers in the village: Rural Benin between democratisation and decentralisation. *Africa* 73, no. 2: 145–73.

Bierschenk, T., S. Brüntrup-Seidemann, and V. Hoffmann. 1999. Role and dynamics of indigenous NGOs in rural development in South Benin. In: Universität Hohenheim. *Report of results (1997–1999) of the Special Research Programme 308 "Adapted Farming in West Africa".* November. Stuttgart: Universität Hohenheim.

Bigg, T., and D. Satterthwaite, eds. 2005. *How to make poverty history: The central role of local organizations in meeting the MGDs.* London: IIED.

Bignante, E., E. Dansero, and C. Scarpocchi. 2007. The global/local nexus in local development strategies in developing countries. Paper presented at the Sixth Pan-European Conference on International Relations, University of Turin, Italy, September 12–15, 2007.

Biney, J. 2004. Profile article: The creation of the Apex Farmers' Organization of Ghana. *Global Forum on Agricultural Research (GFAR)* 10 (August). Available at the egfar.org website.

Bingen, J. 2003. *Community-based producer organizations: A contribution to the West Africa Regional Program Action Plan for the Initiative to End Hunger in Africa.* Bethesda, MD: Abt Associates Inc.

———. 2004. *A comparative review of multi-stakeholder arrangements for representing farmers in agricultural development programmes and policy-making in sub-Saharan Africa.* East Lansing: Michigan State University; Rome: FAO.

Bingen, J., and L. Munyankusi. 2002. *Farmer associations, decentralization and development in Rwanda: Challenges ahead.* Agricultural Policy Synthesis. Rwanda Food Security Research Project/MINAGRI, no. 3E (April). Available at the aec.msu.edu website.

Bingen, J., A. Serrano, and J. Howard. 2003. Linking farmers to markets: Different approaches to human capital development. *Food Policy* 28: 405–19.

Bingen, R. J. 1998. Cotton, democracy and development in Mali. *The Journal of Modern African Studies* 36, no. 2: 265–85.

Birchall, J. 2003. *Rediscovering the cooperative advantage: Poverty reduction through self-help.* Geneva: ILO.

Bird, K., D. Booth, and N. Pratt. 2003. *Food security crisis in Southern Africa: The political background to policy failure.* Forum for Food Security in Southern Africa.

Blaikie, P. 2006. Is small really beautiful? Community-based natural resource management in Malawi and Botswana. *World Development* 34, no. 11: 1942–57.

Boone, C. 2003. Decentralization as political strategy in West Africa. *Comparative Political Studies* 36, no. 4 (May): 355–80.

Booth, D. 2005. *Missing links in the politics of development: Learning from the PRSP experiment.* Working Paper no. 256. London: ODI.

Borgin, K., and K. Corbett. 1982. *The destruction of a continent—Africa and international aid.* San Diego: Harcourt Brace Jovanovich.

Bornstein, L. 2003. Management standards and development practice in the South African aid chain. *Public Administration and Development* 23: 393–404.

Bosc, P-M., D. Eychenne, K. Hussein, B. Losch, M-R. Mercoiret, P. Rondot, and S. Mackintosh-Walker. 2002. *The role of rural producer organizations in the World Bank rural development strategy.* Rural Strategy Background Paper no. 8. March. Washington DC: The World Bank.

Boserup, E. 1965. *The conditions of agricultural growth.* Chicago: Aldine.

Botchway, K. 2001. Paradox of empowerment: Reflections on a case study from Northern Ghana. *World Development* 29, no. 1: 135–53.

Braathen, E. 2006. *A participatory pathbreaker? Experience with poverty reduction strategy papers from four South African countries.* Working Paper no. 2006:122. Blindern: Norwegian Institute for Urban and Regional Research (NIBR).

Bratton, M. 1989. The politics of government-NGO relations in Africa. *World Development* 17, no. 4, 569–87.

Braverman, A., J. L. Guasch, M. Huppi, and L. Pohlheimer. 1991. *Promoting rural cooperatives in developing countries. The case of sub-Saharan Africa.* World Bank Discussion Papers no. 121. Washington DC: The World Bank.

Brent, J. 2004. The desire for community: Illusion, confusion, and paradox. *Community Development Journal* 39, no. 3: 213–23.

Bryceson, D. 1999. *Sub-Saharan Africa betwixt and between: Rural livelihood practices and policies.* ASC Working Paper 43. Leiden: Afrika-Studiecentrum, University of Leiden.

———. 2002. The scramble in Africa: Reorienting rural livelihoods. *World Development* 30, no. 5: 725–39.

Bryceson, D., and J. Fonseca. 2006. Risking death for survival: Peasant responses to hunger and HIV/AIDS in Malawi. *World Development* 34, no. 8, 1664–66.

BTI (Bertelsmann Transformation Index). 2006a. Country report: Senegal. Available at http://bti2006.bertelsmann-transformation-index.de/82.0.html?L=0.

———. 2006b. Country report: Mali. Available at http://bti2006 .bertelsmann-transformation-index.de/78.0.html?L=0.

———. 2006c. Country report: Ghana. Available at http://www .bertelsmann-transformation-index.de/62.0.html.

———. 2006d. Country report: Nigeria. Available at http:// www.bertelsmann-transformation-index.de/fileadmin/pdf/en/ 2006/WesternAndCentralAfrica/Nigeria.pdf.

———. 2006e. Country report: Benin. Available at http://bti2006 .bertelsmann-transformation-index.de/81.0.html?L=0.

———. 2006f. Country report: Burkina Faso. Available at http:// bti2006.bertelsmann-transformation-index.de/84.0.html?L=0.

———. 2006g. Tanzania. http//:www.bertelsmann-transformation-index.de 2006-10-03

———. 2006h. Zambia. http//:www.bertelsmann-transformation-index.de 2006-10-03

———. 2006i. Kenya. http//:www.bertelsmann-transformation-index.de 2006-10-03.

———. 2006j. Botswana. http//:www.bertelsmann-transformation-index.de 2006-10-03

———. 2006k. Malawi. http//:www.bertelsmann-transformation-index.de 2006-10-03

Buhere, K. 2007. Keep civil society out of reform talks. *Kenya Times.* Available at the timesnews.co.ke website.

Calderisi, R. 2006. *The trouble with Africa: Why foreign aid isn't working.* New York and Basingstoke: Palgrave Macmillan.

Campbell, B. M., M. K. Luckert, and M. Mutamba. 2003. Household livelihoods in semi-arid regions: Is there a way out of poverty? *Currents* 31/32 (October): 4–10.

Carroll, T. F. 1992. *Intermediary NGOs: The supporting link in grassroots development.* West Hartford, CT: Kumarian Press.

CBR (Centre for Basic Research). 1994. *Non governmental organisations (NGOs) in East Africa: Report of a survey on training needs.* Consultancy Reports no. 1. Kampala, Uganda: CBR.

Cheru, F. 1995. Structural adjustment, poverty alleviation and democratization—conflicting objectives. In Melin 1995, 41–59.

Chhotray, V. 2004. The negation of politics in participatory development projects, Kurnool, Andra Pradesh. *Development and Change* 35, no. 2: 327–52.

Chimangeni, I. 2007. *Economy-Zambia: Maize production (almost) a success story.* Inter Press Service News Agency. Available at the ipsnews.net website.

Chirwa, E., A. Dorward, R. Kachule, I. Kumwenda, J. Kydd, N. Poole, C. Poulton, and M. Stockbridge. 2005. Walking tightropes: Supporting farmer organisations for market access. *Natural Resource Perspectives*, no. 99 (November). ODI/DFID.

Chowdhury, N., C. Finlay-Notman, and I. Hovland. 2006. *CSO capacity for policy engagement: Lessons learned from the CSPP consultations in Africa, Asia, and Latin America*. Working Paper no. 272. London: ODI.

Clapham, C. 1985. *Third world politics: An introduction*. London: Croom Helm.

Clarke, G. 2006. Faith matters: Faith-based organisations, civil society, and international development. *Journal of International Development* 18: 835–48.

Cleaver, F. 2005. The inequality of social capital and the reproduction of chronic poverty. *World Development* 33, no. 6: 893–906.

Cleaver, F., and A. Toner. 2005. *"How participation evolves": An exploration of participation in community-based water management in Tanzania*. Bradford Centre for International Development, University of Bradford, UK.

Clifford, B. 2001. Marketing rebellion: Insurgent groups, international media, and NGO support. *International Politics* 38, no. 3: 311–33.

Cline-Cole, R., and E. Robson, eds. 2005. *West African worlds: Paths through socio-economic change, livelihoods, and development*. Harlow: Pearsons.

Comaroff, J. L., and J. Comaroff, eds. 1999. *Civil society and the political imagination in Africa: Critical perspectives*. Chicago: The University of Chicago Press.

CONGOMA. 2002. Council for non-governmental organizations in Malawi. Available at the congoma.org website.

Conway, T., C. Moser, A. Norton, and J. Farrington. 2003. Rights and livelihood approaches: Exploring policy dimensions. *Currents* 31/32 (October): 18–24.

Conyers, D. 2007. Decentralisation and service delivery: Lessons from sub-Saharan Africa. *IDS Bulletin* 38, no. 1. Brighton: Institute for Development Studies.

Cooley, A., and J. Ron. 2002. The NGO scramble: Organizational insecurity and the political economy of transnational action. *International Security* 27, no. 1 (Summer): 5–39.

COPAC (Committee for the Promotion and Advancement of Cooperatives). 1981. *Cooperative Information Note No 9: Republic of Upper Volta*. Rome: COPAC.

———. 2000. *Strategic alliances: Cooperatives, farmers' and rural workers' organizations*. Geneva: COPAC.

Coquery-Vidrovitch, C. 1997. The nation-state in Africa. *European Review—Interdisciplinary Journal of the Academia Europea* 5, no. 1 (January): 55–73.

Coughlin, P. 2006. *Agricultural intensification in Mozambique: Infrastructure, policy, and institutional framework*. Lund, Sweden: EconPolicy Research Group, Lda. Maputo/Afrint.

Couture, J-L., P. Lavigne Delville, and J-B Spinat. 2002. Institutional innovations and water management in Office du Niger (1919–1999): The Long Failure and New Successes of a Big Irrigation Scheme. *Coopérer aujourd'hui* 29 (February). Group de recherge et d'échanges technologiques (GRET).

Cracknell, M. 1995. *Cooperatives: Has their time come—or gone?* Available at the fao.org website.

———. 2000. *Forming sustainable small farmer group associations (SFGAs)—More difficult than first thought.* ACC Network on Rural Development and Food Security. July. Available at the rdfs.net website.

Crook, R. C. 2003. Decentralisation and poverty reduction in Africa: The politics of local-central relations. *Public Administration and Development* 23, no. 1: 77–88.

CSPR (Civil Society for Poverty Reduction). 2005. *Targeting small scale farmers in the implementation of Zambia's Poverty Reduction Strategy Paper (PRSP).* Lusaka: CSPR.

Cuellar, M., H. Hedlund, J. Mbai, and J. Mwangi. 2006. The National Agriculture and Livestock Extension Programme (NALEP). Phase I impact assessment. Sida Evaluation 06/31. Stockholm: Sida, Department for Africa.

Dauda, C. L. 2006. Democracy and decentralisation: Local politics, marginalisation and political accountability in Uganda and South Africa. *Public Administration and Development* 26: 291–302.

Defoer, T. 2006. Improving the productivity of ACP family farm systems. *Knowledge for Development.* Available at the knowledge.cta.int website.

deGrassi, A. 2005. *Political studies of agricultural policy processes in Africa, 1975–2005: Review, critique, and recommendations.* Available at the future-agricultures.org website.

deGrassi, A., and P. Rosset. 2003. *A new green revolution for Africa? Myths and realities of agriculture, technology, and development.* Available at the ocf.berkeley.edu website.

de Honoré, M. 2004. Methodologies for poverty alleviation in Burkina Faso: The experience of INADES formation. In Diakonia, 55–62.

de Janvry, A., and E. Sadoulet, 2002. *Some hypotheses for the analysis of producer organizations in Senegal and Burkina-Faso and strategies for empirical testing.* An interim report to the World Bank. Berkeley and Los Angeles: University of California.

———. 2004. *Organisations Paysannes et Développements Rural au Sénégal.* La Banque Mondial and Norwegian Trust Fund for Environmentally and Socially Sustainable Development. Mimeo.

Delion, J. 2000. *Producer organization—donor partnerships in project implementation in Africa: Risks and precautions from a social perspective.* AKIS Discussion Paper. New York: World Bank.

De Renzio, P. 2006. The primacy of domestic politics and the dilemmas of aid: What can donors do in Ethiopia and Uganda? *Opinions*, no. 65. February. ODI. Available at the odi.org.uk website.

De Sardan, J-P. O. 2004. Local powers awaiting decentralisation (Niger). Paper presented at the workshop entitled Decentralisation in Practice: Power, Livelihoods, and Cultural Meaning in West Africa. Uppsala. May 4–6. Uppsala: Department of Cultural Anthropology and Ethnology, Uppsala University/IIED.

———. 2005. *Les povoirs locaux et le rôle des femmes à Namaro.* Etudes et Travaux, n° 37. Laboratoire d'études et recherches sur les dynamiques sociales et le développement local (LASDEL). Niamey.

———. 2007. Interview in *Le Républicain* (Niger) (January 17), 7 and 12.

Destrait, F. 2003. Legitimacy and representativity of farmers' organisations. *Farming Dynamics*, no. 1 (December): 1–8.

Develtere, P., and B. Fonteneau. 2001. *Member-based organisations for social protection in health in developing countries.* Leuven: Hoger instituut vor het arbeid, Katholieke Universiteit.

De Vylder S., G. Axelsson-Nycander, and M. Laanatz. 2001. *The least developed countries and world trade.* Sida Studies no. 5. Stockholm: Sida.

DFID. 2006. Project record: Management and control—essential features for continued access by small-scale growers to EU fresh produce markets. *Research for Development.* Available at http://www .research4development.info.

DFID/CPHP. 2005. *The Harvestor* 2, no. 1 (April-June).

Diakonia. 2004. *Conference Report: West African Conference on Civil Society and Economic Policy.* January 29–31, 2002. Ouagadougou. Diakonia/ACDEP/ERUODAD.

Diaz, J. M. 2003. *Empowering rural producer organizations within the World Bank initiatives: A capitalisation study.* Uganda case study. New York: The World Bank.

Dichter T. W. 2003. *Despite good intentions: Why development assistance to the Third World has failed.* Amherst: University of Massachusetts Press.

Dieklich, S. 1998. Indigenous NGOs and political participation. In Hansen and Twaddle 1998, 145–58.

Divine. No date. Kuapa Kokoo. Available at the divinechocolate.com website.

Djurfeldt, G. 2006. Foreword. In Akande 2006, vi–vii.

Djurfeldt, G., H. Holmén, M. Jirström, and R. Larsson, eds. 2005. *The African food crisis: Lessons from the Asian Green Revolution.* Wallingford, Oxon, UK: CABI Pub.

Docking, T. W. 2005. International influence on civil society in Mali: The case of the cotton farmers' union, SYCOV. In Igoe and Kelsall 2005, 197–221.

Driscoll, R., and A. Evans. 2005. *Second generation poverty reduction strategies.* London: ODI.

Duhu, J. 2005. Strengthening civil society in the South: Challenges and constraints—A case study of Tanzania. *The International Journal of Not-for-Profit Law* 8, no. 1 (November): 42–53.

Dumont, R. 1964. *Afrikas dåliga start*. Stockholm: Utrikespolitiska Institutet/Rabén and Sjögren.

Dunn, J. R. 2004. USDA co-op development efforts support commercial farming in Ghana. *Rural Cooperative Magazine* (May/June). Available at the rurdev.usda.gov website.

Eade, D. 2000. *Development, NGOs, and civil society*. Oxford: Oxfam GB.

Eade, D., and E. Ligteringen. 2001. *Debating development: NGOs and the future*. Oxford: Oxfam.

Earle, L. 2007. *International NGOs and indigenous social movements*. Oxford: Intrac.

Earthscan. 1995. *The reality of aid: An independent review of international aid*. London: Earthscan Publications.

———. 1997. *The reality of aid: An independent review of development cooperation*. London: Earthscan Publications.

Ebrahim, A. 2003. Accountability in practice: Mechanisms for NGOs. *World Development* 31, no. 5: 813–29.

ECIDP. 2001. *The European Community International Development Programme and support to civil society organisations: Notes on the direct funding of Southern NGOs*. Discussion Paper no. 28.11.01.

Edwards, M. 2005. *Have NGOs 'made a difference?' From Manchester to Birmingham with an elephant in the room*. Global Poverty Research Group Department of Economics Working Paper 28. Oxford: Oxford University.

Edwards, M. E., and D. Hulme. 1992. *Making a difference: NGOs and development in a changing world*. London: Earthscan.

Eicher, C. K., and J. M. Staatz. 1998. *International agricultural development*. Baltimore: The Johns Hopkins University Press.

Ellis, F., and A. Freeman. 2004a. Rural livelihoods and poverty reduction strategies in four African countries. *The Journal of Development Studies* 40, no. 4 (April): 1–30.

———. 2004b. *Rural livelihoods and poverty reduction strategies in four African countries*. Mimeo.

Ellis, F., and G. Bahiigwa. 2003. Livelihoods and rural poverty reduction in Uganda. *World Development* 31, no. 6: 997–1013.

Ellis, F., M. Kutengule, and A. Nyasulu. 2003. Livelihoods and rural poverty reduction in Malawi. *World Development* 31, no. 9: 1495–1510.

Esman, M. J., and N. T. Uphoff. 1988. *Local organizations—Intermediaries in rural development*. Ithaca, NY: Cornell University Press.

Essama, S. 2005. Burkina Faso: The zaï technique and enhanced agricultural productivity. *IK Notes* (May). Available at the worldbank.org website.

Fafchamps, M., and T. Owens. 2006. *Is international funding crowding out charitable contributions in African NGOs?* GPRG-WPS-055, Global Poverty Research Group. Available at the gprg.org website.

Fahamu. 2006. *Report on a survey of CBOs in Southern Africa,* October 2003. Fahamu. Available at the fahamu.org website.

FAO. 2005. Twenty-third Regional Conference for Africa, March 1–5, 2004. Available at the fao.org website.

Farrington, J., and A. Bebbington. 1993. *Reluctant partners? Non-governmental organizations, the state and sustainable agricultural development.* London: Routledge.

FDSC. 2001. *Definition of civil society.* Civil Society Development Foundation. Available at the fdsc.ro website.

Ferguson, A. E., and W. O. Mulwafu. 2004. *Decentralization, participation and access to water resources in Malawi.* Madison: University of Wisconsin-Madison.

Ferguson, A., and W. Mulwafu. 2007. If government failed, how are we to succeed? The importance of history and context in present-day irrigation reform in Malawi. In van Koppen, Giordano, and Butterworth 2007, 211–27.

Firtus, M. 1999. A brief note on the need for rural institutions as an instrument in agrarian transformation in Africa. *DPMN Bulletin* 6, no. 1. November. Available at the dpmf.org website.

Flygare, S. 2006. *The cooperative challenge: Farmer cooperation and the politics of agricultural modernisation in twenty-first century Uganda.* Acta Universitatis Upsaliensis. Uppsala Studies in Economic History 79. Uppsala, Sweden: University of Uppsala.

Fowler, A. 1988. *Non-governmental organizations in Africa: Achieving comparative advantage in relief and micro-development.* Discussion paper no. 249. Sussex: IDS.

Friis-Hansen, E. 1994. Hybrid maize production and food security in Tanzania. *Biotechnology and Development Monitor* (June): 12–13.

——, ed. 2000. *Agricultural policy in Africa after adjustment.* CDR Policy Paper. Copenhagen: Centre for Development Research.

Friis-Hansen, E., and J. Boesen. 2001. *Agricultural technology and poverty—socio-economic constraints and opportunities for generation and dissemination of new technology among poor farmers.* Copenhagen: Centre for Development Research.

Fukuyama, F. 2005. *State building: Governance and world order in the twenty-first century.* London: Profile Books.

Fulginiti L. E., R. K. Perrin, and B. Yu. 2004. Institutions and agricultural productivity in Sub-Saharan Africa. *Agricultural Economics,* 31, 169–80.

Galvan, D. 2007. The social reproduction of community-based development: Syncretism and sustainability in a Senegalese farmer's association. *Journal of Modern African Studies* 45, no. 1 (March).

Garland, E. 1999. Developing bushmen: Building civil(ized) society in the Kalahari and beyond. In Comaroff and Comaroff 1999, 72–103.

Gazibo, M. 2005. Foreign aid and democratization: Benin and Niger compared. *African Studies Review* 48, no. 3: 67–87.

Ghazala, M., and V. Rao, 2004. Community-based and –driven development: A critical review. *The World Bank Research Observer* 19, no. 1. New York: The World Bank.

Giddens, A. 1984. *The construction of society.* Oxford: Polity Press.

GIPC. 2006. *Ghana investment profile: Cash crops.* Ghana Investment Promotion Centre. Available at the gipc.org.gh website.

Goldstein, A., and C. Kauffmann. 2006. Is more money enough to fix Africa's transport infrastructure? *Policy Insights* 21 (May). OECD Development Centre. Available at the oecd.org website.

Golooba-Mutebi, F. 2005. Witchcraft, social cohesion and participation in a South African village. *Development and Change* 36, no. 5: 937–58.

Goodman, J. 2001. *Farmer's clubs and associations.* Discussion Paper. April. Concern Worldwide.

Graffham A. 2007. *Public and private standards: Trends in the horticulture export sector from Sub-Saharan Africa.* Information Sheet. Available at www.regoverningmarkets.org.

Guèye, B. 1999. *Whither participation? Experience from Francophone West Africa.* Dryland Issue Paper no. 87. Dakar: International Institute for Environment and Development (IIED).

Gyimah-Boadi, E. 1996. Civil society in Africa. *Journal of Democracy* 7, no. 2: 118–32.

Gyllström, B. 1991. *State administered rural change: Agricultural cooperatives in Kenya.* London: Routledge.

Göteborgs Posten. 2005. Göteborgs stads miljöpris till kaffekooperativ från Rwanda. Available at the vartgoteborg.se website.

Hagberg, S. 2004. Political, economic and cultural practices of decentralisation in West Africa. Paper presented at the workshop entitled Decentralisation in Practice: Power, Livelihoods, and Cultural Meaning in West Africa. Uppsala. May 4—6. Uppsala: Department of Cultural Anthropology and Ethnology, Uppsala University/IIED.

———. 2006. "It was Satan that took the people": The making of public authority in Burkina Faso. *Development and Change* 37, no. 4: 779–97.

Hägerstrand, T. 1983. Presence and absence: A look at conceptual choices and bodily necessities. *Regional Studies* 18, no. 5. 373–80.

Haggblade, S. 2005. From roller coaster to rocket ships: The role of technology in African agricultural success. In Djurfeldt et al. 2005, 139–59.

Hansen, H. B., and M. Twaddle, eds. 1998. *Developing Uganda.* Athens: Ohio University Press.

Harley, A. R., P. Rule, and V. John. 2006. *Report on a survey of CBOs in Southern Africa.* Centre for Adult Education, University of KwaZulu-Natal, FAHAMU.

Harris, M. 1979. *Kannibaler och Kungar: Om kulturernas ursprung.* Stockholm: Prisma.

Harrison, E. 2002. "The Problem with the Locals": Partnership and participation in Ethiopia. *Development and Change* 33, no. 4: 587–610.

Hårsmar, M. 2004a. *Heavy clouds but no rain: Agricultural Growth theories and peasant strategies on the Mossi Platteau, Burkina Faso.* Acta Universitatis Agriculturae Sueciae 439. Uppsala: Swedish University of Agricultural Sciences.

———. 2004b. Decentralisation in practice: Power, livelihoods, and cultural meaning in West Africa. Paper presented at the seminar entitled Decentralisation, Institutions, and Local Powers. Uppsala. May 4–6.

———. 2006. Neither diversification nor accumulation: Peasant strategies among the Mossi people of Burkina Faso. In Havnevik, Negash, and Beyene 2006, 84–101.

Harvey, C., J. Jacobs, G. Lamb, and B. Schaffer. 1979. *Rural employment and administration in the third world.* Saxon House: ILO.

Haskell, J. 2004. Boosting the giant: USDA assistance effort helping Nigerian producers to help themselves with user-owned cooperatives. Available at the findarticles.com website.

Hassim, S. 2004. *Voices, hierarchies, and spaces: Reconfiguring the women's movement in Democratic South Africa.* Political Studies. Johannesburg, South Africa: University of Witwatersrand.

Haubert, M. 2002. Organisations paysannes et développement local dans les pays postcoloniaux. In *Le strategies per lo sviluppo locale in Africa,* ed. E. Luzzati, M. Pallottino, and D. Schunk, 94–126. Quaderni 5. Turin: L'Harmattan Italia, Centro Piemontese di Studi Africani.

Hauer, M. 2006. *Parisdeklarationen och det civila samhället.* Hauer Consulting.

Havnevik, K. 2003. Recent experiences with community based forest management in Babati District, Nortern Tanzania. *Currents* 31/32 (October), 37–41.

Havnevik, K., T. Negash, and A. Beyene. 2006. *Of global concern: Rural livelihood dynamics and natural resource governance.* Sida Studies No. 16. Stockholm: Sida.

Havnevik, K., D. Bryceson, L-E Birgegård, P. Matondi, and A. Beyene, eds. 2007. *African agriculture and the World Bank: Development or impoverishment?* Policy Dialogue no. 1, Uppsala: The Nordic Africa Institute.

Hazell, P., and S. Fan. 2002. The importance of public investments and institutions for the functioning of food markets in developing countries. In Lutz 2002, 99–116.

Hearn, J. 1999. *Foreign aid, democratisation and civil society in Africa: A study of South Africa, Ghana, and Uganda.* Discussion Paper no. 368. Brighton: Institute of Development Studies.

———. 2007. African NGOs: The new compradors? *Development and Change* 38, no. 6: 1095–1110.

Heemskerk, W., and B. Wennink. 2004. *Building social capital for agricultural innovation: Experiences with farmer groups in sub-Saharan Africa.* Amsterdam: The Royal Tropical Institute.

Heinisch, E. L. 2006. West Africa versus the United States on cotton subsidies: How, why, and what next? *Journal of Modern African Studies* 44, no. 2: 251–74.

Herbst, J. 2000. *States and power in Africa: Comparative lessons in authority and control.* Princeton, NJ: Princeton University Press.

Hesselbein, G., F. Golooba-Mutebi, and J. Putzel. 2006. *Economic and political foundations of state-making in Africa: Understanding state reconstruction.* Working Paper no. 3. London: Crisis State Research Centre, Development Studies Institute (DESTIN).

Hettne, B. 1971. *Utvecklingsstrategier i Kina och Indien.* Lund: Studentlitteratur.

———. 1992. The future of development studies. Paper presented at the fortieth anniversary of ISS. The Hague: Institute of Social Studies.

Hillhorst, T., and C. Toulmin. 2000. *Sustainability amidst diversity: Options for rural households in Mali.* Dryland Issue Paper (E97). Dakar: IIED.

Hillhorst, T., D. Bagayoko, D. Dao, E. Lodenstein, and J. Toonen. 2005. *Building effective local partnerships for improved basic social services delivery in Mali.* Amsterdam: The Royal Tropical Institute (KIT).

Hitimana, L. 2004. *Case study on agricultural innovation and cotton production in Ghana.* Paris: Sahel and West Africa Club (SWAC).

Holdcroft, L. E. 1978. *The rise and fall of community development in developing countries, 1950–65: A critical analysis and an annotated bibliography.* East Lansing: MSU Rural Development Papers, Michigan State University.

Holmén, H. 1990. *State, cooperatives, and development in Africa.* Research Report no. 86. Uppsala: The Scandinavian Institute of African Studies.

———. 1991. *Building organizations for rural development: State and cooperatives in Egypt.* Lund, Sweden: Lund University Press.

———. 1994. Co-operatives and the environmental challenge. In Holmén and Jirström 1994, 37–62.

———. 1995. What's new and what's regional in the new regional geography? *Geografiska Annaler* 77B, no. 1: 47–63.

———. 2005. The state and agricultural intensification in sub-Saharan Africa. In Djurfeldt et al. 2005, 87–112.

Holmén, H., and M. Jirström. 1994. *Ground level development: NGOs, co-operatives and local organizations in the third world.* Lund Studies in Geography 56. Lund, Sweden: Lund University Press.

———. 1996. *No organizational fixes: NGOs, institutions, and prerequisites for development.* Publications on agriculture and rural development, no. 4, Department for Natural Resources and the Environment. Stockholm: Sida.

―――. 1999. The challenge to cooperatives as tools for development in post-structural adjustment Africa. In Holmén and Luzzati 1999, 111–31.

―――. 2009. Look who's talking! Second thoughts about NGOs as representing civil society. *Journal of Asian and African Studies* 44, no. 4.

Holmén, H., and E. Luzzati, eds. 1999. *Grassroots' organizations, decentralization, and rural development: African experiences in the 1990s.* Proceedings from a workshop. Turin: ILO.

Hoogvelt, A. 2001. *Globalization and the postcolonial world: The new political economy of development.* Baltimore, MD: The Johns Hopkins University Press.

Hoon, P. N. 2004. Personal markets and impersonal communities? Prospects for community conservation in Botswana. Paper presented at the Breslauer Symposium on natural resource issues in Africa. Los Angeles and Berkeley: University of California, Center for African Studies. Available at http://repositories.cdlib.org/cas/breslauer/hoon2004a.

Hopkins, R., D. Neven, and T. Reardon. 2005. *Case studies of farmer organizations linking to dynamic markets in Southern Africa: The Lubulima Agriculture and Commercial Cooperatives Union.* East Lansing, MI: Michigan State University.

Hospes, O. 1999. Savings at the grassroots in Western Province, Zambia: A matter of policy-making, rain-making, or witch-making? In Holmén and Luzzati 1999, 273–310.

Hudock, A. 2000. Interview: The case for empowering Southern NGOs. Woodrow Wilson Center, *Global Policy Forum.* Available at the globalpolicy.org website.

Huizer, G. 1997. Zambia: People's participation and large-scale cooperatives. *SD dimensions* (May). Available at the fao.org website.

Human Rights Watch. 2001. *Uganda: Freedom of associations at risk: The proposed NGO bill and current restrictions on NGOs in Uganda.* Available at the hrw.org website.

Hussein, K. 2004. Importance of cotton production and trade in West Africa. Paper presented at the WTO Africa Regional Workshop on Cotton. March 23–24. Sahel and West Africa Club (SWAC).

Hydén, G. 1970. Cooperatives and their socio-political environment. In Widstrand 1970, 61–80.

―――. 1983. *No shortcuts to progress: African development management in perspective.* London: Heinemann.

―――. 1995. The economy of affection revisited: African development management in perspective. Paper presented at a special resource course entitled "Improved Natural Resource Management—the Role of Formal Organizations and Informal Networks and Institutions," Hotel Solfrid, Jyllinge, Denmark, October 23–26. Mimeo.

————. 2006. Introduction and overview to the special issue on Africa's moral and affective economy. *African Studies Quarterly—The Online Journal for African Studies* 9, nos. 1–2 (Fall).

————. 2008. After the Paris Declaration: Taking on the issue of power. *Development Policy Review* 26, no. 3: 259–74.

Ibeanu, O., and A. A. Nzei. 1998. *Women cooperatives and power redistribution in rural Nigeria: A case study of Nsukka, Enugu State.* Ibadan: Nigerian Institute of Social and Economic Research (NISER).

ICA (International Co-operative Alliance). 1998. *A report on status of SACCOs in Kenya.* International Co-operative Alliance, Regional Office for Africa. Available at the icaafrica.coop website.

————. 2000a. *A report on cashewnut marketing in Tanzania.* International Co-operative Alliance, Regional Office for East, Central, and Southern Africa. Available at the icaafrica.coop website.

————. 2000b. *Tanzanian cotton industry.* International Co-operative Alliance, Regional Office for East, Central, and Southern Africa. Available at the icaafrica.coop website.

————. 2000c. *Tanzania SACCO survey.* International Co-operative Alliance, Regional Office for East, Central, and Southern Africa. Available at the icaafrica.coop website.

————. 2003. *Proceedings of the third ICA regional workshop on agricultural marketing.* Kenya School of Monetary Studies. June 18–20, 2003.

ICARE. 2001. *Results ICARE Durban Plus 5 poll.* Available at the icare.to website.

ICCSL. no date. *Ghana projects.* International Center for Civil Society Law. Available at the iccsl.org website.

ID21. 2005. *Making decentralisation work for rural people in Mali.* Available at the id21.org website.

————. 2006. *Fighting hunger and poverty in Ethiopia.* Available at the id21.org website.

————. 2007. *Ugandan NGOs act as sub-contractors for international development agencies.* Available at the id21.org website.

IFAD (International Fund for Agricultural Development). 2000. *Benin—Cooperation among the government, IFAD, and NGOs.* Rome: IFAD.

————. 2001. *Assessment of rural poverty: Western and Central Africa.* Rome: IFAD.

————. 2005. Benin—Country programme evaluation. Executive summary. Rome: IFAD. Available at the ifad.org website.

IFAP (International Federation of Agricultural Producers). 2004. *Reducing hunger in Africa (MDGS): Views from farmers' organisations in Africa, members of IFAP.* Available at the ifap.org website.

————. 2005. *Case study on farmer-to-farmer extension system in Kenya.* Available at the ifap.org website.

IFPRI (International Food Policy Research Institute). 2003. *Trade policy and food security.* Washington DC: IFPRI.

Igoe, J. 2004. Has the aid industry disempowered Tanzanian pastoralists? *ID21 Research Highligh.* Available at the id21.org website.

——. 2005. Preface. In Igoe and Kelsall 2005: xi–xii.

——. 2006. Becoming indigenous peoples: Difference, inequality, and the globalization of East African identity policies. *African Affairs* 105, no. 420: 399–420.

Igoe, J., and T. Kelsall, eds. 2005. *Between a rock and a hard place: African NGOs, donors, and the state.* Durham, NC: Carolina Academic Press.

IISD (International Institute for Sustainable Development). No date a. *Six-S: Category of activity.* Winnipeg: IISD. Available at the iisd.org website.

——. No date b. *Six-S (Se Servir de la Saison Sèche en Savane et au Ssahel),* Burkina Faso. Winnipeg: IISD. Available at the iisd.org website.

IJCSL. 2004. Zambia—government bans civil society organization. *IJCSL Newsletter* 2, issue 1 (December). 2006–10–19. International Center for Civil Society Law.

IJCSL Newsletter. 2004. Volume 1, Issue 9 (August).

——. 2006. Volume 3, Issue 8 (July).

IK Notes. 2005. Indigenous innovation in farmer-to-farmer extension in Burkina Faso. *IK Notes,* no. 77 (February). Available at the worldbank.org website.

ILO/ICA. 2003. *The role of cooperatives in designing and implementing poverty reduction strategies.* Report on a regional workshop. Dar es Salaam, Tanzania. June 4–, 2003.

Isinika, A. C., G. C. Ashimogo, and J. Mlangwa. 2005. From Ujamaa to structural adjustment—agricultural intensification in Tanzania. In Djurfeldt et al. 2005, 197–218.

James, R., with J. Oladipo, M. Isooba, B. Mbozi, and I. Kusiima. 2005. *Realities of change: Understanding how African NGO leaders develop.* Praxis Paper no. 6. Oxford: INTRAC.

Jones, E. 2005. Pa Pa Pa—the best of the best: Kuapa Kokoo promoting co-operative values and principles. *The Co-operative College Newsletter* 10 (June).

Jütting, J., E. Corsi, C. Kauffmann, I. McDonnell, H. Osterreider, N. Pinaud, and L. Wegner. 2005. What makes decentralisation in developing countries pro-poor? *The European Journal of Development Research* 17, no. 4 (December): 626–48.

Juul, K. 2006. Decentralization, local taxation and citizenship in Senegal. *Development and Change* 37, no. 4:821–46.

Kaarhus, R., and R. Nyirenda. 2006. *Decentralisation in the agricultural sector in Malawi—policies, processes and community links.* Noragric Report no. 32 (May). Ås: Norwegian University of Life Sciences.

Kabumba, I. 2007. Conflicts between elected and appointed officials in districts. In Asiimwe and Nakanyike 2007, 28–40.

Kachule, R. 2004. *Rural producer organisations and policy formulation in Malawi.* Working Paper no. 127. Blindern: Norwegian Institute for Urban and Regional Research (NIBR).

Karega, R. G. M. 2002a. Addressing poverty through civil societies: Challenges and realities. *DPMN Bulletin* 9, no. 2 (May). Available at the dpmf.org website.

————. 2002b. The role of women's informal associations in the process of poverty reduction in Kenya. *DPMN Bulletin* 9, no. 2 (May). Available at the dpmf.org website.

Kareweh, E. 2004. Economic policy campaigning and advocacy: The experience of the General Agricultural Workers' Union in Ghana. In Diakonia, 52–54.

Karl, M. 2002. *Participatory policy reform from a sustainable livelihoods perspective: Review of concepts and practical experiences.* Rome: FAO, Livelihood Support Programme.

KDDP (Killifi District Development Programme). 2004. *Where there is self-governance.* Final Report. December. Nairobi: GTZ

Kelly, V., A. A. Adesina, and A. Gordon. 2003. Expanding access to agricultural inputs in Africa: A review of recent market development experience. *Food Policy* 28, 379–404.

Kelsall, T. 2001. Donors, NGOs, and the state: Governance and "civil society" in Tanzania. In Barrow and Jennings 2001, 133–48.

Khemani, S. 2004. *Local government accountability for service delivery in Nigeria.* Development Research Group. New York: The World Bank. Draft.

Khor, M. 2006. *The impact of globalisation and liberalisation on agriculture and small farmers in developing countries: The experience of Ghana.* Third World Network (TWN). April.

Kibora, A. S. 1999. Le défi coopératif et le développement en Afrique. In Holmén and Luzatti 1999, 149–72.

Kilby, P. 2006. Accountability for development: Dilemmas facing non-governmental organizations. *World Development* 34, no. 6: 951–63.

Kirsch, O., A. Benjacov, and L. Schujmann. 1980. *The role of self-help groups in rural development projects.* Saarbrücken/Fort Lauderdale: Breitenbach Publ.

Klein, N. 2003. Bush to NGOs: Watch your mouths. *Common Dreams News Center.* August 10. Available at commondreams.org website.

Koch, D-J., A. Dreher, P. Nunnenkamp, and R. Thiele. 2008. *Keeping a low profile: What determines the allocation of aid by non-governmental organizations?* Working Paper no. 1406. March. Kiel Institute for the World Economy.

Korten, D. C. 1980. Community organization and rural development: A learning process approach. *Public Administration Review* 40, no. 5 (September-October): 480–511.

Kötter, H. 1984. Objectives and strategies of agricultural development in the Third World. In *Co-operation as an instrument for rural development in the Third World*, ed. J. Wörtz. Zeitschrift für die Landwirtschaft in der Tropen und Subtropen. Beiheft no. 17: 8–18.

Kouyaté, S., A. K. Coulibibaly, A. Traoré, S. Diarra, A. Calvo, and B. Domenico, eds. 2006. *Décentralisation, organisations endogènes, ressources environnementales, technologies appropriées*. Bamako: Jamana.

Kreuger, O. A., M. Schif, and A. Valdes. 1988. Agricultural incentives in developing countries: Measuring the effects of sectoral and economy wide policies. *The World Bank Economic Review* 2, no. 3: 255–71.

Krishna, A., N. Uphoff, and M. J. Esman, eds. 1997. *Reasons for hope: Instructive experiences in rural development*. West Hartford, CT: Kumarian Press.

Kumar, C. 2005. Revisiting "community" in community-based natural resource management. *Community Development Journal* 40, no. 3 (July): 275–85.

Kumwenda, I., and S. Mingu. 2005. *Follow up study on farmer organizations in Malawi*. Imperial College, London/Bunda College, University of Malawi.

Kurata, P. 2008. Ethiopia: Country launches commodity exchange to develop agriculture. All Africa Com. October 31. Available at the www:allafrica.com website.

Kuznets, S. 1973. Modern economic growth: Findings and reflections. *The American Economic Review* 63, no. 3 (June): 247–58.

Laidlaw, A. F. 1978. Cooperatives and the poor: A review from within the cooperative movement. In *Cooperatives and the poor*, 51–90. London: ICA.

Larsen, A. 2003. Decentralization in Namibia: A case study of the Erongo Region. *The Interdisciplinary Journal of International Studies* 1.

Larsson, R. 2001. *Between crisis and opportunity—Livelihoods, diversification, and inequality among the Meru of Tanzania. Lund Dissertations in Sociology* 41. Lund.

———. 2005. Crisis and potential in smallholder food production—evidence from micro level. In Djurfeldt et al. 2005, 113–38.

Larsson, R., H. Holmén, M. Hammarskjöld. 2002. Agricultural development in sub-Saharan Africa. Afrint working paper no. 1. Department of Sociology. Lunk, Sweden: Lund University.

Larsson-Lidén, L. 2006. Land reform, food security and grassroots movements' scope for survival in Zimbabwe. In Havnevik, Negash, and Beyene 2006, 147–64.

Lecomte, B. J., and A. Krishna. 1997. Six-S: Building upon traditional social organizations in francophone West Africa. In Krishna, Uphoff, and Esman 1997, 75–90.

Le Coq, J. F. 2003. *Farmers' and rural organisations capacity building: The case of the "Agricultural Services Sub-sector Investment Project"*

(AgSSIP) and its producer organisation support component, Ghana. Cirad. Mimeo.

Le Meur, P-Y. 2006. State making and the politics of the frontier. *Development and Change* 37, no. 4: 871–900.

Lentz, C. 2006. Decentralization, the state, and conflicts over local boundaries in Northern Ghana. *Development and Change* 37, no. 4: 901–19.

Lewis, D. 2001. *Civil society in non-Western contexts: Reflections on the "usefulness" of a concept.* Civil Society Working Paper no. 13. London: Centre for Civil Society, London School of Economics and Political Science.

Leysens, A. J. 2006. Social forces in Southern Africa: Transformation from below? *Journal of Modern African Studies* 44, no. 1: 31–58.

Liebhardt, J. 2005. White gold or fool's gold: What will a rollback of U.S. cotton subsidies mean for farmers in Burkina Faso? *Multinational Monitor* 26, nos. 5–6 (May/June). Available at the multinationalmonitor.org website.

Lipton, M. 1989. *Why poor people stay poor.* Baltimore: The Johns Hopkins University Press.

Livernash, R. 1992. The growing influence of NGOs in the developing world. *Environment* 34, no. 5 (June): 12–20, 41–43.

Lockwood, M. 2005. *The state they're in: An agenda for international action on poverty in Africa.* Burton-on-Dunsmore: ITDG Publishing.

Löwenheim, O. 2008. Examining the state: A Foucauldian perspective on international "governance indicators." *Third World Quarterly* 29, no. 2, 255–74.

Lutz, C., ed. 2002. *Food markets and food security in West Africa.* CDS Research Report no. 15.

Luzzati, E. 1999. Grassroots development and multipurpose cooperatives in Africa today. In Holmén and Luzzati 1999, 133–47.

———. 2002. Coopératives communautaires et cooperatives des intérêts dans le Delta du Fleuve Sénégal: Le cas de Ronk. In *A cura di, Lavoro, genere e sviluppo locale in Mali e in Senegal,* ed. E. Benenati et al. Italy: L'Harmattan.

———. 2003. Le mouvement paysan au Sénégal: du coopérativisme communautaire au syndicalisme rural. In *Développement local et développement durable,* Université Gaston Berger de Saint-Louis, Juliet.

Luzzati, E., and C. Altare. 2006. Coopératives, enterprises communautaires et économie solidaire au Sénégal. Le cas des foyers de Asescaw. In Kouyaté et al. 2006, 120–41.

Lyon, F. 2003. Community groups and livelihoods in remote rural areas of Ghana: How small-scale farmers sustain collective action. *Community Development Journal* 38, no. 4 (October): 323–31.

Lyon, F., and G. Porter. 2005. The social relations of economic life and networks of civic engagement: "Social capital" and targeted development. In Cline-Cole and Robson 2005, 191–205.

Mabogunje, A. 1989. *The development process: A spatial perspective.* London: Unwin Hyman.

Mackintosh, M. 1992. Questioning the state. In *Development policy and public action,* ed. Marc Wuyts, Maureen Mackintosh, and Tom Hewitt, 61–89. Oxford: Oxford University Press,

Mafeje, A. 2003. *The agrarian question, access to land, and peasant responses in sub-Saharan Africa.* Civil Society and Social Movements Programme Paper no. 6. Geneva: UNRISD.

MAFS. 2008. The Ministry of Agriculture and Food Security, Malawi. Database on farmer organizations at the malawiagriculture.org website.

Mahmoud, Y. M. 2007. *Chinese development assistance and west african agriculture: A shifting approach to foreign aid?* Lund, Sweden: Department of Social and Economic Geography, Lund University.

Mana, K. 1995. Democracy in Africa: A basic problem. In Melin 1995, 21–27.

Manji, F. 2000. Collaboration with the South: Agents of aid or solidarity? In Eade 2000, 75–79.

Manji, F., and A. Naidoo. 2006. Introduction. In *Report on a survey of CBOs in Southern Africa.* FAHAMU. Available at the fahamu.org website.

Mansuri, G., and V. Rao. 2004. Community-based and –driven development: A critical review. *The World Bank Research Observer* 19, no. 1: 1–39.

Manuh, T. 1998. Women in Africa's development. *Africa Recovery.* Briefing Paper no. 11 (April). Available at the un.org website.

Materu, J. S. 2002. Decentralization policies and practices in West Africa. UN-HABITAT. Available at the unhabitat.org website.

Mazrui, A. 2002. Who killed democracy in Africa? Clues of the past, concerns of the future. *DPMN Bulletin* 9, no. 1 (February). Available at the dpmf.org website.

Mbeki, M. 2005. *Perpetuating poverty in sub-Saharan Africa.* London: International Policy Press.

McKeon, N. 1999. Grassroots development and participation in policy negotiations: Bridging the micro-macro gap in Senegal. In Holmén and Luzzati 1999, 331–54.

McKeon, N., M. Watts, and W. Wolford. 2004. Peasant associations in theory and practice. Civil Society and Social Movements Programme Paper no. 8. May. Geneva: UNRISD.

McMahon, J. 2007. Developments in the regulations of NGOs via government counter-terrorism measures and policies. Policy Briefing Paper 11. Oxford: INTRAC.

Meinzen-Dick, R., L. Pandolfelli, S. Dohrn, and J. Athens. 2005. Gender and collective action: A conceptual framework for analysis. Paper presented at the international research workshop entitled "Gender and Collective Action," Chiang Mai, Thailand, October 17–21.

Meisel, N., and J. O. Aoudia. 2008. *Is "good governance" a good development strategy?* Working Paper no. 58 (January). Paris: Agence France de Développement.

Melin, M., ed. 1995. *Democracy in Africa: On whose terms?* Stockholm: Forum Syd.

Mercoiret M-R., B. Goudiaby, S. Marzartoli, D. Fall, S. Gueye, and J. Coulibaly. 2001. Empowering producer organizations: Issues, goals, and ambiguities. In Rondot and Collion 2001, 20–28.

Metcalfe, S. 1997. The CAMPFIRE program: Community-based wildlife resource management in Zimbabwe. In Krishna, Uphoff, and Esman 1997, 273–88.

Michael, S. 2004. *Undermining development: The absence of power among local NGOs in Africa.* African Issues. Bloomington: Indiana University Press.

Michener, V. J. 1998. The participatory approach: Contradiction and co-optation in Burkina Faso. *World Development* 26, no. 12, 2105–18.

Milligan, S., and T. Binns. 2007. Crisis in policy, policy in crisis: Understanding environmental discourse and resource-use conflict in northern Nigeria. *The Geographical Journal* 173, no. 2, (June): 143—56.

Mistry, P. S. 2005. Reasons for Sub-Saharan Africa's development deficit that the Commission for Africa did not consider. *African Affairs* 104/417, 665–78.

Mitlin, D., S. Hickey, and A. Bebbington. 2007. Reclaiming development? NGOs and the challenge of alternatives. *World Development* 35, no. 10: 1699–1720.

Mloza-Banda H. R., B. C. Munthali, S. Chimphonda, and A. Likupe. 2003. *Agricultural transformation in Malawi: The role and status of farmers' organisations.* RELMA. Available at the relma.org website.

Mohamadou, A. 2004. *Foncier agro-pastoral, conflits et gestion des aléas climatiques au Niger: cas de Dakoro et d'Abalak.* Etudes et Travaux, n° 26. Laboratoire d'études et recherches sur les dynamiques sociales et le développement local (LASDEL). Niamey.

Moore, M. 2006. Good government? Introduction. *IDS Bulletin* 37, no. 4 (September): 50–56.

Moser, C. M., and C. B. Barrett. 2005. The complex dynamics of smallholder technology adoption: The case of SRI in Madagascar. *Agricultural Economics* (November): 373–88.

Mtinda, E. O. 2006. *Sustainability of rural water supply and sanitation services under community management approach: The case of selected villages in Tanzania.* Linköping, Sweden: The Tema Institute, Linköping University.

Mulat, D., and A. Teketel. 2003. *Afrint study: Ethiopian agriculture: macro and micro perspective.* Addis Ababa: University of Addis Ababa.

Munene, H. 2005. Why NGO corruption in Africa is unsettling. *The New Times* (Kenya). August 24.

Münkner, H. H. 1983. *The legal status of pre-cooperatives.* Bonn: Friedrich-Ebert Stiftung.

Murunga, G. R. 2000. Civil society and the democratic experience in Kenya: A review of "Constitution-Making from the Middle: Civil Society and Transition Politics in Kenya, 1992–1997," by Willy Mutunga [Nairobi: Sareat and Mwengo, 1999]. *African Sociological Review* 4, no. 1: 97–118.

Närman, A. 1995. *Education and nation building in Kenya: Perspectives on modernization, global dependency and local development alternatives.* Göteborg University Series B, no. 88. Gothenburg.

NCBA. 2004. *Producer trade companies boost profits in Southern Africa.* National Cooperative Business Association. Available at the ncba.coop website.

Ndegwa, S. N. 1996. *The two faces of civil society: NGOs and politics in Africa.* West Hartford, CT: Kumarian Press.

New Agriculturist. 2004. Country profile: Ghana. *New Agriculturist Online.* Available at the new-agri.co.uk website.

———. 2006. *News Brief 0602:* Zambia's crop export hit by strong kwacha. Available at the www.new-ag.info website.

Ngoma, J. 2008. *Effects of climate change on maize production in Zambia.* Department for Water and Environmental Studies. Linköping, Sweden: The Tema Institute, Linköping University.

Nkonya, E. 2002. Uganda crop trader characteristics and their marketing constraints. *Eastern Africa Journal of Rural Development* 18, no. 1: 23–39.

Nkwachukwu, O. 2003. "Conventional" notion of civil society, international civil society organisations, and the development of civil society in Africa. Paper presented at the International Civil Society Forum at Ulaanbaatar, Mongolia, September 8–9. Mimeo.

Nkwake, A. 2007. Local government and NGO partnerships. In Asiimwe and Nakanyike 2007, 278–88.

Nolutshungu, T. 2008. Neo-colonialist NGOs. *The Daily Times* (Malawi), April 30.

North, D. 1990. *Institutions, institutional change, and economic performance.* Cambridge: Cambridge University Press.

NSSD. 2003. National strategies for sustainable development. Burkina Faso: The NSSD Sustainable Development Report.

Nunnenkamp, P. 2008. The myth of NGO superiority. *Development and Cooperation/Entwicklung und Zusammenarbeit* 35 (May).

Nunnenkamp P., J. Weingarth, and J. Weisser. 2008. *Is NGO aid not so different after all? Comparing the allocation of Swiss aid by private and official donors.* Working Paper No. 1405, March. Kiel Institute for the World Economy.

Oakley, P. 1999. *A review of Danish NGO activities in developing countries: Overview report.* Copenhagen: Danida.

Odhiambo, G. 2003. Inventory of farmers' organisations in Kenya. Paper presented at the Regional Seminar on Farmers Cooperation. Lilongwe, Malawi. March 24–27.

OECD (Organisation for Economic Co-operation and Development). 2008. *Civil society and aid effectiveness: Synthesis of findings and recommendations.* DCD/DAC/EFF(2008)6/REV1 (30 May).

Offenheiser, R. C. 1999. *Enhancing NGO effectiveness in Africa: Re-evaluating the potential for genuine partnerships.* Working Paper no. 4. Oxfam America.

Ogunbayo, O. S. 2003. Formal and informal financial services. *Urban Agriculture Magazine* 9 (April): 39.

Okome, M. O. 1999. State and civil society in Nigeria in the era of structural adjustment programs, 1986–93. *West Africa Review* 1, no. 1. Available at the icaap.org website.

Onibon, A., B. Dabiré, and L. Ferroukhi. 1999. *Local practices and the decentralization and devolution of natural resource management in French-speaking West Africa. Unasylva* 199. Available on the fao.org website.

Onsander, S. 2007. Swedish development cooperation through Swedish and local NGOs. *Perspectives* 7 (March). Center for African Studies, Gothenburg University.

Onyando, R. M. 1999. *Are NGOs essential for Kenya's development?* Nomadnet. November 20. Available at the netnomad.com website.

Oppong-Manu, I. 2004. *Cooperatives and cooperative education in Ghana: Perspectives from a cooperative educator.* Mimeo.

Østerberg, D. 1978. *Sociologins nyckelbegrepp och deras ursprung.* Göteborg: Korpen.

Otim, J. J. 2003. *The ACU experience.* RELMA. Available at the relma.org website.

Oudet, M. 2002. *Which strategy should be adopted to fight poverty?* ABC Burkina. Available at the abcburkina.net website.

Ouedraogo, A., and H. Sawadogo. 2005. Indigenous innovation in farmer-to-farmer extension in Burkina Faso. *IK Notes*, no. 77 (February). Available at the worldbank.org website.

Ouedraogo, B. 1989. The Africa prize for leadership for the sustainable end of hunger. Address by Dr. Bernard Lédéa Ouedraogo. Available at the africaprize.org website.

Oxfam. 2006. Kuapa Kokoo today. Available at the oxfam.org website.

Oya, C. 2006. From state dirigisme to liberalisation in Senegal: Four decades of agricultural policy shifts and continuities. *The European Journal of Development Research* 18, no. 2 (June): 203–34.

Oyugi, W. 2004. The role of NGOs in fostering development and good governance at the local level in Africa with a focus on Kenya. *Africa Development* 29, no. 4: 19–55.

Pact. 2003. *Strengthening civil society participation in the governance process.* South Africa: Pact Country Programs. Available at the pactworld.org website.

PAFP (Pan African Farmers Platform). 2008. *Final Declaration.* Addis Ababa: PAFP.

Pagaran, E. 1994. Agro-industries, co-operatives and rural development in the Philippines. In Holmén and Jirström 1994, 108–36.

Pandolfelli, L., S. Dohrn, and R. Meinzen-Dick. 2007. Gender and Collective Action: Policy Implications from Recent Research. *CAPRi,* CgiAR Systemwide Program on Collective Action and Property Rights. *Policy Brief,* no. 5, January. Available at the Capri.cgiar.org website.

Pantanali R. 2004. *IFAD approach to community driven development in West and Central Africa—Lessons from experience.* Draft Consultancy Report, June (mimeo).

Perrett, H. 2004. *Community development funds: Some emerging lessons for project design.* Main Report. August. PT/IFAD.

Pesche, D. 2001. Can producer organizations be strengthened by provision of funding and human resources? In Rondot and Collion 2001, 32–37.

Pieterse, J. N. 1998. My paradigm or yours? Alternative development, post-development, reflexive development. *Development and Change* 29: 343–73.

Pimbert, M. 2004. *Institutionalising participation and people-centered processes in natural resource management: Research and publications highlights.* London: IIED/IDS.

———. 2005. Supporting locally determined food systems: The role of local organizations in farming, environment, and people's access to food. In Bigg and Satterthwaite 2005, 129–55.

Platteau J-P. 2000. *Institutions, social norms, and economic development.* The Netherlands: Harwood Academic Publishers.

———. 2004. Monitoring elite capture in community driven development. *Development and Change* 35, no. 2: 223–46.

Platteau, J-P., and F. Gaspart. 2003a. *Disciplining local leaders in community-based development.* Namur: Centre for Research on the Economics of Development (CRED).

———. 2003b. The risk of resource misappropriation in community-driven development. *World Development* 31, no. 10: 1687–1703.

PMA. 2000. *Plan for modernisation of agriculture: Eradicating poverty in Uganda.* Kampala: Ministry of Agriculture, Animal Industry, and Fisheries (MAAIF)/Ministry of Finance, Planning, and Economic Development (MFPED).

Pollard, A., and J. Court. 2005. *How civil society organisations use evidence to influence policy processes: A literature review.* London: ODI.

Power, M., G. Mohan, and C. Mercer. 2006. Postcolonial geographies of development: Introduction. *Singapore Journal of Tropical Geography* 27, 231–34.

Practical Action. 2005. *The crisis in African agriculture: A more effective role for EC aid?* Practical Action/PELUM. Available at the africanvoices.org.uk website.

Public Agenda. 2006. *The NPP government and decentralization in Ghana.* Available at the www.ghanaweb.com website.

Putnam, R. D. 1993. *Making democracy work.* Princeton, NJ: Princeton University Press.

Rättvisemärkt. 2006. Kuapa Kokoo. *Världsbutikernas nyhetsbrev,* no. 7. Available at the rattvisemarkt.se website.

RDFS. 2003. Interview with Mr. Ndiogou Fall (President of FONGS). *UN System Network on Rural Development and Food Security.* Available at the rdfs.net website.

RELMA. 2003. *Farmers get organized.* Available at the relma.org website.

Riddell R., A. Bebbington, and L. Peck. 1995. *Promoting development by proxy — The development impact of government support to Swedish NGOs.* London: ODI.

RIMISP, ICCO, and IDRC/CRDI. 2007. *WDR2008 Civil Society Consultation: Final Report.* Toronto: RIMISP, ICCO, and IDRC/CRDI.

Robinson, M. 2006. *The political economy of governance reforms in Uganda.* IDS Discussion Paper no. 386. Brighton: Institute of Development Studies, University of Sussex.

Roche, C. 1991. ACORD's experience in local planning in Mali and Burkina Faso. *RRA Notes* 11 (London: IIED): 33–41.

Rondot, P., and M. H. Collion, eds. 2001. *Agricultural producer organizations: Their contribution to rural capacity building and poverty reduction.* Washington DC: The World Bank.

Ruijs, A. 2002. The effect of institutional improvements on cereal trade in Burkina Faso: Infrastructure, market information, and credit. In Lutz 2002, 149–82.

Rusike J., and J. P. Dimes. 2004. Effecting change through private sector client services for smallholder farmers in Africa. In *New Directions for a Diverse Planet: Proceedings of the Fourth International Crop Science Congress.* Brisbane, Australia. Sept. 26–Oct. 1. Available at the cropscience.org.au website.

Ruttan, V. W., and Y. Hayami. 1998. Induced innovation model of agricultural development. In Eicher and Staatz 1998, 163–78.

Salzer, W. 2003. *The untapped potential: Self-governing communities for public service provision in rural areas: The Kilifi experience.* Available at the kddp.com website.

Sandberg, S. 1992. De fattiga måste komma oss nära. *Volontären,* no. 2: 8–9.

Sanyal, B. 1994. *Cooperative Autonomy: The dialectic of state-NGO relationships in developing countries.* Geneva: International Institute for Labour Studies.

Schmale, M. 1993. *The role of local organizations in third world development.* Aldershot: Avebury.

Schreiber, C. 2002. *Sources of innovation in dairy production in Kenya.* ISNAR Briefing Paper no. 58. December. International Service for National Agricultural Research.

Schumpeter, J. 1951. *The theory of economic development—An enquiry into profits, capital, credit, interest, and the business cycle.* Cambridge, MA: Harvard University Press.

Schweigmann, C. 2003. *Food security: Opportunities and responsibilities or: The illusion of the exclusive actor.* CDS Research Report no. 19. ISSN 1385–9218.

Scott, J. C. 1985. *Weapons of the weak: Everyday forms of peasant resistance.* New Haven, CT: Yale University Press.

Scott, N. 2006. Review article of S. Freidberg (2004): "French beans and food scares: Commerce and culture in an anxious age." *Journal of Modern African Studies* [Oxford University Press] 44, no. 4 (December): 650–51.

Sebastian, B. 2003. Farmers' organisations in Rwanda—Building of a new structure. RELMA. Available at the relma.org website.

Seckinelgin, H. 2006. The multiple worlds of NGOs and HIV/AIDS: Rethinking NGOs and their Agency. *Journal of International Development* 18: 715–27.

Seini, W., and V. Nyanteng. 2003. *Afrint macro study: Ghana macro report.* Legon: Institute of Statistics, Social and Economic Research (ISSER). Available at http://www.soc.lu.se/afrint.

Seward, P., and D. Okello. 2000. *SCODP's mini-pack method: The first step towards improved food security for small farmers in Western Kenya.* Available on the ifpri.org website.

Shaw, S. 1990. Burden of hope: Africa in the 1990s. *New Internationalist* 208 (June). Available at the newint.org website.

Shepherd, A. 1998. *Sustainable rural development.* Hong Kong: MacMillan.

Shivji, I. G. 2006. The silences in the NGO discourse: The role and future of NGOs in Africa. *Pambazuka News,* Special Report 14. Fahamu. Oxford, Cape Town, Nairobi.

Sida. 2002. *Good governance.* Stockholm: Sida.

———. 2003. *Support to small-scale farming through NALEP.* Stockholm: Sida.

———. 2004. *Sida's policy for civil society.* Stockholm: Sida, Department for Cooperation with Non-governmental Organizations and Humanitarian Assistance and Conflict Management.

————. 2007. *Sida's support to civil society.* Stockholm: Sida, Department for Cooperation with Non-governmental Organizations and Humanitarian Assistance and Conflict Management.

Sikpa, A. 2005. Financing agricultural trade: The agrotrade approach. In *Private enterprise and the post-harvest sector.* GASGA Executive Seminar Series no. 7. Chatham, UK: The National Resource Institute. Available at the fao.org website.

Simon, D., and C. Radoki. 1990. Conclusions and prospects: What future for regional planning? In *Third World Regional Development: A Reappraisal,* ed. D. Simon, 249–60. London: Paul Chapman Books, 1990.

Sinclair, M. 1995. *The development impact of the Swedish government's support to NGOs: Kenya case study.* London: ODI.

Smith, G. E., and S. E. Rice. 2004. WTO hands a critical victory to African farmers. *Global Envision.* Available at the globalenvision.org website.

Smith, J. 2006. Non-governmental organizations in development: Adapt or perish. ID21 Research Highlight. Available at the id21.org website.

Snrech, S. 2001. Donors and farmers organizations: Lessons learned from ongoing experiences in the Sahel. In Rondot and Collion 2001, 46–56.

Snyder, K. A. 2008. Building democracy from below: A case from rural Tanzania. *Journal of Modern African Studies* 46, no. 2: 287–304.

Soulama, S. 2003. Le Groupement Villageois: Pertinence d'une Organisation d'Economie Sociale au Burkina Faso. *Revue Economie et Solidarités* 34, no. 1. Quebec: Presses de l'Université du Québec, CIRIEC.

Souley, A., and E. K. Hahonou. 2004. *Les associations cantonales dans le Tagazar et le Tondikandia.* Etudes et Travaux, n° 24. Laboratoire d'études et recherches sur les dynamiques sociales et le développement local (LASDEL). Niamey.

Spore. 2005. Farmers' organisations: Services and setbacks. Spore 115 (February). Available at the cta.int/spore website.

SRTV. 2006. *Pärleporten* (The Pearly Gate). Swedish Television. Channel 2. December 11.

Stöhr, W. B., and F. Taylor F., eds. 1981. *Development from above or below? The dialectics of regional planning in developing countries.* Chichester: Wiley.

SWAC (Sahel and West Africa Club). 2005. *The family economy and agricultural innovation in West Africa: Towards new partnerships.* (March). SWAC.

Swartzendruber, J. F., and B. B. Njovens. 1993. *African NGO participation in natural resource policy reform.* Washington DC: World Resources Institute, Center for International Development and Environment.

Tambulasi, R. I., and H. M. Kayuni. 2007. Decentralization opening a new window for corruption. An accountability assessment of Malawi's four years of democratic local governance. *Journal of Asian and African Studies* 42, no. 2:163–83.

Tandon, R. 2001. Riding high or nosediving: Development NGOs in the new millennium. In Eade and Ligteringen 2001, 44–59.

TANGO (Tanzania Association of NGOs). 2007. NGOs need to be more transparent and open up to government. Available at the tango.or.tz website.

Tangri, R. 1999. *Parastatals, privatization, and private enterprise: The politics of patronage in Africa.* Oxford: James Currey; Kampala: Fountain Publishing; Trenton, NJ: Africa World Press.

Taylor, M. P. 2003. Ghana: Building Better Co-op Law: Countries Struggle to Undo Colonial-age Statutes. NCBA Clusa International Program. *Cooperative Business Journal* (June).

Tefft, J. 2004. Building on successes in African agriculture: Mali's white revolution: Smallholder cotton from 1960 to 2003. *2020 Vision,* Focus 12, Brief 5 (April). Washington DC: IFPRI.

Temudo, M. P. 2005. Western beliefs and local myths: A case study on the interface between farmers, NGOs, and the state in Guinea-Bissau rural development interventions. In Igoe and Kelsall 2005, 253–77.

Teorell, J., and A. Hadenius. 2006. Democracy without democratic values: A rejoinder to Welzel and Inglehart. *Studies in Comparative International Development* 41, no. 3 (Fall): 95–111.

Thiéba, D. 2004. Experience with devolution of natural resource management and issues for the decentralisation process. In Bagré et al. 2004, 17–30.

Tibblin, A. 2006. Samarbete ger högre utdelning. Stockholm: SCC. Available at the utangranser.se website.

Tiffen, P., J. MacDonald, H. Maamah, and F. Osei-Opare. 2004. From tree-minders to global players: Cocoa farmers in Ghana. In *Chains of fortune: Linking women producers and workers with global markets,* ed. M. Carr, 11–44. London: The Commonwealth Secretariat.

Times of Zambia. 2005. ZCF chief tells coops to stay out of politics. *Times of Zambia.* Available at the times.co.zm website.

Toborn, K. 1992. The Naam movement in Burkina Faso. *IDRCurrents* 4 (October): 23–26.

Tokuori, T. 2006. The economy of affection and local enterprises in Africa: Empirical evidence from Burkina Faso and Senegal. *African Studies Quarterly—The Online Journal for African Studies* 9, nos. 1–2 (Fall).

Tönnies, F. 1963. *Community and society.* New York: Harper Torchbooks, Harper and Row.

Toulmin, C., and B. Guèye. 2003. *Transformations in West African agriculture and the future of family farms.* Issue Paper no. 123. December. London: IIED.

Touré, B. A. 2004. Influencing the Mali Poverty Alleviation Strategic Framework: The experience of OAMES. In Diakonia 2004, 15–22.

Transparency International. 2005. TI 2005 Corruption Perceptions Index 2005. Available at the transparency.org website.

Tripp, A. M. 2001a. Women and democracy: The new political activism in Africa. *Journal of Democracy* 12, no. 3 (July): 141–55.

———. 2001b. Women's movements and challenges to neopatrimonial rule: Observations from Africa. *Development and Change* 32: 33–54.

Tripp, R. 2001. GMOs and NGOs: Biotechnology, the policy process, and the presentation of evidence. Overseas Development Institute. *Natural Resource Perspectives* 60 (September).

Tschirley, D., B. Zulu, and J. Shaffer. 2004. *Cotton in Zambia: An assessment of its organization, performance, current policy initiatives, and challenges for the future.* Working Paper no. 10, Food Security Research Project. Available at the aec.msu.edu website.

Uemura, T. No date. Sustainable rural development in Western Africa: The Naam movement and the Six 'S'. *SDdimensions.* Available at the fao.org website.

UN. 2004. *Economic report on Africa 2004—Unlocking Africa's trade potential.* Addis Abeba: UN Economic Commission for Africa.

UNCDF (United Nations Capital Development Fund). 2003. Countries and regions: Benin. Available at the uncdf.org website.

———. 2004. Countries and regions: Burkina Faso. United Nations Capital Development Fund. Available at the uncdf.org website.

UNCTAD (United Nations Conference on Trade and Development). 2006. *Doubling aid: Making the "Big Push" work.* New York and Geneva: UNCTAD.

UNRISD. 1975. *Rural cooperatives as agents of change: A research report and a debate.* Geneva: UNRISD.

Uphoff, N., M. J. Esman, and A. Krishna. 1998. *Reasons for success: Learning from instructive experiences in rural development.* West Hartford, CT: Kumarian Press.

Utviklingsfondet. No date. *Promising practices: Lead Farmer Project.* Oslo: Utviklingsfomdet.

van Koppen, M., M. Giordano, and J. Butterworth. 2007. *Community-based water law and water resource management reform in developing countries.* Wallingford: CABI International.

Vaughan, S., and K. Tronvoll. 2003. *The culture of power in contemporary Ethiopian political life.* Sida Studies no. 10. Stockholm: Sida.

Verhagen, K. 1984. *Cooperation for survival.* Amsterdam: Royal Tropical Institute/ICA.

von Wright, G. H. 1994. *Myten om framsteget.* Trondheim: Bonniers.

Wadala, A. 2007. The politics of decentralisation in Uganda. In Asiimwe and Nakanyike 2007, 41–60.

Watson, E. E. 2003. Examining the potential of indigenous institutions for development: A perspective from Borana, Ethiopia. *Development and Change* 34, no. 2: 287–309.

Webster, N. 2004. *Understanding the evolving diversities and originalities in rural social movements in the age of globalization.* Civil Society and Social Movements Programme Paper no. 7. February. Geneva: United Nations Research Institute for Social Development (UNRISD).

Weinberger, K., and J. P. Jütting. 2001. Women's Participation in Local Organizations: Conditions and Constraints. *World Development* 29, no. 8: 1391–1404.

Wellard K., and J. G. Copestake. 1993. *Non-governmental organizations and the state in Africa—Rethinking the roles in sustainable agricultural development.* London: Routledge.

Wennink, B., and W. Heemskerk. 2006. *Farmers' organizations and agricultural innovation: Case studies from Benin, Rwanda, and Tanzania.* Bulletin 374. Amsterdam: The Royal Tropical Institute.

Wennink, B., S. Nederlof, and W. Heemskerk. 2007. Access of the poor to agricultural services: The role of farmers' organizations in social inclusion. *Development Policy and Practice.* Bulletin 376. Amsterdam: The Royal Tropical Institute.

Whaites, A. 2000. Let's get civil society straight: NGOs, the state, and political theory. In Eade 2000.

Widstrand, C. G. 1970. *Cooperatives and rural development in East Africa.* Uppsala: The Nordic Africa Institute.

Wiesmann, D. 2006. *2006 Global Hunger Index.* Washington DC: International Food Policy Research Institute (IFPRI).

Wiggins, S., and E. Cromwell. 1995. NGOs and seed provision to smallholders in developing countries. *World Development* 23, no. 3: 413–22.

Winter, P. 2001. A glossary for new Samaritans. In Barrow and Jennings 2001, 31–44.

Woltz, A. 2005. *The role of agriculture and rural development in achieving the Millennium Development Goals: A joint donor narrative.* Bonn: GDPRD.

Wonani, C. 2004. *The gender dimension of rural producer organization in Zambia.* Working Paper 2004:133. Oslo: Norwegian Institute for Urban and Regional Research (NIBR).

World Bank. 2001. Rural decentralization in Burkina Faso: Local level institutions and poverty eradication. *A World Free of Poverty,* no. 178. March. Available at the worldbank.org website.

———. 2004. Building agricultural policy and institutional capacity. In *Agriculture investment sourcebook, Module 01.* Available at the worldbank.org website.

————. 2006a. *Bridging the north-south divide in Ghana*. Draft summary. Equity and Development, World Development Report. Background papers.

————. 2006b. *Doing business*. Available at the doingbusiness.org website.

————. 2007. *World Development Report 2008*. Washington DC: World Bank.

Wright-Revolledo, K. 2007. *Diverse state-society relations: Implications of implementing the Paris Declaration*. Oxford: Intrac.

Xinhua. 2007. Zambia threatens to de-register inactive farmers' co-operatives. *People's Daily Online*. Available at the english.people-.com.cn website.

Yaro, J. A. 2006. Is deagrarianisation real? A study of livelihood activities in rural northern Ghana. *Journal of Modern African Studies*, 44, no. 1, 125–56.

Young C., N. P. Sherman, and T. H. Rose. 1981. *Cooperatives and development: Agricultural politics in Ghana and Uganda*. Madison: The University of Wisconsin Press.

Zaidi, S. A. 1999. NGO failure and the need to bring back the state. *Journal of International Development* 11: 259–71.

Zeleza, P. T. 2006. Foreword. In Amutabi 2006, xiii–xv.

Zoundi, J. S. 2004. *Case study on agricultural innovation and the cotton sub-sector in Mali*. Paris: Sahel and West Africa Club (SWAC).

Index

About the Author

Hans Holmén is an associate professor in social and economic geography at the Tema Institute, University of Linköping, Sweden. He has been a member of cooperatives, a board member of a condominium and students' union, trustee in a labor union (blue collar), and a staff member of a Jordanian NGO. In the 1980s he researched cooperatives and development, and since the early 1990s he has studied NGOs and development. He has worked as a consultant for the Swedish Cooperative Centre (SCC), the Swedish Aid Agency (SIDA), and UNSO/UNDP. Since 2001 Holmén has researched rural development and food production in sub-Saharan Africa.

Also from Kumarian Press...

Foreign Aid and Development:

Surrogates of the State: NGOs, Development and Ujamaa in Tanzania
Michael Jennings

Aiding Violence: The Development Enterprise in Rwanda
Peter Uvin

The World Bank and the Gods of Lending
Steve Berkman

Development Brokers and Translators: The Ethnography of Aid and Agencies
Edited by David Lewis and David Mosse

New and Forthcoming:

Rights-Based Approaches to Development: The Potential and Pitfalls
Edited by Sam Hickey and Diana Mitlin

How the Aid Industry Works: An Introduction to International Development
Arjan de Haan

A Fragile Balance: Re-examining the History of Foreign Aid, Security and Diplomacy
Louis Picard and Terry Buss

Civil Society under Strain: Counter-Terrorism Policy, Civil Society and Aid Post-9/11
Edited by Jude Howell and Jeremy Lind

Visit Kumarian Press at **www.kpbooks.com** or call **toll-free 800.232.0223** for a complete catalog.

green press

INITIATIVE

Kumarian Press is committed to preserving ancient forests and natural resources. We elected to print this title on 30% post consumer recycled paper, processed chlorine free. As a result, for this printing, we have saved:

4 Trees (40' tall and 6-8" diameter)
1,981 Gallons of Wastewater
1 Million BTU's of Total Energy
120 Pounds of Solid Waste
411 Pounds of Greenhouse Gases

Kumarian Press made this paper choice because our printer, Thomson-Shore, Inc., is a member of Green Press Initiative, a nonprofit program dedicated to supporting authors, publishers, and suppliers in their efforts to reduce their use of fiber obtained from endangered forests.

For more information, visit www.greenpressinitiative.org

Environmental impact estimates were made using the Environmental Defense Paper Calculator. For more information visit: www.papercalculator.org.

Kumarian Press, located in Sterling, Virginia, is a forward-looking, scholarly engagement and *an awar...*

HC 800 .H64 2010
Holmen, Hans.
Snakes in paradise